SEARCH FOR THE
TRUTH

SEARCH FOR THE TRUTH

BLACK WOMAN FAILED BY THE STATE OF GEORGIA

MICHELLE GRAVES

gatekeeper press™

Columbus, Ohio

SEARCH FOR THE TRUTH

Black Woman Failed by the State of Georgia

Published by Gatekeeper Press

2167 Stringtown Rd, Suite 109

Columbus, OH 43123-2989

www.GatekeeperPress.com

The cover design, interior formatting, typesetting, and editorial work for this book are entirely the product of the author. Gatekeeper Press did not participate in and is not responsible for any aspect of these elements.

Library of Congress Control Number: 2022943583

ISBN (paperback): 9781662930522

ACKNOWLEDGMENTS

To the Horsford boys, you have continued to give me the strength to fight for your mom whether you know it or not. The pain I've watched you endure along with that of Tamla's parents over the loss of their daughter is unbearable. A parent should never have to bury their child, and a child should never bury their mother. Though Tamla was only a friend and not a family member, someone had to have Tamla's back, and while everyone else was grieving, I turned my pain into finding out why this happened.

This book is not only for the Horsford family, but for the others who suffered tragic losses in Forsyth County: Linda Henderson and Kenny Brown to name a few. I write for those who may have also suffered tragedy in Forsyth County but were too afraid to do anything about it. Tamla and the others deserved better; whether Black, White, or otherwise, everyone deserves to get the same investigation our officers and agents took an oath to provide.

Thank you to Wayne Beyea for supporting me and unknowingly giving me motivation. Most of all, thanks for Chapter 4 from your book *Blind Justice*. Thank you to my new friend, Darcy who introduced me to Wayne and has become a huge support system for me whether she knows it or not. It is amazing how tragedy can bring people together, however unfortunate that we share in the grave injustice done to our loved ones in Forsyth County, Georgia.

Thank you to the complete strangers who have heard about Tamla's case and supported me on social media. To those who have helped get her story out there with your podcasts and blogs, thank you.

Most of all, thank you to my friends and family who have supported me and dealt with all the time that was taken from them while I worked on this book and Tamla's case. My kids sacrificed a great deal of time with their mother while I worked hard defending myself in court, defending my own child, deflecting felonies being committed against me, etc.

Thank you for those who did not get spooked and run away like the others.

Thank you to Nile Capello from *Rolling Stone* who did two very good stories about Tamla's death and the inept investigation attempted by the Forsyth County Sheriff's Office. I know she is continuing to work, as the others are, to figure out how to get justice for Tamla!

I want to thank all those who have supported me and encouraged me along this long and difficult journey. Your messages have kept me going at times, so continue to send those encouraging words. Those doing readings, podcasts, etc. to see if you can get to the truth and get the story out there, THANK YOU! Together we can figure out the TRUTH about WHAT HAPPENED TO TAMLA HORSFORD.

....

Please check out the author's website, **tamlahorsford.net**
for more details about the case.

Email: **contact@tamlahorsford.net**

PREFACE

As you read this book, I felt a little history into where exactly this story originated is crucial. Forsyth County (Cumming, Georgia) is not to be confused with Forsyth, Georgia, the city. Forsyth County, Georgia, is a historically racist town and Oprah Winfrey marched as recently as 1987 through the town.

In 1912, a Black boy who was accused of raping a young White girl was lynched in the middle of downtown. The book titled, *Blood at the Roots,* by Patrick Phillips gives an account of his personal experience as a White boy growing up in Forsyth County, Georgia. Unlike the rest of the kids, he was nice to the Black kids, and was chastised for it. Patrick grew up in Atlanta prior to moving to Forsyth County so he was unaware of the racism that existed there.

In January 2021, a new memorial was placed in front of the sheriff's office commemorating the 1912 lynching. Shortly after the lynching, more than one hundred Blacks were forced out.

There was a town called Oscarville where all the Blacks lived; it was flooded and became Lake Lanier in an effort to cleanse the town. Blacks were even chased out of town by Whites who went door to door. For seventy-five years, Forsyth County remained all-White.

Today, Forsyth County is only 4.4 % Black, 77.6 % White, and 15 % Asian.

CHAPTER 1
"The Real Tamla Horsford"

Tamla was born in St. Vincent and the Grenadines, however, grew up as a young girl in New York City and South Florida. She was street-smart, to say the least. That is why I suspect her manner of death did not occur by the hands of just one person. It is my opinion Tamla was attacked by at least two or more people.

Tamla was my neighbor and best friend but besides that, Tamla was a mother of five and a damn good one! A woman who spent every single day at her kids' schools volunteering her time to help with yearbook pictures, picture day photos, working as a room mom, on the school dance committee, and selling chicken biscuits for both the middle and elementary school, to raise money for the Parent-Teacher Organization. She ate lunch every day with her younger boys and helped with field day. Anything and everything she could do to help; she was willing to offer her time. Yet she was still available to attend my kids' sporting events, graduations, graduation parties, going away parties, etc. Tamla was the definition of a good friend. A woman who gave you the shirt off her back if you mentioned you liked it and Tamla never met a stranger.

I met Tamla through my kids. She watched out for them at the bus stop in the morning without even knowing me as I had to leave early for work. My kids were adamant I meet this new woman on our street. Tamla's boys and my kids were already friends and had classes together, so the connection began with them. When Tamla and I first met, it was like we had known each other forever and immediately became remarkably close friends and neighbors—a woman I visited with every single day, even multiple times a day until her death. Tamla introduced me to all her family members and friends. Whomever was visiting Tamla, I met them. When Tamla passed, it comforted me that I had already met Tamla's closest friends, with whom I keep in touch. I suppose Tamla was laying out a framework for the future unknowingly. My daughter Julia wrote a letter about Tamla that I read at her funeral. It was beautiful to see what Tamla looked like through the eyes of a child.

CHAPTER 2
"November 3, 2018"

————

It was a cool, overcast Saturday afternoon in Cumming, Georgia, when Tamla texted me to come over around 3:00 p.m. When I arrived, Tamla Horsford, a mother of five boys and my best friend, was getting ready for a sleepover party. The usual shenanigans were going on, with five boys between four and fifteen, the environment was always boisterous. There was nothing unusual about Tamla vacuuming, cooking, talking with me, and folding laundry at the same time. She gave multitasking a new meaning. The same was true on this Saturday. Tamla had prepared a breakfast casserole, cleaned the house, made dinner, and started a bonfire with her husband and kids prior to leaving that evening in preparation for this sleepover. It was a birthday party for new friend, Jeanne. Tamla met Jeanne through her son's football team, August 2018.

As Tamla and I attempted to hang out that afternoon, we discussed this party and who was attending. Tamla even joked and asked me to be her plus one, and I replied, "Those are not my kind of people." I had casually met one of the attendees through another friend, Tina—and Tamla and I both were not fond of Jenn. We sat on the porch that afternoon, joking and laughing about how the party would go. I never once imagined it would be the last time I would see this woman, my friend. I spent about an hour with Tamla and said, "See you tomorrow" as I left, anticipating the good gossip we would exchange about the party. The women at the party were not Tamla's regular crowd and she didn't know most of them. When Tamla described the plan for the evening, it was supposed to be an all-women sleepover, so no one had to drive home after drinking. Tamla and I spoke about her not spending the night and that she was probably going to come home. Tamla rarely stayed away from home overnight, away from her children.

CHAPTER 3
"The Party"

Tamla arrived at the party at 8:34 p.m. according to her location history obtained from her phone. The party began around 7:00 p.m., but Tamla, as usual, was preparing her family for the evening and arrived fashionably late. Since it was a birthday party, Tamla arrived with a bottle of Tequila for Jeanne as a gift, which she rudely refused because Tequila made her "throw up" in her mouth after smelling it. There were twelve people present including four men not previously mentioned in the "Girls Sleepover" invite. One of the men, Jose, age twenty-seven, was employed as a pre-trial officer for the Forsyth County Court system. He was there as Jeanne's boyfriend, the forty-five-year-old, newly divorced, birthday girl. Jeanne was "dating" Jose for a year but was not divorced until July 2018.

In addition to Jose, Tom, Mike, and Gary were the other three men present. It was originally believed that Jose and Tom stayed in the basement all night. However, Gary, who was also in attendance, told the Georgia Bureau of Investigation (GBI) that Jose and Tom were in the kitchen when he arrived with his wife between 7:30 and 8:00 p.m. Gary said he saw Tamla who was already drunk, but Tamla did not arrive until 8:34 p.m. and Gary said he only stayed fifteen to twenty minutes. Tamla could not have been drunk upon arrival so perhaps Gary lied to the GBI? In a second interview, Gary told the agent he dropped his wife off around 2:30 or 3:00 p.m. in the afternoon. According to Jeanne's statement in the report from the scene, Mike was also present. Mike was unreachable through the early morning and into the next day while his wife, Jenn, was texting him.

Everyone was drinking heavily that evening. Several people smoked marijuana with Tamla. Stacy also smoked cigarettes with Tamla that evening along with Marcy, according to Tom and Bridgett. (Stacy denied ever smoking in later interviews.) Stacy told the GBI that Bridgett was wearing a necklace full of Xanax for her "anxiety." Stacy was the only one who told the GBI Tamla was all over the place on the deck and would not sit down. Stacy also said she was "aggravated" with her that night and made Tamla at least one drink. Bridgett's necklace was never mentioned in the county investigation. Bridgett did tell the GBI that she had access to Tamla's bottle and her (Bridgett's) fingerprints would be on it. Stacy was quick to give an accusatory account of that night with Marcy smoking and taking at least one shot of Tamla's Tequila, which Marcy denied. Bridgett told the GBI "my morning regimen" consists of Adderall, Prozac, Xanax, and Wellbutrin. Everyone consumed alcohol and at least two people at the party were on Xanax but they did not wind up in the backyard. The Xanax never made it to Tamla's liver, according to the autopsy performed by Dr. Shaker, so it was taken shortly before injury and/or death. The police and GBI suggested Tamla got the Xanax prior to the party or at the party, but that does not match up to the digestive process.

In a video where a birthday song was sung, Tamla had a joint behind her ear. It was not yet smoked, which according to several statements was at 10:30 p.m. verified by the time stamp on the video from Jeanne's phone. This was also the time Tom and Jose went to the store to get ice, yet according to Tom they did not get anything. Jeanne and Jose both told the police Jeanne and Tamla got into an argument about her smoking marijuana there, and Jose could get in trouble being in "law enforcement."

Jose stated he did not know Tamla had marijuana but overheard an argument. The birthday song video showed everyone in the kitchen, including Jose and Jeanne with Tamla (who had the joint behind her ear) singing. Paula, Nichole, Stacy, Marcy, Tom, Jose, and Jeanne claimed ignorance that Tamla had marijuana, yet all were shown standing next to it in the kitchen. Stacy told the GBI the joint was smoked before the birthday song, yet it was still behind Tamla's ear during the birthday song, per the video.

As the evening progressed, the partygoers all engaged in a game of *Cards Against Humanity*. Tamla called her husband at 9:23 p.m. and received a Facetime call from her stepdaughter at 12:32 a.m., which lasted about three minutes. Tamla was still a mother and wife, that never changed, even away from home. During the Facetime call, Paula can be heard in the background telling Tamla to "Hurry up and take her turn" and again asking, "What is she doing, Jose? Tell her to take her turn." Jose tells Tamla, "Hurry up girl, get a black card!"

What happened after that phone call and into the next hour is unknown? The Facetime call was at 12:32 a.m. An hour before that call at 11:26 p.m., Jose took a video of Tamla and Jenn in the kitchen, with Tamla standing on one foot trying to speak to Jenn, who was visibly intoxicated and falling. Then Jose said, "That makes three of us," and the video ended. The video was specifically focused on Tamla filmed from across the room outside the kitchen. The other video Bridgett said Jose took of the girls dancing was never entered into evidence. Consequently, Jose told the GBI, "I will do my best" not to delete anything off my phone. It was later found he'd deleted everything from 2018.

Bridgett texted her husband Gary, who left the party earlier, to come and get her, "She had enough." The text continues with her asking her husband to get her the next day, and then she mentions shoe sizes. It is important to know Tamla's shoes were not collected from the scene as evidence and were returned by Stacy November 12, 2018, to Tamla's home. Stacy dropped the shoes off secretly behind a cabinet in the kitchen when she signed up to bring food to the house. Tom, Stacy's husband, told the GBI he remembered seeing Tamla's boots she wore to the party there at Jeanne's in the morning; however, Stacy, Tom's wife, told the GBI, she was not sure if Tamla was wearing the shoes at the party. Stacy also told the GBI Leander, Tamla's husband, was "distraught" when she brought the shoes back. I was there when Stacy brought the shoes and Leander was not distraught. I was at Tamla's and had ironically just cleaned up water behind the cabinet where the shoes were left. Brady, Tamla's boy, had spilled water on the floor behind the cabinet so I knew the boots had not just been there.

Partygoers began mysteriously vacating the party that was supposed to be a sleepover. Bridgett was picked up at 1:47 a.m. Bridgett told police, "Tamla's DNA would be all over her" because Tamla kissed her goodbye and walked her to the door, and police never mentioned anything about testing for DNA. However, Gary told police no one walked his wife Bridgett to the door.

The glass front door is evident in the crime scene photos and real estate photos. Also, Kelly Aldrich, Investigator from the GBI mentioned to Gary that the door was glass. Bridgett immediately told Tyler Sexton she didn't put anything in Tamla's drink when he brought up the Xanax. Bridgett was immediately giving alibis before any such thing was suggested. One of Jeanne's Attorney's, Z. Smith suggested Bridgett left via the garage door at 1:40 a.m., during Jeanne's interview with the GBI. Jeanne told officer Waldrop on scene the same. Attorney Z. Smith provided a letter to the GBI stating Bridgett went out the garage door at 1:40 a.m. Jeanne, however, later said Bridgett left out the front door at 1:47 a.m.

Jeanne couldn't account for the garage door opening and closing multiple times between 1:32 a.m. and 1:40 a.m. which police did not include in the investigation, but it was heard on the body cam and the officer wrote it down. On the body camera at the scene, Jeanne suggested Jose went to get water when the door opened and closed multiple times, but Jose said, "Who, me?" Jeanne and Jose initially told police Jose went to get his phone charger from the basement at 1:30 a.m., and nothing about water. The aunt told police at the scene she had Jeanne bring her cell phone to the basement, which no one else ever mentioned. When asked about Jose getting his charger, Jeanne told the GBI that he came back "quicker than expected and they were having sex." Jose told police in his statement it was 1:30 a.m. when he saw Tamla coming back from the basement to get his charger. Jose said he went straight up stairs and back to bed, then later said he saw Tamla in the kitchen eating at the island but did not see Bridgett. Bridgett said Tamla was sitting on a barstool at the island eating while she was waiting for her husband to get her. If Jose did not see Bridgett and she was already gone, then the time was after 1:47 a.m. when Jose saw Tamla alone in the kitchen. From pictures inside the house, it would have been impossible for Jose coming from the basement to see Tamla in the kitchen at the island unless he walked into the kitchen and around the wall. If the back door opened at 1:50 a.m. according to statements, then Jose would have only had a 3-minute window to see Tamla alone before she went on the deck and died supposedly. In the 911 call, Jose said he saw Tamla alone in the kitchen at 1:00 a.m., but the house was very rowdy in the video during Tamla's Facetime call with her stepdaughter at 12:32 a.m., and everyone said they went to bed soon after at 1:30 a.m.

The door in the kitchen never closed at 1:40 a.m., so it too was left open all night, like the deck door was left open at 1:57 a.m. A good deal of action was going on for everyone to be asleep except Bridgett and Tamla with doors opening and closing for twenty minutes. Stacy and her husband Tom stated they left at 8:30 a.m. the morning of the fourth with a Crock-Pot in hand, and no one was awake. However, Madeline, the aunt who lived with Jeanne, told police Stacy and her husband, Tom, left in the "early morning hours."

At this point, Jeanne was allowed to bust in the door offering Dunkin' Donut gift cards and donuts. So obviously Jeanne was allowed to leave the scene of a crime during "interviews," not interrogations. Jeanne continued to interrupt her aunt's interview two additional times. Two years later, the neighbor corroborated Stacy and Tom leaving at 9:00 a.m. with a Crock-Pot in hand.

The text I received from Tina said the "2 men there in the morning would not let the women see," the women being Jenn, the aunt, and Jeanne. Jeanne told police she followed Jose downstairs and "stood in the gravel where she could see." If Jeanne were in the gravel, she would have been standing over Tamla because Tamla was not "out in the grass" as described by the aunt and Jose in the 911 call.

Tamla was positioned partially under the deck in the photos, contrary to where the body imprint was and how she was originally described by Jose on scene November 5, 2018. Jeanne told police that Jose had told her about the cut or scratch, but she did not see it. If she did not observe it when she went down to see Tamla, then how did Jose see it? Jose was adamant he did not touch her arm or check her pulse. The injury was hardly a cut, it was a compound fracture.

Marcy suggested she left at 4:10 a.m. and did not set an alarm. She just "woke up" and went home for her second day at her new job at the Coach Outlet store when she spoke to Tyler Sexton on February 20, 2019. However, Jeanne was adamant Marcy set an alarm to go to work. The written statement provided at the scene by Marcy mentioned setting an alarm. T. Sexton prompted Marcy to recall setting an alarm when he called her just minutes before the press release, and she miraculously recalled she must have woken up just before the alarm went off.

Marcy also said the TV in the living room was loud, but in a second interview did not recall the TV being loud. Marcy had another slip of words when she said she saw the living room nice and put together at 4:15 a.m., but she'd left at 4:10 a.m. in the written statement taken at the scene. Was it common to attend an all–nighter before your second day as a sales associate for the Coach Outlet? Marcy continued to probe Sexton about the case, and he told her about the press release and it being an accident. Keep in mind, Tamla's family arrived at the sheriff's office to watch the press release but were not allowed inside. The family still did not know the determination of investigation, but the partygoers all did! The case was closed on February 20, 2019, the same day Marcy, Gary, and Bridgett were all interviewed a first, second, and third time. Marcy admitted to taking Xanax and then lied about how she found out about the party. Marcy said she was invited at another birthday party at Marlowe's Tavern, and she did not recall receiving an evite. However, the evite was in the case file with her RSVP! Marcy told the GBI she'd left at 5:00 a.m. Kelly Aldrich, Investigator from the GBI, chalked it up to the time change and the door notification not updating. If that were the case, who left out the front door at 4:10 a.m., because there is no 5:00 a.m.? Additionally, who left at 1:47 a.m. if Bridgett left at 2:47 a.m. (not 1:47 a.m.) when her husband's phone showed the text message with the time?

Jenn and Paula both suggested they were up alone and no one else was awake when Paula left at 7:45 a.m. Stacy and Tom suggested they left at 8:30 a.m. and no one was awake. Jenn called her husband Mike to get her at 7:32 a.m. According to Jenn, the aunt came tearing up the stairs from the basement when she was on the phone with her husband.

Why was Jose allowed to determine Tamla deceased, and able to keep everyone from the body? I still wonder why a kid who worked as a tech at Goodyear and a fry cook at Zaxby's (the only jobs he was not fired from) before his short stints as a probation officer and court officer deemed him the only one allowed to call 911?

When Mike was interviewed, he said police told him to wait outside and not to come in, so he parked up the street. His wife, Jenn, said he had to come in and he stayed in the dining room area because he got there at the same time as the police. The aunt said she got up at 8:30 a.m. in her written statement at the scene but said 8:50-9:00 a.m. in her transcribed statements. Mike said his wife first called him about 8-8:30 a.m. just to say she was up, but she said she had been communicating with him all night to get her. Why did she not get an Uber or Lyft home?

On body cam, you could hear Officer Waldrop ask Sergeant C. Miller why he was there because it was his beat, and he was close to the call.

There were also cleaning supplies photographed about five feet behind Tamla's body and just outside the basement door which Tamla would have stumbled past.

No one considered this evidence or asked about it?

Stories changed multiple times from the police body camera at the scene, to the first witness statements, to the third interviews in 2020, to the GBI, in addition to several court appearances. The coroner's death certificate reports Tamla's injury at 1:30 a.m. before the time change at 2:00 a.m. and time of death 10:47 a.m. which is significant considering the ambulance was cancelled en route just after 9:07 a.m. The coroner arrived at 9:47 a.m. and Tamla was not rolled over nor had her pulse been checked by anyone until the GBI photographer took her photo. Jimmy Brown, the photographer, started photos at 10:10 a.m. and I do not know what time the ones of Tamla's face were taken. Detective Christian told Leander Horsford that his wife "walked down the stairs, tripped, and fell and landed in the grass." Between the stairs and the grass is a six-foot area of gravel she catapulted over, and she knocked over the table with the empty cleaning bottles left out. The bottles were what resembled Murphy's Oil Soap, Pine-Sol, and glass cleaner located five feet behind Tamla's body. Would Tamla have walked all the way across the deck and down a flight of stairs to smoke a cigarette to trip over the garden border rather than remain upstairs on the deck in her socks? Furthermore, the crime scene photos show Tamla's cigarettes and lighter on a table on the upstairs deck. The story provided to the family and law enforcement was that at 1:30 a.m., prior to daylight savings time, which occurred at 2:00 a.m. that morning, Tamla wanted to leave and go home. According to Jeanne, Jose refused to allow Tamla to leave, and according to statements by Stacy, Bridgett, and Tom, they would not allow Tamla to leave. In fact, Stacy said she was ADAMANT Tamla did not leave! Stacy also told police she was AGGRAVATED with Tamla over Tamla saying she made "wimpy" drinks.

CHAPTER 4
"The 911 Call"

The 911 call was made at 8:59 a.m., at least an hour and a half after the discovery of Tamla in the backyard by the aunt. During the 911 call, Jeanne handed the phone over to Jose, who takes over the call introducing himself like the dispatcher was a friend of his. Immediately he suggested suicide and a cut on Tamla's right wrist for which he couldn't explain the origin.

Later, "this cut" was found to be a compound fracture with the ulna bone protruding through the bottom of Tamla's arm. Veins and arteries are located on the underside of the wrist, yet no sign of blood was present except for a small area on her cuff at the wrist. Ironically, the sleeve was turned over, so the clean side was on the topside of Tamla's wrist. Tamla's arm was twisted behind her as well so you could not see the injury. It was apparent the small presence of blood had been washed; you could see three rings of dark red to light pink blood. The sleeve with the bloodstain had been turned over so the stain could not be seen. No one knew her arm was injured based on photos and statements except Jose. The arriving Sergeant, C. Miller, told GBI he did not know Tamla's arm was fractured until they rolled her over.

There was red clay all around this wound with no red clay present anywhere in the backyard. During the 911 call, dispatch asked Jose several times if Tamla was breathing, and he continued to avoid the question and said, "She is not moving." He didn't check for a pulse, but he said he'd tried to "access her." Jose, trained in CPR, neglected to provide any lifesaving measures and blocked lifesaving services from getting to Tamla. Jose said Tamla's "leg was stiff and did not move like you would think." According to Sheriff Freeman, every officer's patrol car had an AED. Jose told the GBI he did not check her pulse or roll her over, "that death freaked him out." Tamla was not blue in photos to indicate she was deceased or had been for some time. Sheriff Ron Freeman boasted on a Facebook post about his men saving a man who hit a telephone pole and was deceased on scene. They spent thirty minutes administering care and were able to revive him while EMS was on the way, and how all police vehicles have AED devices in them. Tamla lay in a backyard for twelve hours in 38° weather with a traumatic brain injury which can result in spasticity that can affect the way muscles move. The stiffness Jose described is quite common in someone who has suffered a stroke, which in Tamla's case was present with the subarachnoid hemorrhage she suffered.

According to Lauren McDonald, the coroner in 2018, now Georgia State Representative, said Tamla had 150 ml (about 5.07 oz) of blood on her brain, and the enormous hematoma in her right temple—with a blunt object marking present—could have attributed to her "stiffness" but did not mean she was dead. Someone should have checked her pulse and/or breathing, which no one did.

Throughout the 911 call, Jose told a different story than he did in his initial statement. Aside from accusing Tamla of committing suicide, he told police only four people had left from the previous night, when in fact nine people had left.

Jose said he last saw Tamla at 1:00 a.m. alone in the kitchen, but his interview statement said 1:30 p.m. It was stated by multiple people they played cards until 1:00 a.m. and no one went to bed until 1:30 a.m. or later.

The dispatcher never mentioned the ambulance was on its way, they should be pulling in, etc. Only the officer arrived. According to Jose and the EMS report, the ambulance was cancelled by Sergeant C. Miller. Miller was the "arriving officer" for Forsyth County Sheriff's Office. Immediately, Jeanne and Jose suggested Tamla fell off the deck. Yet in their first story to me and according to the police, Tamla fell face-first with both hands behind her back from tripping over a metal garden border in the yard. Detective Christian also said this to Tamla's husband. Sheriff Freeman tried to tell me I was grieving and did not hear correctly. I explained I did not hear anything; I saw the scene the following day. We were told by Jeanne and Jose on scene and in Jose's statement that the police did not think she fell, but that was not true. At the scene on the body cam, that was what everyone said except a few officers who questioned the position of her body and arm. On arrival, law enforcement all stated a fall. On the 911 call, Jose and Jeanne both suggested a fall. Jeanne also told the public "No one fell off my deck," and her ex-husband also told the police on scene he "built the deck for his kids to be safe." However, no one seemed to know what had happened in the interviews given a few days later. At least two partygoers suggested Tamla fell down the stairs and even provided times she fell, but no one called 911 and police did not investigate that theory. Would Tamla not have been found at the bottom of the stairs if that were the case?

According to the private pathologist, Dr. Adel Shaker, who was hired by the family, the wound was determined to be postmortem or near death. We have since learned from the GBI file that Dr. Koopmeiners, the GBI medical examiner, said the fracture occurred "right at death," to explain no blood at the wound. Considering she died at 10:47 a.m., someone had to break her arm while everyone was standing there.

Dr. Koopmeiners also took back the cervical vertebrae 2 (C2) injury reported on an official autopsy report police used to give the reason for death. Dr. Koopmeiners agreed with Dr. Shaker: Tamla's neck experienced subluxation or was "twisted." Dr. Koopmeiners later said it was "hyperextended" from the fall! She died from the combination of her other injuries. Tammy had no life-threatening injuries other than she was debilitated from the head injuries and blunt trauma.

Tamla never being rolled over on scene could have easily contributed to her suffocation in my opinion. Detective Christian told Leander Horsford at his home the day Tamla passed, "Maybe the cold did it, (It was 38° outside and Tamla had on a fleece onesie, shorts, socks, and a tank top) and she passed out and never regained consciousness." Christian told his girlfriend Tamla died from positional asphyxiation. Forensic Investigator C. Robinson also stated Tamla died of suffocation.

It doesn't seem logical that she froze to death, or she just passed out and never regained consciousness. What caused her to pass out in the first place? Jeanne and Stacy both told people Tamla fell face first and did not try to stop herself. Unless Tamla was unconscious when she fell, she would have braced herself. Also, Tamla's arms were not by her side, so that raises more questions. Could Xanax, which she was not used to taking and that possibly someone may have slipped in her drink have caused her to pass out? Is that why they did not call police?

Did police or GBI account for the pill bottles the women had at the scene to see how many were missing from their bottles, or call doctors to see if anyone needed to fill their prescriptions early? Unfortunately, no. Instead, Stacy alluded I gave Tamla the Xanax by suggesting Tamla stopped by my house on way to the party, a known lie per Tamla's location history and my statement to the police. I went to her house earlier that day. Stacy also suggested I was going through a divorce. I was divorced in 2010, and Agent Aldrich knew thatbecause she'd investigated my daughter's abuse allegations against her father in a separate case going on at the same time, which was a total conflict of interest.

No one attempted CPR or turned Tamla over until the photographer was done with the crime scene photos. Why did no one roll Tamla over until 10:47 a.m., even though the coroner had arrived at 9:47 a.m. and Detective Mike Christian arrived at 10:15 a.m.? The county report even states no one turned Tamla over until Crime Scene Investigator Fujimura, who worked for Forsyth County, was done with photos. I will never understand why no one turned this woman over. If I found an unconscious body in my yard, friend or foe, I would attempt CPR and whatever else I could to avoid a death at my home.

Jose and Jeanne immediately said in the 911 call that Tamla was outside and drinking alone after they all went to bed. Jose admitted to not checking Tamla's pulse even though dispatch asked him to, and he alleged to never have moved her arm or turned her over because "death freaked him out." Jose couldn't recall how many times he met Tamla, whether once or four times. In the 911 call he said once. In his interview he said four times. The GBI asked him twice how many times he'd met Tamla and he never could provide a straight answer. Jose spent fifteen minutes on a phone call with the GBI detective whose only question was how many times he had met Tamla and he never gave a straight answer. Jose accessed Tamla's case file three times over the course of the police investigation and once prior to anyone being interviewed initially by police outside of the statements at the scene. On November 7, 2018, Jose accessed Tamla's file, the same day the autopsy results had come back about the initial injuries. Detective Christian went back to Jeanne's house on November 7, 2018, to reassess the scene. Jose was put on administrative leave for accessing the file a few weeks later and fired December 20, 2018, for accessing my personal information, after I found my driver's license number on the magistrate arrest warrants filed against me. Of course, Jose denied any of this when interviewed.

The police still deny anyone giving Jose access to the case file and tried to convince me "not even the deputies on the road have access" per Detective T. Sexton.

Everyone was allowed back in the home two hours after Tamla died, so for three days things were available for tampering.

Evidence that was not destroyed before police arrived was most certainly destroyed three days later. The house was immaculate in crime scene photos, and it was not that way in videos and pictures throughout the night, not to mention Jose said he cleaned up.

CHAPTER 5
"November 4, 2018"

As police arrived on the scene, it was clear Forsyth County had never worked a possible murder scene, much less one of this magnitude. You could hear the officers on the body cam trying to tell one another where to run the crime scene tape, suggesting that another officer was beginning to do it incorrectly. Officer Waldrop apparently never worked a death before. In my opinion, that is why Jose got Sergeant C. Miller to the scene before the dispatched officer arrived to cancel the ambulance. Officer Waldrop was trying to do everything by the book, and he likely would not have cancelled the ambulance and possibly would have checked Tamla's pulse.

You can hear Officer Waldrop tell Jose, his friend and colleague, to not allow anyone on the deck or in the backyard. Jose was allowed a questionable degree of control over a crime scene where he was directly involved. Several officers could be heard at the scene talking about their relationship with Jose and how their wives worked with one partygoer. Officer Miller told Jeanne's mother (who called him directly) that she could not come to the house because it was a crime scene, and he would arrest her. Miller went on to reassure her that Jeanne was okay because he was friends with her, and they had mutual friends as well.

Additional officers arrive, including Detective Christian, who went on to mention how he knew Jose from his county position and the gym where they worked out together. Nichole knew both Jose and the lead detective from the gym and introduced Jeanne to Jose. Christian went on to say how good Jose was at what he did. Investigator Andy Kalin, the lead county investigator, had landed Jose his job as a court officer with Forsyth County. Jose spoke about Andy as his friend, and they were on a first-name basis, although Andy denied this.

Conflicts of interest were abundant in this case. For instance, Andy Kalin told the GBI that Jose was liked by the District Attorney (DA) and all the Assistant District Attorneys (ADAs). The same DA felt no prosecution was necessary in this case and refused to allow me to press charges against Jose for accessing my information, for which Jose was fired. Consequently, James Dunn, the ADA during this case, became a state court judge. I had a phone call with Andy Kalin (November 8, 2018, unrecorded of course) about his personal relationship with Jose. He was going to get cameras and shoes, none of which turned up on record. I even spoke of this conversation with Detective T. Sexton and H. Wheeler, Victim's Advocate, November 19, 2018, during my interview. Andy Kalin later told me shoes were not part of the crime scene. The tops of the boots Tamla wore could be seen in one of the crime scene photos.

If Sheriff Ron Freeman wanted to avoid backlash and trusted there was no foul play in Tamla's case, he should have stepped back and allowed the GBI to stay on the case initially due to all the conflicts of interest and relationships involved.

As more interested officers arrived on scene, you could hear the conversation of two officers on the body cam identified as Officer Spriggs and an unidentified officer who states that the position of her arm and body does not look right, questioning the theory everyone at the scene believed was a fall from the deck. You never once hear anyone mention Tamla may have tripped and fallen at ground level over a garden border. Why would Detective Christian even suggest tripping at the ground level if everyone on audio at the scene stated a fall from the balcony was the cause—even Jeanne and Jose on the 911 call. Detective Mike Christian never made contact with the body as the investigator of the crime. Mike Christian would have known he had been lied to at the scene if he followed proper protocol and examined the body and scene for evidence. As a result of Jose's position and relationships, there was no investigation. Jeanne admitted on the 911 call that she did not know if Tamla was breathing because no one rolled her over. Then why cancel the ambulance? Why not roll her over when Jose went to "assess" her so CPR could be attempted? He was CPR certified. Now we know Mike Christian told Leander at his home on November 4, 2018, that "maybe the cold did it" and "she passed out and never regained consciousness." He never had any contact with the body or examined the scene around the body. Mike Christian told Leander it looked like his wife "walked down the flight of stairs, tripped, and fell and landed in the grass." What about the six feet of gravel that met the stairs and the foot of mulch before ever reaching the grass? The disturbed landscaping was in the photos taken by the GBI, as I stated above, and could be seen on the story *11 Alive* in Atlanta, which aired May 13, 2022. As I told Sheriff Freeman, Jeanne made a scene at her house to corroborate the story of Tamla tripping at ground level. If Tamla did not trip and fall, how did the rocks get from the gravel into the mulch since Jeanne just had her landscaping done "three weeks ago" as she stated?

Officer Waldrop and Sergeant C. Miller could be heard laughing about Waldrop stating Tamla did not have a valid driver's license because she kept her Florida license. Sergeant C. Miller was laughing, asking "Are you going to give her a ticket?" Tamla kept her Florida license (which was valid) because they did not know how long they would stay in Georgia as her family was still in Florida. She had expressed an interest in returning there. Another officer could be heard telling Officer Waldrop her license was valid. It was just in Florida. Waldrop goes on to make a big deal about it not being a valid license because it was not a Georgia one. The police did not care there was a Black deceased woman at an all-White house. They just callously were joking about a ticket, which was deplorable.

At the scene, Jeanne admitted Tamla's husband had been calling her phone all morning, but they refused to answer it. However, no time was wasted calling Bridgett, who called everyone else and so on. No one ever thought to call Leander Horsford. They waited until 11:45 a.m., when police went to the house to notify him of his wife's passing. Oddly though, Jeanne told police, "I called you first," referring to Nichole, but Nichole wasn't called until 9:30 a.m. Bridgett would have been the first notified at 9:00 a.m. with "She's Dead" according to her statement to the GBI. Also at 9:00 a.m., Jeanne was supposed to be on the phone with 911.

As the day progressed and Tamla's friends were notified by family of her passing, I immediately went to the home to comfort the children.

Jeanne, Jose, and Tom showed up at Tamla's residence, and Leander recalled Tom acting different and telling Leander he "was sorry. Not sorry for his loss. Just sorry," unlike everyone else. Tom was the only male to attend the funeral or viewing. On November 4, 2018, Jeanne came back to Tamla's with Bojangles for the family for dinner.

Jeanne's ex-husband, Mr. Meyers, told the GBI he got the phone call Tamla was deceased while at the Waffle House. Apparently, Jeanne's mother, called the ex-husband and told him he needed to get to the house. Meyers said he saw the women separated outside when he arrived. You could see the women together in the reflection of the glass front door in one of the crime scene photos and in the patrol car camera from the scene. Mr. Meyers discussed his interaction with law enforcement on scene during his interview with the GBI. Meyers had no right to be at the house, much less conversing with law enforcement at a crime scene, especially when the husband of the deceased was not allowed. Jeanne's mother called police and asked to come to the home and was told she could not because it was a crime scene.

Jeanne's ex attacked me, Tamla's cousin, and Tamla's aunt via Facebook messenger accusing Tamla of irresponsible behavior. Meyers went on about how Tamla was high as a kite and the toxicology report would show it, just like his ex-wife mentioned. Her toxicology would prove it was not a crime. What did these people know about how the toxicology screen would come out? His ex-wife also told police to "wait for the toxicology, it will prove an accident."

Tamla's alcohol level should not have been the determining factor on accident or homicide. Many other factors in addition to alcohol, including the presence of medication Tamla was not prescribed have also contributed to her death. The whereabouts of such medication should have been determined, along with origin of every injury, but we are still waiting on those explanations as well.

Meyers even admitted he had a DUI himself, and he had the audacity to call Tamla an alcoholic. He referenced friends from Florida who attended Tamla's funeral that had been in AA. Just because someone's friend was in AA does not mean they were in the program.

Why wasn't Leander notified when police arrived, and why was he not allowed on scene with the number of officers there? What could he possibly have done to not afford him the right to see his wife one last time? Officer Waldrop lied to Leander when he told him his wife was already on her way to the GBI when Leander requested to go to the scene. Officer Waldrop had just gotten off the phone with someone at the scene who told him they were still processing her; it could be heard on his body cam.

Officer Waldrop told Tamla's mother, who you could tell was upset on the phone with him, that the GBI was at the scene and had taken over the investigation. Ron Freeman, who was the sheriff, and Detective T. Sexton said they did not need the GBI for this case and that "they" (referring to Forsyth County) "Investigate a lot of murders and do not need the GBI." Ron Freeman pulled the GBI off this case and reaffirmed to me in a recording that the GBI could not do anything unless he or the DA requested them.

Neither investigation through the GBI nor the county ever produced a re-creation of the body falling off the balcony and landing the exact way Tamla did. The deputy coroner Keith Bowen specifically mentioned in the police report that the body may have been "pushed or fallen" from the balcony. As a former GBI employee, the forensic expert I hired lied and refused to provide proof of his video, which he'd said he had, of a mannequin that landed just like Tamla. I even took him to court, and he still would not produce said video. This man told me he didn't need to investigate further because he knew Dr. Eisenstat and agreed with him. I wonder what he thought when his friend took back the C2 injury he agreed with? The counsel for the sheriff's office refused to provide the agency name and/or investigative report that Andy Kalin, the lead detective for all investigations in the county, told Bridgett was hired and why he'd had to call her and ask her more questions. Mike Christian also told his girlfriend about this "unknown agency" in Social Circle, Georgia. In fact, Andy and Tyler Sexton made three calls the day they closed the case on February 20, 2019, as a result of this unknown agency investigation per their own open record conversations with the witnesses. According to counsel, there are no responsive documents and no other agency that did an investigation, so their attorney basically called Andy a liar.

Detective Christian returned to the home where Tamla passed, three days later on November 7, 2018. Flags were put down where the police said there were divots in the ground to indicate where the body was. This was not done the day of, so he was "guesstimating" the position of the body. Mike only returned after the initial injuries came out in the autopsy report. There were no divots in the ground when I was there on November 5, 2018, and I was present with Dianne, Steven (our neighbor), Jeanne, Jose, the aunt, Jeanne's mother, and Nichole. We all walked all over the backyard, particularly in the area Mike put the flags and indicated "divots" were present. That is where we stood and were shown the rocks in the mulch.

The huge imprint of Tamla's body still in the grass seen in the top right of crime scene photos not under the deck where she was photographed was the only visible marking in the grass.

On the 7th, Fujimura, crime scene investigator, expressed in the report that "marker 4 was not present on Sunday, the day of discovery." A piece of gumbo (with shrimp) was on the ground, near where her head would have been. Oddly enough, no one interviewed by police in the transcribed statements said Tamla was drunk, or that they saw her throw up to cause her to go over the balcony, nor did anyone mention a piece of food near the body. No one said they saw Tamla take shots except Jeanne, who said it at the scene.

Detective Mike Christian's phone call with Dr. Koopmeiners was November 7, 2018, about 2:00 p.m. after his visit to Jeanne's. Christian told Dr. Koopmeiners it did not appear the body fell from the balcony by the position, but rather from ground level. Dr. Koopmeiners said, "The fall had to occur from much higher and not ground level." Immediately these individuals knew something else had happened other than what they were led to believe by the partygoers.

At 8:20 a.m., November 7, 2018, there was an internal GBI email I obtained by open records, which confirmed that Dr. Koopmeiners had already determined

Tamla to have died from "an accidental fall from the balcony." Even email recipients were surprised, and this was the medical examiner's excuse for not testing Tamla's bottle of tequila. Keith Bowen asked twice for the bottle to be tested for "poison, antifreeze, etc.," and was both times denied. Ironically, two years later, the GBI decided they would test the bottle and it was clear of all poison. Of course, it was two years later.

Lauren McDonald, coroner, described how his office worked with the medical examiner to determine the cause of death. There was a text about this as well. On February 6, 2019, McDonald called Leander Horsford, Tamla's husband, and described the traumatic blunt force injuries. This phone call was recorded. The timeline did not match. The medical examiner determined it was an "accident" less than twenty-four hours into the autopsy, but the police waited months to release the information to the family and close the case.

There was still no answer to who moved Tamla's arm. Tamla's arm was not only out to the side, but in a slightly open fist, which was contrary to what Jeanne and Jose described multiple times to police. Jeanne was adamant both arms were back by Tamla's sides. She even told a neighbor she'd had a camera that showed the position. Sergeant C. Miller did not move it either because no one checked her pulse or went near her. C. Miller told the GBI maybe he moved it when he checked her pulse. However, he did not check her pulse because it was not documented in the report. Also, he'd said he saw what appeared to be a deceased female and went inside, having had no contact.

To date, no one can explain how Tamla's arm was moved. Jose, however, was the one who'd told the police and everyone else at the scene that Tamla was dead. No officer on scene did their due diligence and looked over the body, checked for a pulse, nothing.

Jose told the police he threw away the cigarette butts at the scene and dumped the ashtray while he was "cleaning up" in the morning. More concerning was

30

that Bridgett told the police she threw away the cigarette butts and dumped the ashtray after the police left, because it was a constant reminder to Jeanne. Jose admitted not allowing anyone near the body and that was said in Tina's text message to me. Shortly after I learned of Tamla's death, Tina, who was also best friends with Jenn and her husband Mike, was the first one to call me the afternoon of November 4.

Tina was a friend of Tamla's prior to this event. She even started the GoFundMe for the family. I have a voice mail about how she called and notified the school about Tamla's passing as well. Tina sent my posts to Jenn, who sent them to their attorney for Magistrate Court and they were used in court, which proved useless. I had been friends with Tina for nine years, and our daughters were best friends. After Tamla's death, we never spoke again, and our daughters never spent time together out of school again.

Tom did not admit to being there in the morning, contrary to the neighbor who mentioned the couple with the Crock-Pot still there at 9:00 a.m. and Tina, who said her friend Jenn reported two men were there in the morning. Jose initiated the story of Tamla standing on the propane tank, slipping, and falling off the deck. Bridgett confirmed this in her statement, and Mike Christian noted in his report the top of the propane tank had been dusted off. Tom, Jose, and Jeanne all talked about trying to get the firepit lit, so they had to "switch tanks because one was empty." Jeanne made this comment in her statement: "Jose had been asking her all week, who was coming to the party?" From what we now know from the GBI interviews with Jose (all six of them), he was allowed to manipulate the scene simply because of who he was and who he knew at the scene. At the scene, no one was examined for any cuts, bruising, scrapes, etc., to clear everyone of any wrongdoing. There were no breathalyzers or drug screens to test for any substances the partygoers were under to rule out any foul play. Not even after the initial autopsy report came back and Christian went back to the house did anyone get examined. Detective Christian had two toxicology reports run about the marijuana, yet multiple people smoked there, and Jeanne's son used it for his seizures. In fact, Lauren McDonald, coroner and now State Representative of Georgia, told Leander on February 6, 2019, that he had not recognized one of the components to the THC found in Tamla's tox screen.

I am not a scientist, but it makes me wonder if Tamla had liquid marijuana drops given to her at some point, which would show different on a toxicology screen than straight marijuana? Remember, Jeanne's son used the drops for seizures as stated by Bridgett. Jeanne had blood pressure medication, which could cause someone to pass out if they didn't have blood pressure issues, or it could make their pressure rise, which could cause a stroke. But that was never told to police. It was only told to the GBI two years later.

Police reported Tamla did not die immediately and may have even "gotten up and/or moved or crawled" and then "collapsed" where she was found, according to Detective Tyler Sexton. So, Tamla did not try to get to the basement window or door to holler for help since she was able to get up and move? Why would she be facing away from the house she would have gone to for help? Was she, in fact, running to get away from someone? Tamla would not have gone so far to smoke when she had been on the balcony upstairs smoking all night. These are all questions a police department should have examined but didn't in this case.

Messages from Jeanne to Dianne on November 4, 2018, at 2:31 p.m. said that "Tamla wandered outside for a cigarette in the night and died." At 2:33 p.m. on November 4, 2018, Dianne received a text message from Paula that said, "We all went to bed and at 1:57 a.m." "Tamla fell down the back deck steps and died," and "police are doing an autopsy." Two completely different accounts from two different people two minutes apart.

Detective Christian told Leander his wife "walked down the steps then tripped and fell into the grass." A text by Stacy was found by GBI that stated Tamla "fell down the stairs and hit her head." If everyone went to bed, how did you know it was 1:57 a.m. when she fell unless the partygoers had already spoken about their story because that door time was on Jeanne's phone from her alarm system. Who went out the door to the garage at 1:40 a.m. and left it open?

Was it left open so someone would have a way back in? Jose said he saw Tamla in the kitchen alone at 1:30 a.m. The doors opened multiple times between 1:32 a.m. and 1:40 a.m. So, did he sneak out and wait for Tamla to smoke?

I recently found emails between A. Page, who was Sheriff Freeman's secretary, where Freeman, Detective Sexton, and Detective Kalin, were all laughing and making jokes about my concerned emails in this case. Tamla's case was a bigger circus than Barnum & Bailey's as far as Forsyth County was concerned. There was a comment found on Facebook that stated, "You are my favorite Goober," referring to Detective Christian and posted by Detective L. Belafi, who was Aldrich's other best friend

According to the POST file on Christian, Detective Christian can attempt reinstatement in two years. Per the report, Christian was named a "predator" by POST, (Peace Officer's Standards and Training) which certifies police. I am sure Mike's ability to be reinstated effected the decision by Aldrich and Freeman not to press charges. Mike knew too much in the Horsford case for that, just read his texts from "murder covering up land."

Christian sent texts to at least one girlfriend that implied Black people deserved it when their homes were vandalized. A text referred to Tamla as "the porch lady." In another, he referred to himself multiple times as a "racist cracker bastard." The article about the texts and pictures he sent of Tamla from the scene were in *Rolling Stone* on September 29, 2021. Aldrich and Freeman refused to press charges against Christian, but POST thought the behavior so bad, he lost everything. Of course, he was warned about the internal affairs investigation by his friend and colleague, Deputy Chief Grady Sandford, who was arrested and fired for distributing child pornography. Sandford advised Detective Christian to resign to keep his pension before he was fired. Freeman and Aldrich, along with the DA, were okay with the fact Mike Christian used his position to prey on victims of crimes who were vulnerable and compromised an open death investigation. I mean, you can hear him flirting with Jeanne, telling her to "get out of his head" when she tells him she is going to "charge him rent" and handing out gift cards.

Christian sent pictures to women he was having affairs with, performing lewd acts in bathrooms at work, taking nude pictures at work, having sex in county cars in car washes on work time, and taking women to abandoned crime scenes and homes for sale that were vacant to which he somehow had access. (The entire report is available open record via a request to POST). Investigator Kelly Aldrich oversaw the investigation of Detective Christian, which was another conflict of interest. Her best friend was L. Belafi, who was close to Christian, and Aldrich sat in the sheriff's office with all these people not at the GBI headquarters. You can see the story about Mike Christian on a February 4, 2020, WSB-TV Facebook story post by Mike Petchenik.

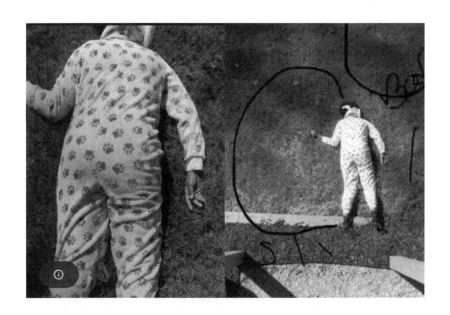

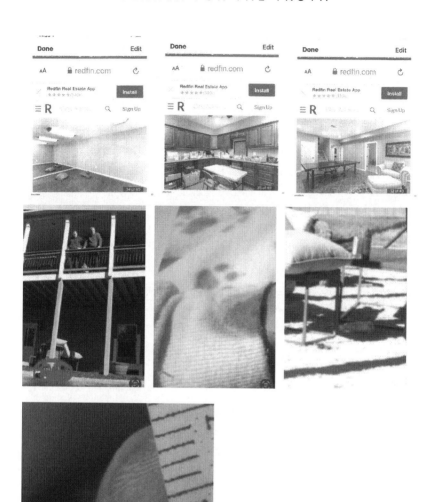

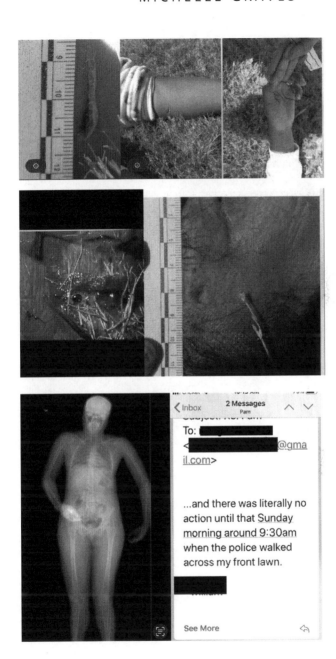

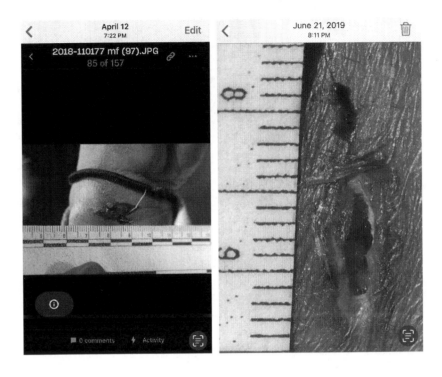

SEARCH FOR THE TRUTH

CASE SUPPLEMENTAL REPORT
NOT SUPERVISOR APPROVED

Printed: 02/19/2019 08:42

Forsyth County Sheriff`s Office

OCA: **2018110177**

THE INFORMATION BELOW IS CONFIDENTIAL - FOR USE BY AUTHORIZED PERSONNEL ONLY

Case Status: ACTIVE/PENDING   Case Mng Status: ACTIVE   Occurred: 11/04/2018

Offense: DECEASED PERSON

Investigator: CHRISTIAN, M. E. (B2775)   Date / Time: 11/06/2018 10:04:14, Tuesday

Supervisor: SEXTON, T. R. (B2683)   Supervisor Review Date / Time: NOT REVIEWED

Contact: Reference: Supplemental Follow-up

On Sunday, November 04, 2018 at approximately 0900 hours, FCSO Uniform Patrol responded to a medical call at   . A female at that location had been found unresponsive and cold to the touch in the backyard of the residence.

This female was identified as Tamla Iana Horsford, B/F   1978. This identification was made both anecdotally and by her Florida Driver License which had been found in her purse inside the residence.

Tamla had attended a combination birthday and football party at the residence the night before. She was a guest at the residence which is owned by Jeanne Meyers. Tamla resides in the   Subdivision and was just spending the night at the residence after the party.

Tamla was anecdotally the last guest to go to bed that night. After saying good night to the host and another friend, she went out onto the back deck of the residence around 0200. This is borne out by the log on the burglar alarm at the residence.

The morning of the 4th, Tamla was seen laying in the backyard by Madeline Lombardi, the Aunt of Meyers. Lombardi went upstairs and got Meyers and her friend Jose Barrera to come check on Tamla.

Barrera called 911. At the request of the 911 operator, he touched Tamla trying to find a pulse or signs of life. None were found.

Responding FCSO Deputies found Tamla face down in the back yard. She was obviously deceased. The fire department and EMS were cancelled.

Tamla was found lying face down in the back yard. She was laying almost immediately at the base of an elevated back porch. Tamla was clad in a one-piece pajama set which was white and had a dog print on it. Tamla`s right wrist was dislocated as if she had tried to brace herself from a fall. Additionally, there were two defects on Tamla`s shins which corresponded with a metal landscape which was part of the yard and was located near her feet. This landscape divider was a piece of metal approximately one eight of an inch thick which would have made cuts corresponding to what was seen on Tamla`s shins. Tamla was lying face down head downhill from her body. Her right arm was by her side. Her left arm was somewhat out from her body and bent at the elbow.

Statements gleaned from the guest state Tamla had consumed a large quantity of alcohol and had used marijuana at the party.

Tamla was photographed and examined on scene with the aid of FCSO CSI Specialist M. Fujimura. Forsyth County Deputy Coroner K. Bowen represented the Coroner`s Office and acted as a liaison

Investigator Signature   Supervisor Signature

40

Forsyth County Sheriff's Office

Crime Scene Unit

Crime Scene Report

Crime Scene Specialist: M. Fujimura

Case Investigator: Christian   Case Number: 2018-110177

Type of Incident: Death Investigation   Date Duties Performed: 11/07/2018

Location Duties Performed: ███ ████████████████████████

Brief description of duties performed:

On November 07, 2018 I responded to ████████████████ in follow up of a death investigation per the request of Detective Christian. Approximate arrival time was 1619 hours.

In the back yard of the residence evidence markers (EM) #1 and #2 were placed at divots in the earth. EM #3 was place at the approximate location of the head of the decedent. EM #4 was placed at an unknown substance located within the grass of the back yard. Overall photographs were taken at ground level as well as from above, the second level deck, for spatial relation. The divots, head location and unknown substance were photographically documented with a scale. A propane tank observed at the rail line of the upper deck was photographically documented in place. It was observed that the top of the tank appeared to have had the buildup of dirt removed.

The scene was departed at approximately 1655 hours.

No further action was taken at this time.

Forsyth County Sheriff's Office

OCA: **2018110177**

THE INFORMATION BELOW IS CONFIDENTIAL - FOR USE BY AUTHORIZED PERSONNEL ONLY

Case Status: ACTIVE/PENDING	Case Mng Status: ACTIVE	Occurred: 11/04/2018
Offense: DECEASED PERSON		

Investigator: CHRISTIAN, M. E. (B2775)   Date / Time: 11/06/2018 10:04:14, Tuesday

Supervisor: SEXTON, T. R. (B2683)   Supervisor Review Date / Time: NOT REVIEWED

Contact: Reference: Supplemental Follow-up

---

sofa.
From there we preceded to the back deck. There I was shown the body of Tamla Horsford.

TAMLA HORSFORD
Investigation into the death of Tamla Horsford was aided by FCSO CSI Specialist, M. Fujimura and Forsyth County Deputy Coroner. K. Bowen.
Tamla was located in the back yard in a prone position. She was laying with her head away from the residence and her feet toward the residence. Her left arm was at an approximately 40 degree angle from her body and the forearm and hand were bent further toward her head in the approximately 10 o'clock position. Her right arm was straight and by her side with the hand approximately six inches from the leg. Her legs were straight behind her with both feet pointing to the right.
Tamla was clad in a one piece pajama outfit consisting of a white fleece hooded outfit with dog paw prints on it and a set of ears affixed to the hood. The outfit was clean with a small dirty spot on the right buttocks of the outfit.
Tamla's body was sketched and measured. Additionally the height of the main level porch was noted as well as the height of the rail.
Multiple photographs were taken by CSI Fujimura.
With the permission of Deputy Coroner Bowen, Tamla was turned over. Most notable when Tamla was turned over was the fact she had come to rest face down. Her head had not been canted to one side or the other.
Tamla's right wrist was fractured or dislocated. There was a large bump where her wrist met her hand as well as a cut over the bump as if the bone had cut the skin from the inside.
There were matching defects on both of Tamla's shins. These corresponded with a piece of metal landscape edging which stood up approximately one inch from the surrounding ground.
Other than the broken wrist and cuts on her shins, no obvious signs of injury presented themselves.
Tamla Horsford was turned over to Coroner Bowen who in turn transported her to the GBI for autopsy.
Additionally, Tamla Horsford's property was inventoried. This was done by CSI Fujimura and myself. In her purse was located a small amount of marijuana and rolling papers. The marijuana was taken by CSI Fujimura for destruction.

JOSE BARRERA
On Sunday, November 4th, 2018 I spoke with Jose Barrera regarding this incident. Jose stated the residence is the home of his girlfriend Jeanne Meyers. He said Meyers had thrown a birthday/ football party at the house. He said she had invited a bunch of her girlfriends over and it was mostly a girl's night. Jose said the only other male there was Thomas Smith. Jose said he and Smith had been downstairs watching the LSU Football game until halftime. He said they had come upstairs at halftime and found food and never went back downstairs.
Jose stated he and Meyers went to bed around 1:30 in the morning and Tamla was still awake. He

---

Investigator Signature   Supervisor Signature

Page 10

Cpl Miller: "And she's fi...She's fine. **I actually know your daughter. We have some mutual friends together** and I've been in here talkin' with her and she's fine. She is fine..."

Cpl Miller: ..."I'm just trying to be very respectful to you. I know it's your home and if you try to barge your way in unfortunately you will be taken into custody and I do not want that to happen."

Jeanne's mother: *inaudible*

Notice he refers to it as a *crime scene

Cpl Miller: "I understand that but right now we are in control of this property because it's an active crime scene."

Cpl Miller: I understand. I understand but this is an active crime scene right now . Even if you show up here you would have to stay inside your vehicle. We can't let you inside the house.

Jeanne's mother: *inaudible*... "I own that house. *inaudible*"

Cpl Miller: "With what's going on right now I do request that you do not come up here. Everybody is fine as far as your daughter and Jose and everybody else there goes.

Jeanne's mother: *inaudible*

CHAPTER 6
"The Cover Up"

———

Police were not called until 8:59 a.m. the morning of November 4, 2018, and EMS was cancelled en route to the scene by first arriving Officer Sergeant Corey Miller. A sergeant who made $70,000 a year in 2018, who cancelled EMS with NO CONTACT with Tamla Horsford ever! Corey was not the officer dispatched by 911 as read earlier. No pulse was taken, the body wasn't rolled over, there was no check for breathing done, etc. This officer did not even know Tamla's arm was broken until they rolled her over.

Jeanne admitted in the 911 call that she did not know if Tamla was breathing because she had not rolled her over. Corey just walked inside and started talking to people after he "observed" the body.

When the police arrived, all partygoers were mysteriously gone from the sleepover except Jenn, Jose, and the aunt.

At some point in the evening Nichole and Sarah left, yet there were never any alarm notifications to Jeanne's phone to corroborate their departure. In fact, Jeanne suggested under oath that they left together for childcare and Nichole did not drink. Bridgett suggested they left for new puppies they both had. According to Nichole, she left alone and merely called Sarah, and they spoke on the phone their entire way home to ensure they both made it safely.

Funny thing, all these women stated this was a sleepover with close friends and everyone was staying over to not drink and drive. Nichole had two dogs, one that was five months old and one that was three years old in March 2021. Tamla died in November 2018. I cannot confirm or deny if Sarah had a dog that was a puppy in November 2018. Nichole gave police multiple times she left, which included 9:30 p.m. when Paula arrived, 10:30 p.m. after the birthday song, and she was there when Tamla spoke to her stepdaughter, which was at 12:32 a.m. Nichole confirmed this in her statement. Tom told police "It was 11:30 when a couple people left." I still don't understand why Nichole would have to leave for a dog, but not her kids. The husband would watch them, but not the dog?

The scene of the crime was in no way preserved and the partygoers were all allowed back in the home only two hours after police arrived, as that is all the time they spent combing the scene. Three days had gone by before police returned to the scene, and considering evidence was tossed at the scene, one can only imagine what was done in three days.

There were never any photographs taken of the home's basement. The only photos were found online when Jeanne put it up for sale immediately following the close of the case. The aunt hauled ass back to Louisiana and has since moved to another state according to her Facebook.

Jose went to get his phone charger from the basement at the same time Tamla (according to the death certificate) was injured.

We now know from the GBI interviews that Jose and Tom were both in the kitchen when Gary arrived with his wife, Bridgett. In fact, Gary hung out in the kitchen with Jose while he was there. The funny thing, though, was that Jose said Gary was not at the party. Gary was not interviewed by the police until the day they closed the case, and he was at the scene the day his wife went back to be interviewed.

The GBI interviewed him two to three times. Later you will read how Gary's stories did not match. Surprise, surprise!

The crippled aunt resided in the basement and mentioned that Tamla had spent time with her down there getting ice and smoking marijuana with Stacy.

This is when Tamla and Marcy had the conversation about Marcy keeping her Florida license for the Disney discount. Police officers were heard laughing at the scene regarding Tamla having a Florida license and joking about a ticket because her license was not valid for Georgia. Jose said at 10:30 p.m. they came up to sing "Happy Birthday" and then stayed upstairs the rest of the evening. Tom told police the two came upstairs to sing "Happy Birthday" and went back downstairs to watch football. Photos and videos showed the men in the living room and kitchen area playing a card game at midnight. Gary put the men upstairs when he arrived between 7:30 and 8:00 p.m. The two men supposedly went to get ice at 10:30 p.m., and Nichole and Sarah left. No notifications of these door times were taken as evidence from Jeanne's phone or provided by Jeanne to the police in either investigation. The police did not bother to get the neighbor's Ring camera footage, or they could have confirmed these departures. The neighbor to the right confirmed he had a camera and saw police in his yard the morning Tamla died.

Neither the police nor the GBI got a receipt for the ice, asked what car was taken, or asked who drove. Nothing was investigated or questioned by police or the GBI. The cameras at the store could have been obtained as well, or at least reviewed. The police should have searched the large trash receptacles behind the store for possible evidence.

Tom told the police he did not get anything at the store because his wife Stacy called him asking for ginger beer. The store did not have any, so "they did not get anything." The neighbor to the right (if you are looking at the house from the street) said other neighbors called police and asked questions and were told there was no information to tell. The aunt told the police she had ice in her fridge in the basement, and Jeanne was believed to have had a refrigerator in the garage as well. Jeanne told the GBI that Tom and Jose had had a cooler of beer in the basement that they were drinking from. Why did Jeanne never mention this in the first investigation?

Bridgett asked on her way to the party if they needed ice for the evening and was told "No" per her November 14, 2018, interview with police. According to her, Bridgett arrived between 7:30 and 8:00 p.m., but her husband told the GBI he'd dropped her off about 2:30 p.m. in the afternoon.

Tom told the GBI he had four Crown Royal and Cokes but did not drink much that evening or often. Tom told police in his first interview that he did not remember what Jose was drinking, but he was drinking beer. More discrepancies ignored by Kelly Aldrich and the Forsyth Sheriff's Office. Tom even told the GBI two years later he and Jose went back to the basement after the birthday song.

Sheriff Ron Freeman, who was a friend of Stacy, told Tamla's father in an open record interview on January 31, 2019, that he could not get search warrants for phones in this case. Why not? The GBI got search warrants. However, two years later, all the evidence had been destroyed. The police never interviewed the neighbors at the time of the initial investigation.

The GBI interviewed them two years later, and the neighbors had a great deal of information that confirmed previous stories.

The police told Tamla's father in February 2019 in an additional conversation at Kurt St. Jour's (Tamla's father) request that what they thought was a camera was really a light.

Jeanne asked Mike Christian, who was the lead Investigator during her first interview, about the neighbor's camera. Two years later, the neighbor interviewed told the GBI that Jeanne told her specifically that her camera caught "Tamla falling face first and she did not try to catch herself." Jeanne later denied this. I have since found out through one of the six interviews the GBI had with Jose that he'd installed Jeanne's alarm system, cameras etc., and he had the same system.

The home was photographed in immaculate condition at the scene. There was no sign of there ever being a party at this residence in the GBI photos, contrary to the photos and videos from the phones of people from the party. So, there were no cameras from November 1–7, according to Christian, but the email is from August.

No door notifications of the evening except 1:47 a.m., 1:49 a.m., 1:50 a.m. and 1:57 a.m. entered evidence, no mention of the garage door and back door being left open, and only Jenn and Jeanne said the back door was open. No one else confirmed that story. In fact, Marcy told police the door was not open when she left at 4:10 a.m. in her first interview.

The garage door opened at 1:39 a.m., closed at 1:40 a.m., opened at 1:40 a.m., and then never closed. After 4:10 a.m., there are no more notifications to establish whether these people were lying or not, and there are no door notifications prior to 1:32 a.m. What happened to all the notifications from the start of everyone arriving, Nichole and Sarah leaving, the trip to the store, etc.?

How can a woman who was eating gumbo according to Jose and Bridgett at 1:47 a.m. when Bridgett left, fall off a balcony alone at 1:57 a.m.? Tamla managed to walk Bridgett to the door, right? Bridgett said she would not have left Tamla alone if she were messed up. Bridgett left three minutes before the back door opened.

The first thing Jeanne told the police in her interview (and it was heard on the body cam footage at the scene) was how Tamla came in and immediately started taking shots of tequila from the bottle she brought, including a shot of Fireball Whisky to "catch up" since she arrived late. Five days later, Jeanne told police that the bottle of Tequila was brought as a gift which she rudely refused to accept because she does not like Tequila. Consequently, Tamla was the only one at the party who brought "NOTHING" to drink for herself that night. The story of Tamla passing her bottle around for everyone to "smell" the tequila is another lie. Nichole passed the bottle around for everyone to "smell" while Tamla was on the deck smoking. In fact, no one was able to coordinate their statement from the scene to the interview's days and weeks later or the GBI interviews two years later.

All those involved, even people not previously interviewed by Forsyth County, had different accounts for the scene.

The truth is the truth and should not waiver, no matter how much time has passed. There were people traipsing all over the scene, including Jeanne's ex-husband, who had no legal business there.

The husband of the deceased was not allowed to be there to identify his wife. Then Jeanne's ex should not have been there either! The police were there. If it were an accident, why not let the husband view the scene liked he asked? Why not tell him immediately? Why make the man wait until noon to know his wife was dead?

Lead Detective Mike Christian told the family during one of their first requested meetings with the police that he was not at the scene and was "on call." However, the crime scene photos taken by the GBI clearly show Mike Christian and Sergeant Miller conversing, leaning on the balcony railing where Tamla was said to have fallen by Jose, thus disturbing the scene. Mike was also on the body camera footage at the home of Tamla on November 4, 2018. Mike texted his girlfriend from the scene. These texts were recently printed in the September 29, 2021, issue of Rolling Stone magazine where he described himself as a "racist cracker bastard" and said that Tamla died from "positional asphyxiation," further confirming the belief that Tamla was allowed to purposely lie dying with no help to save her life.

Christian told his girlfriend he believed the body had been moved, which supports what he told the GBI medical examiner.

Christian told Dr. Koopmeiners on November 7, 2018, that it "did not appear the body fell from the balcony by the position." This conversation was six hours after Dr. Koopmeiners determined an accidental fall from the balcony with no police investigation whatsoever. Christian accused Tamla and me of being "lovers" to explain my passion and tenacity for getting justice for her. The sheriff's office kept this case open for three months claiming they were waiting on the GBI medical examiner to complete the autopsy report. However, the GBI medical examiner, Andrew Koopmeiners, determined Tamla died of an "accidental fall from a balcony" on November 6, 2018.

Immediately following the end of her autopsy, and by 8:20 a.m. on November 7, 2018, "accidental fall from a balcony" was in the system according to an email to Lisa Holt of the GBI, which was prior to any investigation by the police or anyone at the party being interviewed by police. According to Andrew Koopmeiners's autopsy report, he did not start Tamla's autopsy until November 6, 2018, at 1300 hours. It was clear Tamla was never provided any type of investigation by the police or the GBI. The interviews did not start until November 9, 2018, and Jose accessed the case file November 7, 2018, the same day Dr. Koopmeiners determined it was an "accident." These people knew this had already been determined an "accident," which explained their arrogance in the courtroom in front of Tamla's family.

The sheriff's office failed to place Tamla's case on their major crimes page. When the family called the Forsyth County newspaper days after days Tamla's death, they asked why it was not placed in the newspaper or on the Forsyth County News Facebook page. They were told "There were no details to release by the sheriff's office."

From the start, the county made sure to keep this story out of the public eye. I started commenting on this case on the Forsyth County Newspaper Facebook page to get Tamla's story out once Andrew Popp ran the story about Jose being fired. My account was suspended, and I was no longer able to comment on the county newspaper Facebook page.

Home **About** **Videos** **Posts** **Event:**

Early this afternoon we have an elderly citizen go missing. I know her, she went to my church. She and her late husband were salt of the earth. My wife worked for him as a teen. FCSO as usual pulls out all the resources, patrol, special operations deputies, volunteers, drone teams, K9 teams. Weather is about to get bad, we believe she left on foot hours before and no good idea of a direction. If we don't find her, we'll we are all worried. Two K9 teams partnering with our FC Fire partners head out for a third try. We send K9 Flash right, K9 Buzz to the left. Hundreds of yards later they meet on the middle. Try again, K9 Buzz gives alerts and off they go. We find her in a deep ravine by a creek, injured but alive. Tell me prayers aren't answered. Did I tell you her son in law is a local pastor and I'm quite sure there were many prayers being lifted. Happy faces, better Monday.

Head home for a quick uniform change

Home **About** **Videos** **Posts** **Event:**

Head home for a quick uniform change before Citizens Police Academy tonight and dispatch gives out an accident with injuries just a few miles from me. Off we go, reports said driver was not breathing and blue after hitting a power pole and entrapped. I get there first to an unreal scene, power pole about to collapse, citizens have pulled the driver from the car and are performing CPR underneath live wires that could come down any second. I check, no pulse, a 2nd Deputy, an SRO who was already off duty slides up, we grab his AED (defibrillator) which all Deputies carry as his is closer than mine. I don't want to share personal details, but this driver is lifeless not breathing, no pulse. I've seen this too many times, the prognosis is not good. We apply the AED which the Deputy applies in record time, I look over and a sweet lady is on her knees in a ditch fervently praying for this driver. The AED requires a shock, then more CPR by the

Sharon ›

iMessage
Thursday 9:11 PM

Good Evening Diane, I was planning to attend Tam's funeral on Saturday but after speaking to Jeanne, I'm not sure I would be welcome. I understand that rumors are running rampant and people are making wild allegations concerning her death. That is all very sad to me when in reality all should be mourning the loss of a beautiful woman vs trying to be detectives and looking to place

Sharon ›

her death. That is all very sad to me when in reality all should be mourning the loss of a beautiful woman vs trying to be detectives and looking to place blame. Unfortunately none of us were there and none of us know anything more than an accident occurred and a mother, wife, daughter and sister lost her life. My heart breaks for such a tragic loss. Can you please talk to Lee and let me know if I can/ should attend? Even though I had met her

Sharon ›

a mother, wife, daughter and sister lost her life. My heart breaks for such a tragic loss. Can you please talk to Lee and let me know if I can/ should attend? Even though I had met her only twice, I know she was a good friend to Jeanne and her son is a favorite friend of Reece's. Thanks for interceding on this for me. I would like to pay my respects but don't want to be a distraction.
Best, Sharon

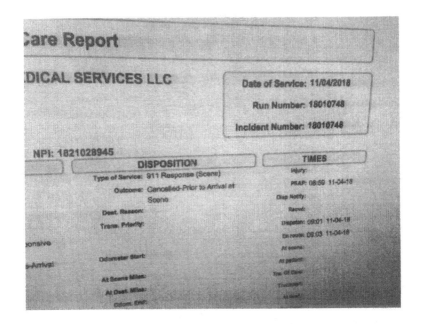

Care Report

DICAL SERVICES LLC

Date of Service: 11/04/2018

Run Number: 18010748

Incident Number: 18010748

NPI: 1821028945

DISPOSITION	TIMES
Type of Service: 911 Response (Scene)	Injury:
Outcome: Cancelled-Prior to Arrival at Scene	PSAP: 08:59 11-04-18
	Disp Notify:
Dest. Reason:	Recvd:
Trans. Priority:	Dispatch: 09:01 11-04-18
	En route: 09:03 11-04-18
Odometer Start:	At scene:
	At patient:
At Scene Miles:	Tm. Of Care:
At Dest. Miles:	Transport:
Odom. End:	At dest:

UPDATE: Two men found dead on boat at Lake Lanier identified as brothers

7/9/22, 7:24 AM   UPDATE: Two men found dead on boat at Lake Lanier identified as brothers -- WSB-TV Channel 2 - Atlanta

Police have identified the men as Scott Landeck, 22, and Brian Landeck, 31, both of Cumming. The two men were brothers, **according to our partners at the Atlanta Journal-Constitution**.

The Forsyth County Sheriff's Office, along with the Cumming Police Department, Forsyth County Fire Department and EMS all responded to the scene.

Police said the believe the men's deaths are a tragic accident. Deputies responded to the park around 11:23 p.m. Officials learned that three family members went out on their boat Friday evening to spend the night. When family members arrived Saturday, the two men were unresponsive. Family members towed the boat to Mary Alice Park.

Mary Alice Park Lake Lanier

By WSBTV.com News Staff
August 08, 2020 at 5:22 pm EDT

FORSYTH COUNTY, Ga. — Police said two men were found dead in a boat at Mary Alice Park on Lake Lanier Saturday.

https://www.wsbtv.com/news/local/forsyth-county/two-men-found-dead-boat-lake-lanier/RHVTENQNYRCVTKWJ5HRBPP4BBM/   1

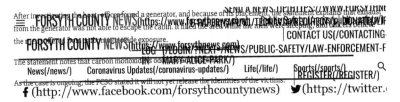

FORSYTH COUNTY NEWS(https://www.forsythnews.com)

LOG IN(/LOGIN/?NEXT=/NEWS/PUBLIC-SAFETY/LAW-ENFORCEMENT-F

CONTACT US(/CONTACTING-

News(/news/)   Coronavirus Updates(/coronavirus-updates/)   Life(/life/)   Sports(/sports/)   REGISTER(/REGISTER/)

f (http://www.facebook.com/forsythcountynews)   (https://twitter.

Local law enforcement found two deceased males in a boat near Mary Alice Park Saturday.

According to a statement published online by the Forsyth County Sheriff's Office, the agency, along with the Cumming Police Department, the Forsyth County Fire Department and EMS responded to a call from Mary Alice Park Saturday in reference to the two bodies found on the boat.

FCSO is currently investigating. At this time, no foul play is suspected, according to the statement.

This story will be updated.

Want more Forsyth County breaking news like this?

Sign up for the Breaking News email alerts from Forsyth County News and get timely updates & special reports.

Email   Required

08-0381-01-20

that he did recall that TAMLA was cold to the touch and rigormortis had started to set in so he cancelled EMS upon his arrival.

February 6, 2019

RE: Tamla Horsford
        DOB: 10/10/1978
        DOD: 11/04/2018

I have been requested by Mr. Leander Horsford to perform an autopsy on his deceased wife Mrs. Tamla Horsford. I performed the second autopsy on November 17, 2018 and based on my findings, I state the following:

I.   Previously autopsied and embalmed body;
II.   No evidence of significant traumatic injuries to the
        a. skull bones (calvarium, base of the skull),
        b. or cervical vertebrae;
III.   Postmortem compound Smith fracture of the right forearm;
IV.   Toxicology positive results in the liver: methanol, 0.420 mg/g ethanol, salicylate, nicotine, and cotinine;
V.   Internal thoraco-abdominal organs and brain are previously bread loafed and dissected in a biohazard bag inside the abdominal cavity

The time elapsed between the date of death November 4, 2018 and date of second autopsy on November 17, 2018 in addition to the dissection of the thoraco-abdominal/brain organs on prior autopsy prevents the precise and accurate determination of the cause of death. A thorough and meticulous investigation should be performed in conjunction with the initial forensic pathologist who examined the body. Comparison of the blood positive Alcohol levels should be compared with the liver results. The absence of hematoma/hemorrhage surrounding the Smith fracture of the right forearm is a sign of peri or postmortem fracture. The absence of subcutaneous/subgaleal hemorrhages or lacerations of the scalp and depressed/linear fracture of the calvarial bone raises the flag to the cause of death as falling from second story of a building.

Adel Shaker signature
Adel Shaker, MD, LLB
Board Certified Anatomic & Forensic Pathologist
February 6, 2019

MICHELLE GRAVES

EVIDENCE OF INJURY

The following injuries are identified on the body:

1. An impacted nasal septal fracture;
2. A patterned contused red abrasion measuring 1.3 x 1.2 cm on the right frontal scalp;
3. Faint red contusion that measures 0.6 x 0.5 cm on the left frontal scalp;
4. Red contusions are found as follows: 1.2 x 0.7 cm at the left upper eyelid, 0.4 x 0.3 cm on the right upper eyelid, 0.7 x 0.5 cm on the upper nasal bridge, and 0.6 x 0.5 cm on the left side of the chin;
5. Lacerated wound that measures 0.9 cm is located at the anterior lower one-third of the right thigh;
6. Linear red abrasion that measures 3.3 cm on the medial left big toe;
7. Linear red abrasion measuring 3.8 cm on the upper one-third of the anterior aspect of the left thigh;
8. Red abrasion measuring 2.1 cm oriented horizontally on the medial aspect of the upper third of the left leg;
9. Multiple red abrasions that range from 0.2 to 0.4 cm on the ventral distal one-third of the left forearm;
10. Parallel red linear abrasions that range from 4 up to 5 cm on the ventral right upper arm;
11. And a sutured wound that measures 3.6 cm in length on the ventral distal one-third of the right forearm, and after removing the suture, it reveals a laceration with compound Smith fracture of the right radius and ulna of the distal one third of forearm.

EVIDENCE OF MEDICAL INTERVENTION

None.

EXTERNAL EXAMINATION

The body has been previously autopsied with a Y-shaped anterior chest and abdominal incision.

BODY HABITUS The body is that of a well-developed, well nourished, African American female, appearing to be in the reported age of 40 years and a height of 66 ¼ inches.

IDENTIFICATION: An identification tag is attached to the right ankle with the following information: Horsford, Tamla DOD: 11/4/2018. Another ID tag is attached to the left big toe with the following information: Tamla Horsford 40Y B F Forsyth County 11/6/18. An ID tag is also located to the left big toe with the following information: Horsford, Tamla DOB 10/10/1978 DOD 11/04/18 @ 1047 hrs. There are black and blue tattoos noticed on the lateral left foot and lower mid back. There is an old healed scar that measures 1.3 cm identified on the left knee.

REPORT OF AUTOPSY

DATE OF AUTOPSY: November 17, 2018   **DATE OF DEATH:** November 4, 2018

NAME: Tamla Horsford   **AGE:** 40 years   **COUNTY:** Jefferson County, AL

RACE: African American   **SEX:** Female   **LENGTH:** 66 ¼ inches

Final Anatomic Diagnosis

I.   Previously Autopsied and Embalmed African American Adult Female

II. Compound Smith Fracture of the Right Forearm

GEORGIA DEATH CERTIFICATE

State File Number: 2018GA008084825

1 DECEDENT'S LEGAL FULL NAME (First, Middle, Last) TAMLA IANA HORSFORD	1a IF FEMALE, ENTER LAST NAME AT BIRTH ST JOUR	2 SEX FEMALE	2a DATE OF DEATH (Mo., Day, Year) ACTUAL DATE OF DEATH 11/04/2018

3 SOCIAL SECURITY NUMBER 193-67-2497	4a AGE (Years) 40	4b UNDER 1 YEAR		4c UNDER 1 DAY		5 DATE OF BIRTH (Mo., Day, Year) 1978
		Mos	Days	Hours	Mins	

6 BIRTHPLACE SAINT VINCENT AND THE GRENADINES	7a RESIDENCE - STATE GEORGIA	7b COUNTY FORSYTH	7c CITY TOWN CUMMING

7d STREET AND NUMBER 4466 AMBASSADOR WAY		7e ZIP CODE 30040	7f INSIDE CITY LIMITS? NO	8 ARMED FORCES? NO

9a USUAL OCCUPATION HOMEMAKER	9b KIND OF INDUSTRY OR BUSINESS DOMESTIC

8 MARITAL STATUS MARRIED	10 SPOUSE NAME LEANDER LAMOT HORSFORD	11 FATHER'S FULL NAME (First, Middle, Last) HURTLAND DELANRDO ST JOUR

12 MOTHER'S MAIDEN NAME (First, Middle, Last) JANICE-ELIZABETH PROVIDENCE POTTS	13a INFORMANT'S NAME (First, Middle, Last) LEANDER LAMOT HORSFOR	13b RELATIONSHIP TO DECEDENT HUSBAND

13c MAILING ADDRESS 4465 AMBASSADOR WAY CUMMING GEORGIA 30040	14 DECEDENT'S EDUCATION HIGH SCHOOL GRADUATE OR GED COMPLETED

15 ORIGIN OF DECEDENT (Italian, Mex, French, English, etc.) NO, NOT SPANISH/HISPANIC/LATINO	16 DECEDENT'S RACE (White, Black, American Indian, etc.) (Specify) BLACK OR AFRICAN-AMERICAN

17a IF DEATH OCCURRED IN HOSPITAL	17b IF DEATH OCCURRED OTHER THAN HOSPITAL (Specify) PLACE OF DEATH

18 HOSPITAL OR OTHER INSTITUTION NAME (If not in either give street and no.) 4450 WOODLET COURT	19 CITY, TOWN or LOCATION OF DEATH CUMMING	20 COUNTY OF DEATH FORSYTH

21 METHOD OF DISPOSITION (specify) CREMATION	22 PLACE OF DISPOSITION CREMATORY OF FORSYTH 150 SAWNEE DRIVE CUMMING GEORGIA 30040	23 DISPOSITION DATE (Mo., Day, Year) 11/21/2018

24a EMBALMER'S NAME BRIAN S TODACK	24b EMBALMER LICENSE NO 4604	25 FUNERAL HOME NAME MCDONALD AND SON FUNL HOME

25a FUNERAL HOME ADDRESS 150 SAWNEE DRIVE CUMMING GEORGIA 30040		

26a SIGNATURE OF FUNERAL DIRECTOR PAUL HOLBROOK.	26b FUN DIR LICENSE NO 6287	AMENDMENTS

27 DATE PRONOUNCED DEAD (Mo., Day, Year) 11/04/2018	28 HOUR PRONOUNCED DEAD 10:47 AM	

29a PRONOUNCER'S NAME KEITH M BOWEN	29b LICENSE NUMBER 9062713	29c DATE SIGNED 11/04/2018

30 TIME OF DEATH 10:47 AM	31 WAS CASE REFERRED TO MEDICAL EXAMINER YES

32. Part I. Enter the chain of events—diseases, injuries, or complications that directly caused the death. DO NOT enter terminal events such as cardiac arrest, respiratory arrest, Or ventricular fibrillation without showing the etiology. DO NOT ABBREVIATE		Approximate interval between onset and death
IMMEDIATE CAUSE (Final disease or condition resulting in death)	A. MULTIPLE BLUNT FORCE INJURIES	MINUTES
	Due to, or as a consequence of	
	B.	
	Due to, or as a consequence of	
	C.	
	Due to, or as a consequence of	
	D.	

Part II. Enter significant conditions contributing to death but not related to cause given in Part I A. If female, indicate if pregnant or birth occurred within 90 days of death ACUTE ETHANOL INTOXICATION	33 WAS AUTOPSY PERFORMED? YES	34 WERE AUTOPSY FINDINGS AVAILABLE TO COMPLETE THE CAUSE OF DEATH? YES

35 TOBACCO USE CONTRIBUTED TO DEATH NO	36 IF FEMALE (range 10-54) PREGNANT NOT PREGNANT WITHIN THE PAST YEAR	37 ACCIDENT, SUICIDE, HOMICIDE, UNDETERMINED (Specify) ACCIDENT

38 DATE OF INJURY (Mo., Day, Year) 11/04/2018	39 TIME OF INJURY 01:30 AM	40 PLACE OF INJURY (Home, Farm, Street, Factory, Office, Etc.) (Specify) RESIDENTIAL HOME	41 INJURY AT WORK? (Yes or No) NO

42 LOCATION OF INJURY (Street, Apartment Number, City or Town, State, Zip, County) 4450 WOODLET COURT CUMMING GEORGIA 30041 FORSYTH	

43 DESCRIBE HOW INJURY OCCURRED DECEASED FELL FROM A RESIDENTIAL DECK	44 IF TRANSPORTATION INJURY NO

45 To the best of my knowledge death occurred at the time, date and place and due to the cause(s) stated. Medical Certifier (Name, Title, License No.)	46. On the basis of examination and/or investigation, in my opinion death occurred at the time, date and place and due to the cause(s) stated. Medical Examiner/Coroner (Name, Title, License No.) /S/ KEITH M BOWEN CORONER 9062713

45a DATE SIGNED (Mo., Day, Year)	45b HOUR OF DEATH	46a DATE SIGNED (Mo., Day, Year) 02/06/2019	46b HOUR OF DEATH 10:47 AM

47 NAME, ADDRESS, AND ZIP CODE OF PERSON COMPLETING CAUSE OF DEATH KEITH M BOWEN 110 E MAIN STREET CUMMING GEORGIA 30040	

48 REGISTRAR (Signature) /S/ GWENDOLYN DUFFIN	49 DATE FILED - REGISTRAR (Mo., Day, Year) 02/08/2019

Form 3903 (Rev. 04/2012), GEORGIA DEPARTMENT OF HUMAN RESOURCES

DO NOT FOLD THIS CERTIFICATE

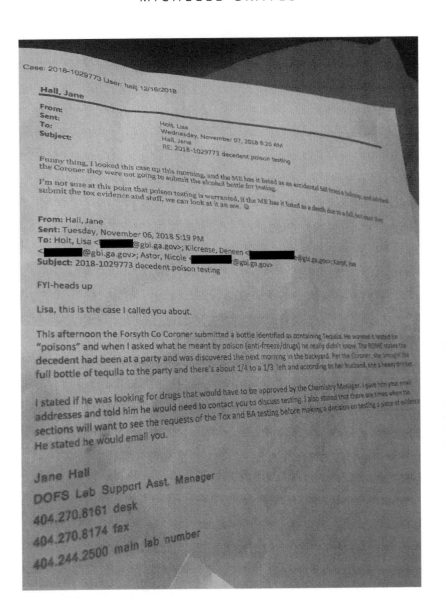

Case: 2018-1029773 User: hallj 12/16/2018

Hall, Jane

From:
Sent:
To: Holt, Lisa
Subject: Wednesday, November 07, 2018 8.20 AM
Hall, Jane
RE: 2018-1029773 decedent poison testing

Funny thing, I looked this case up this morning, and the ME has it listed as an accidental fall from a balcony, and advised the Coroner they were not going to submit the alcohol bottle for testing.

I'm not sure at this point that poison testing is warranted, if the ME has it listed as a death due to a fall, but once they submit the tox evidence and stuff, we can look at it an see. ☺

From: Hall, Jane
Sent: Tuesday, November 06, 2018 5:19 PM
To: Holt, Lisa <██████@gbi.ga.gov>; Kilcrease, Deneen <██████@gbi.ga.gov>; Karpf, Joe
<██████@gbi.ga.gov>; Astor, Nicole <██████@gbi.ga.gov>
Subject: 2018-1029773 decedent poison testing

FYI-heads up

Lisa, this is the case I called you about.

This afternoon the Forsyth Co Coroner submitted a bottle identified as containing Tequila. He wanted it tested for "poisons" and when I asked what he meant by poison (anti-freeze/drugs) he really didn't know. The ROME states the decedent had been at a party and was discovered the next morning in the backyard. Per the Coroner, she brought the full bottle of tequila to the party and there's about 1/4 to a 1/3 left and according to her husband, she a heavy drinker.

I stated if he was looking for drugs that would have to be approved by the Chemistry Manager. I gave him your email addresses and told him he would need to contact you to discuss testing. I also stated that there are times when the sections will want to see the requests of the Tox and BA testing before making a decision on testing a piece of evidence. He stated he would email you.

Jane Hall
DOFS Lab Support Asst. Manager
404.270.8161 desk
404.270.8174 fax
404.244.2500 main lab number

CHAPTER 7
"The Next Day"

———

On November 5, 2018, the day after finding out my best friend was dead, I immediately knew something was not right. I spent every day with this woman. I knew there was no way Tamla would fall off a balcony from intoxication, especially one with a four-foot balcony railing. Also, I was certain she had not tripped at ground level and could not lift her head up because she was too drunk. Tamla would never do anything risky that would compromise her ability to get back to her family.

Thankfully, Tamla and I had a mutual friend we saw on a regular basis, Dianne. Over the years, Dianne happened to be particularly good friends with Jeanne and was supposed to be at the infamous party, but instead was in California on business.

Jeanne had offered Dianne the opportunity to bring any of Tamla's family over who needed closure by visiting the scene. Jeanne did not know this was one of her many mistakes. Investigator Andy Kalin told Internal Affairs that I showed up unannounced and uninvited, stalking Jeanne. This was confirmed as false. Andy wrote a false letter to the police regarding Jose moving Tamla's arm and said I went to the scene and interrogated everyone. He said in the letter that he told me if I did this, the persons involved may not be able to be prosecuted. The Internal Affairs investigation stemmed from my complaint filed December 19, 2018, against Kalin threatening me and pointing his finger in my face to intimidate me. The day I filed a complaint against Jose and asked Mike Christian why he helped the partygoers file false reports of stalking against me, I had the sheriff, internal affairs, three detectives, etc., all trying to keep me from filing a report against Jose or Mike Christian. I asked to speak to Mike. He came down and Investigator A. Kalin stopped me from speaking to him.

Investigator Kalin was still exonerated even after Jose admitted to the police that Jeanne invited people to the house, and I admitted in my interview with Tyler Sexton that Jeanne invited us to the house. In fact, Jeanne threw out another mutual friend that went to the house with us that day, her name was Mandy.

Upon arrival, we were invited in by Jeanne and her mother. We were shown through the kitchen and out onto the infamous balcony. While we walked across the deck clear to the opposite end of the house and down the deck steps, the aunt made a comment that is burned in my brain: "It sounded like people were dancing on tables."

The aunt also commented on Tamla's cigarette butts being crumpled up on the ledge of the balcony, not where they were photographed.

I remember thinking that was odd because Tamla would not do that. She would put them in the ashtray or throw them away, especially at someone else's house.

Tamla's family said the same thing to the police in their recorded conversation with Mike Christian. Crime scene photos showed the cigarette butts balled up outside the ashtray on the firepit. Jose told police he picked up an unlit cigarette and a lighter at the scene on his way down to the body, but he did not know "what he was about to walk up on." According to Jose's statement, he only went to the body when the aunt woke him because he slept through the night.

This 5th day of November, Jose pointed out the large body imprint in the grass and said, "This is where Tamla's body was." He described where her head and feet were, contrary to her position in the photos. In the 911 call, Jose told the dispatcher the police officer (Sergeant C. Miller) could come through the back gate because she was out in the grass. Then says, "Up under the deck." More than twenty-four hours later, you could still see Tamla's body imprint in the grass, not under the deck where the crime scene photos showed her body. Jose said, "The police said if Tamla fell off the balcony, she would have been more over here." Those were Jose's exact words at Jeanne's home. Jose even looked up at the balcony when he made the statement. Jose said Tamla had a cut on her wrist. When Steve asked which wrist, Jose replied immediately, "the right" like he was waiting to give that answer.

While we were at Jeanne's home, she demonstrated against the wall along the stairs how Tamla must have "slid down the wall like this," stumbled through a six-foot section of gravel, tripped over the garden border on the ground, and catapulted out into the yard where she died with both hands behind her back. There was also a table with cleaning supplies she must have knocked over on her way into the grass. Jeanne said, "Maybe she had a medical event, because she had no external injuries." We noticed there was no disturbed gravel to indicate a struggle or that anything took place there. I demonstrated what it might look like to hit that metal border and how you would immediately go down on one knee. You would not catapult unless you had running momentum. Why would Tamla have been running away from the house barefoot?

I made sure to point out that the story made no sense. Jeanne said she, "Just had landscaping done and the house painted, which is why the cameras were not working." Jeanne showed us where the rocks were pushed into the mulch. "This is where she tripped."

Jeanne continued to demonstrate how the crippled, demented aunt stepped out onto the patio outside her basement apartment with her coffee in hand and said "At 7:30 a.m. she went to check the weather and that is when she saw Tamla in the yard."

Jeanne said the aunt specifically went outside and "stood over the body" twice at the scene. However, statements made to the police revealed the aunt said she never went outside. She in fact "walked past the window and saw Tamla in the yard, while making coffee when she went to dump the grinds from the previous day." From the vantage point of the window, there is no way the aunt could see Tamla under the deck where she was positioned when photos were taken. The deck furniture would have made it impossible to see Tamla unless she was "out in the yard" like first stated. Detective Tyler Sexton made sure to emphasize to the aunt, "You did not go outside, right?" The aunt told police she NEVER went outside to the body. In fact, she went and washed her face and said a prayer before running up two flights of stairs twice to get Jose. Mind you, prior to Jose being fired from his position as a probation officer from the city of Cumming and being fired from Forsyth County for "lying," he was fired from Hall County after six months as a probation officer.

Upon our departure from Jeanne's residence on November 5, 2018, at approximately 1:00 p.m. in the afternoon, Jeanne's mother presented a check to Dianne in front of all of us for $9,000 and said, "I want to pay for the funeral." Jeanne's mother also paid for Tamla's stepdaughter, her fiancé, and son to fly to the funeral from Texas.

There were four excessive standing floral arrangements sent to the funeral home on behalf of Jeanne and her mother, Stacy and Tom, Jose and Jeanne, etc. Two years later, Jeanne had the audacity to tell GBI Investigator Kelly Aldrich, that she "felt sorry for a stay-at-home mom who rented a house and had no health insurance," and that is why her mother paid for the funeral. Tom and Stacy rent their current home, Marcy and her boyfriend rent their home. Jeanne's ex-husband also rents his home according to public property records.

CHAPTER 8

"The Funeral"

On November 10, 2018, the family held the funeral for Tamla Horsford at McDonald and Son funeral home, owned and operated by Lauren McDonald, a former coroner and now the state representative for Georgia. Here is some background on Mr. McDonald. Lauren McDonald lost his license to practice and run his funeral home temporarily for a violation I found in public records. In a recorded conversation I had with Mr. Mcdonald, he suggested some "unfriendlys" from Atlanta stole his "unlocked" county vehicle in which he left the keys for a coworker to pick up. During my conversation with Lauren, he said it was his office and the medical examiner that were taking so long with completing the investigation. Meanwhile, the medical examiner put accident November 7th, 2018.

Tamla was so disfigured she was unrecognizable in the open casket. The funeral home made Tamla look like she was in blackface with wet Jheri-Curled hair. When her children and family saw her, they screamed and cried in horror. The image will forever be burned in our minds. When the funeral director, Paul Holbrook, who is now the coroner, was questioned about why Tamla was made to be in blackface, we were told it was due to the severity of her facial injuries that her makeup had to be done so dark. Tamla's lips were reconstructed and did not mirror her mouth at all. Her broken nose had to be reconstructed as well as the side of her face. A deep indention in the right temple was apparent, as was a cut stitched all the way across her right wrist on the underside. We later found out it was to hide the protruding bone from a compound fracture.

Hundreds of guests arrived, forced to witness my disfigured friend. The people from the party arrived, all together of course, playing sweet southern belles, hats and all.

The only male attendant from the party was Tom. The other men—Gary, Mike, and Jose—did not attend. Jose did attend the celebration dinner at the hibachi restaurant following the funeral. Drinks flowing were pictured on Jeanne's son's Instagram dated November 10, 2018; Bridgett was still in her funeral attire. As I was standing in another room speaking with a good college friend who was also friends with Tamla, Jeanne and her mother came by. Jeanne said to her mother, "That's her," referring to me. My friend witnessed this and asked, "Do you need something?" Jeanne and her mother scurried away. They did not attend the reception because they were not invited. After the funeral, the family decided to delay Tamla's cremation and paid to send her body to a private pathologist in Alabama, Dr. Adel Shaker, to get a second opinion of what really happened to Tamla.

It was apparent, they were not going to get the truth out of anyone in Forsyth County or the GBI. Tamla's husband demanded to see his wife after the viewing without the makeup and out of her clothes to document all the injuries to his wife. Scratches, abrasions, cuts, etc., all over her body were recorded by her husband but not documented in the autopsy performed by the GBI medical examiner, Andrew Koopmeiners.

CHAPTER 9
"The Injuries"

———

Tamla's injuries as determined by both the GBI and the private pathologist hired by the family, Adel Shaker, were NOT indicative of a fall. Most of Tamla's injuries were sustained to her face and her cause of death was determined to be "MULTIPLE BLUNT FORCE TRAUMA" as a result of "ACUTE ALCOHOL INTOXICATION." No one else's BAC (blood alcohol content) was tested by the police or the GBI, nor was any type of drug screen conducted to determine all the drugs these people had consumed that evening. Everyone had showered and changed before being questioned.

Dr. Shaker stated in his autopsy that there was no C2 fracture, there was a postmortem Smith fracture of the wrist, no skull fractures to indicate she fell headfirst, and she did not fall face-first because her outfit was unremarkable. Multiple blunt force is a result of being beaten with something, and there was a clear indentation in her right temple where the subdural hematoma was located. Neither the police nor GBI ever determined what instrument made the mark to the right temple where Tamla was hit.

Neither agency addressed how the subdural hematoma was acquired. Not even the forensic expert I hired could say how that injury was obtained. The fall was fourteen feet, how does someone who fell headfirst not have skull fractures?

Neither the GBI nor the county police did any re-creation of the scene with the use of a "dummy" from the balcony to determine trajectory and positioning.

The GBI measured the height of the deck, the railing, the distance from the ground to the top of the railing, and even the depth of the ledge on the balcony railing. No one tossed something resembling a body over to determine an accident, being pushed, etc. Consequently, if Tamla were as intoxicated as they claim, she could have been relaxed and not suffered such tremendous injury.

The GBI failed to ever provide Dr. Shaker with Tamla's blood and fluids, which were requested to determine the true toxicology levels. The police requested Tamla's THC level four times. Lauren McDonald, coroner, mentioned to Leander Horsford that he didn't recognize a certain THC and needed to research it. Of course, we never heard what the unexplained THC complex turned out to be. For the police to run it four times, they did not recognize it either, or the coroner. I find it peculiar a coroner and/or police could not recognize regular THC in a toxicology screen?

According to Deputy Coroner Keith Bowen, except to her arm, Tamla had no injuries significant enough to cause death that were visible when he rolled her over. There was no C2 fracture, so her time of death of 10:47 a.m. meant she died a very long, slow death if she was injured at 1:30 a.m., according to Keith Bowen's notarized and sealed death certificate. Keith Bowen arrived at 9:47 a.m., so why did he wait an hour to pronounce her? Jose said he went to get his phone charger at 1:30 a.m., Bridgett was making gumbo for Tamla at 1:30 a.m., and the door to the garage from the kitchen opened and closed multiple times from 1:32 a.m. to 1:40 a.m. There was an awful lot going on in the house at 1:30 a.m. for no one to have seen or heard Tamla fall off a balcony, especially while eating a bowl of gumbo, smoking a cigarette, and standing on a propane tank!

The injuries first reported by the GBI were 150 milliliters (about 5.07 oz) of blood on the brain, a subdural hematoma in the right temporalis lobe, subarachnoid hemorrhaging, a broken neck at C2, a lacerated heart, a dislocated right arm, multiple scratches, and abrasions on her face. There were deep scrapes and a hole into the front and back of opposite shins but no hole in her pajamas. There was only a small blood stain. Tamla had no reported lacerations to her tongue and no chipped teeth, which would have been apparent from a fall of fourteen feet. Her head "hyperextended," according to Dr. Koopmeiners. In 2020, Dr. Koopmeiners withdrew the C2 fracture. The GBI autopsy left out the lacerated lips, bleeding scratch on her right cheek, and the abrasions to her chin and the bridge of her nose. Tamla's nose was visibly broken, and the dislocated arm Dr. Koopmeiners and Jose referenced was a "compound fracture" with the ulna bone protruding the skin from the underside of the wrist. In fact, Jose was the only one at the scene who knew Tamla's arm was "cut" he said. There is no way he did not see the bone protruding the skin if he remembered which wrist and so many other details. The sleeve was twisted upside down too, the blood from the "cut" was on top of her wrist—not the underside—and her arm was turned up so you could not see the blood.

The stain appeared washed. There were three lighter rings of blood going up the cuff. The sleeve being turned over was why no one at the scene, other than Jose, knew the arm was injured until they finally rolled her over at 10:47 a.m. Tamla could not have fallen so perfectly she hit a spot of water that washed the blood and turned her sleeve over while falling.

There were abrasions between both thighs. It appeared from photos that her jaw was broken, but that was not documented because her face was so swollen.

Her feet had cuts, her fingers and left wrist had cuts, and most significant were the bubbles coming out of Tamla's nose as she was rolled over, which indicated air was still present.

In fact, bubbles were also present in Tamla's mouth, along with drool, blood, etc. Tamla 100% had just taken her last breath or was still taking her last breath. This evidence could corroborate Mike Christian's text to his girlfriend that Tamla died from "positional asphyxiation." My forensic expert, Chris Robinson, said "she suffocated, and it wasn't pretty at the end." So why did the police and Dr. Koopmeiners say she died from an accidental fall from blunt force trauma, not suffocation?

On December 19, 2018, Ron Freeman told me the GBI couldn't do anything without him or the DA telling them to. So, was Ron or Penny the one who told the GBI to say "accident" and called off the fingernails, DNA, rape kit, photos, etc.? Was this why protocol was not followed, and now the GBI has no evidence to prove their original theory or any other theory?

Lauren, who worked for the sheriff's office, told DFCS that Forsyth records "everything with me" because of the tension between us. Investigator Andy Kalin leaned over and pointed in my face and said, "I am going to go to your place of employment and harass you." I said "Go ahead. My coworkers know all about this case and they do not believe you either." I was threatened in the middle of the sheriff's office for simply filing a warranted report about my confidential information being accessed.

I immediately filed a report with Sergeant Garrison, who was in Internal Affairs at the time, about Andy Kalin getting in my face. Sheriff Freeman said it would have been caught on the cameras all over the inside of the building. Ironically, when I filed a request for said video from open record, I was informed by the county attorney that there were "no records found."

Dr. Koopmeiners commented to his colleague at the GBI, Agent Aldrich, that if he had known how big this case would be, he would have taken more pictures of the arm. Dr. Koopmeiners said the arm was the most significant injury. He also could not distinguish between the old and new abrasions, cuts, and/or scratches. His explanation for the lack of blood from the wrist fracture was she'd died immediately on impact when the injury occurred.

The police arrived at 9:07 a.m. and Tamla passed at 10:47 a.m. Dr. Koopmeiners goes on to say, though, that Tamla did not die immediately because now she did not have a broken neck. She died from a combination of the other injuries.

Tamla did not have any injuries that would have proven fatal, especially with EMS assistance. One can only infer Tamla's "twisted" or "hyperextended" neck (what both doctors referred to the neck injury as) may have rendered her unable to lift her head coupled with the brain injury from the blunt force trauma to the right temple.

Dr. Koopmeiners had only worked for the GBI since July 2018 and was only two years out of his fellowship. So, if the GBI did not reopen the case and he was made to answer for his findings, he never would have taken back the broken neck. **Dr. Koopmeiners used that injury to determine an accidental fall and the police used it to determine immediate death from a fall.**

GEORGIA BUREAU OF INVESTIGATION
REGION 8
INVESTIGATIVE SUMMARY

08-0381-01-20

On Tuesday, July 14, 2020, at approximately 12:58 p.m., GBI Special Agent KELLY ALDRICH was located at GBI Headquarters for the purpose of interviewing GBI Chief Medical Examiner Dr. JONATHAN EISENSTAT in regard to TAMLA HORSFORD'S autopsy. HORSFORD was found deceased on November 4, 2018. SA ALDRICH utilized a digital recorder during this interview (see attached).

Dr. EISENSTAT stated essentially the following:

Dr. EISENSTAT had reviewed HORSFORD'S autopsy and agreed with GBI Medical Examiner Dr. ANDREW KOOPMEINERS findings that HORSFORD'S death was an accident. It should be noted that Dr. KOOPMEINERS conducted HORSFORD'S autopsy. HORSFORD'S death was ruled an accident due to her intoxication, injuries, and lack of certain injuries. All of HORSFORD'S injuries could have come from a fall off of a balcony. As far as a lack of certain injuries, Dr. EISENSTAT stated that for signs of any kind of struggle they look for certain external injuries. HORSFORD did not have any broken fingernails, and her fingernails were clean and short. There was no evidence of her grabbing or scratching anything. HORSFORD did not have bruises to her knuckles or external injuries to her neck. There were also no injuries that suggested that HORSFORD had been hit prior to contact with the ground. Dr. EISENSTAT stated that evidence of bruising and bleeding suggested that HORSFORD was alive when she impacted the ground. Dr. EISENSTAT stated it would have been possible for HORSFORD to have bounced slightly when she hit the ground due to the ground not being a completely flat surface.

EXHIBIT ___38___

08-0381-01-20

Dr. EISENSTAT stated that the fact that HORSFORD was so close to the base of the porch suggested a fall. Dr. EISENSTAT stated that if she had jumped or been pushed she would have been further out from the base of the porch.

Dr. EISENSTAT stated if there was ever any new evidence related to HORSFORD'S autopsy that suggested anything more than a fall, he would be happy to review it but due to what Dr. KOOPMEINERS saw during the autopsy Dr. EISENSTAT still agreed with HORSFORD'S death being an accidental fall.

ATTACHMENTS
AUDIO Interview - DR. EISENSTAT

(Attachments)

CONTACT INFO:

EISENSTAT, JONATHAN (DOCTOR)
EMPLOYER:
GBI DIVISION OF FORENSIC SCIENCE
3121 PANTHERSVILLE ROAD
DECATUR, GA 30034

SPECIAL AGENT KELLY N ALDRICH: 7/17/2020
made: 7/13/2020

KA ᴮᴷᴺ

EXHIBIT ___38___

72

MICHELLE GRAVES

GEORGIA BUREAU OF INVESTIGATION
REGION 8
INVESTIGATIVE SUMMARY

08-0381-01-20

On Tuesday, July 14, 2020, at approximately 1:20 p.m., GBI Special Agent KELLY ALDRICH was located at GBI Headquarters for the purpose of interviewing GBI Medical Examiner Dr. ANDREW KOOPMEINERS in regard to TAMLA HORSFORD'S autopsy. HORSFORD was found deceased on November 4, 2018. SA ALDRICH utilized a digital recorder during this interview (see attached).

Dr. KOOPMEINERS stated essentially the following:

Prior to HORSFORD'S autopsy, Dr. KOOPMEINERS was told that HORSFORD was found deceased in a backyard below a balcony that was 25 to 30 feet high. HORSFORD may have fallen or been pushed and had been drinking heavily. No one from the Forsyth County Sheriff's Office attended the autopsy, but Dr. KOOPMEINERS did speak with Forsyth County Sheriff's Office Detective MIKE CHRISTIAN the day after the autopsy.

SA ALDRICH asked Dr. KOOPMEINERS if there were more photographs than what were given to the Forsyth County Sheriff's Office. Dr. KOOPMEINERS stated there were, but said that was all of the photographs that were taken. The reason there were not other photographs was due to a miscommunication with their photographer, and that it is not standard practice to take pictures of minor injuries. SA ALDRICH again questioned Dr. KOOPMEINERS in regard to photographs and there not being pictures with pictures of any of HORSFORD'S major injuries. Dr. KOOPMEINERS stated again that there was a miscommunication with the photographer, and it seemed pretty straight forward in regard to the fact that HORSFORD had fallen and was not pushed, so he did

08-0381-01-20

a standard autopsy. Dr. KOOPMEINERS did not do a sexual assault kit or fingernail clippings on HORSFORD due to it being a standard autopsy. SA ALDRICH asked Dr. KOOPMEINERS why he felt that HORSFORD had fallen instead of being pushed and did a standard autopsy when the information he received was that she could have fallen or been pushed. Dr. KOOPMEINERS stated there was an absence of injuries to middle surfaces of the body, there were no signs of strangulation, and there were minor internal injuries. Dr. KOOPMEINERS did not see any evidence of her being pushed and did not make a final decision until he got toxicology back. Dr. KOOPMEINERS stated that HORSFORD'S level of intoxication led him to believe that she fell.

Dr. KOOPMEINERS stated that his opinion had not changed and he still believed that HORSFORD'S death was an accidental death. Dr. KOOPMEINERS stated that he wished he had taken more photos during the autopsy. Dr. KOOPMEINERS heard through his walls that the autopsy had been reviewed. Dr. KOOPMEINERS stated that nothing he saw during the autopsy would say that HORSFORD was pushed.

Dr. KOOPMEINERS stated that he has only had contact with law enforcement, the Forsyth County Coroner, and MICHELLE GRAVES in regard to the autopsy. Dr. KOOPMEINERS stated that GRAVES sent him emails asking questions, and he tried to have the Forsyth County Coroner deal with GRAVES. Dr. KOOPMEINERS stated that he has not responded to GRAVES due to the fact they can only talk to people who are not family if they have consent from the family to do so. Dr. KOOPMEINERS provided SA ALDRICH with two copies of physical letters that GRAVES sent him and two emails that she sent to him (see attached).

GEORGIA BUREAU OF INVESTIGATION
REGION 8
INVESTIGATIVE SUMMARY

08-0381-01-20

On Tuesday, August 11, 2020, GBI Special Agent KELLY ALDRICH received a telephone call from GBI Chief Medical Examiner JONATHAN EISENSTAT and Medical Examiner ANDREW KOOPMINER. Dr. EISENSTAT stated that he and Dr. KOOPMINER had listened to the Murder Squad Podcast on Spotify relating to TAMLA HORSFORD's death that SA ALDRICH had previously requested that they listen to.

Dr. EISENSTAT and Dr. KOOPMINER stated the following in regards to information from autopsy that was discussed in the podcast:

It was mentioned in the podcast that the independent autopsy that was conducted showed an absence of a hematoma and hemorrhage surrounding HORSFORD's Smith fracture of her right wrist. Dr. EISENSTAT stated that there was blood around the fracture, and that HORSFORD did not survive long enough after the fracture for a hematoma to form.

The absence of subcutaneous subgaleal hemorrhage or lacerations of the scalp was also mentioned. Dr. EISENSTAT said that was not surprising to him due to HORSFORD landing on a grassy surface.

Dr. KOOPMINER addressed the scratches on HORSFORD's arms. He said they were minor and there was no way to tell if they were from HORSFORD's fall or occurred prior to the fall.

EXHIBIT ___67___

GEORGIA BUREAU OF INVESTIGATION
REGION 8
INVESTIGATIVE SUMMARY

08-0381-01-20

On Friday, November 13, 2020, at approximately 12:34 p.m., GBI Special Agent (SA) KELLY ALDRICH received, via the GBI Division of Forensic Sciences website, the following DOFS Reports regarding TAMLA HORSFORD, Leafy Material Drug Identification, Semen Identification, two Poison Determinations, Latent Prints, Drug Identification, Paints and Coating, and AFIS (see attached).

SA ALDRICH reviewed the Leafy Material Drug Identification Report which confirmed the presence of marijuana in the sample tested.

SA ALDRICH reviewed the Semen Identification Report showed that a visual and/or alternate light source examination of the pajama one piece, the tank top, the shorts, and the bra revealed stains characteristic of semen. Chemical examination of the tank top indicated the presence of seminal fluid, but serological examination failed to confirm the presence of seminal fluid. Microscopic examination of the smear prepared from the tank top failed to reveal the presence of identifiable spermatozoa. Chemical examination of the pajama one piece, the shorts, and the bra failed to reveal the presence of seminal fluid. Visual and/or alternate light source examination of the socks failed to reveal stains characteristic of semen.

SA ALDRICH reviewed the first Poison Identification Report which showed that the blood specimen from HORSFORD was negative for Gamma Hydroxybutyric Acid and Ethylene Glycol.

SA ALDRICH reviewed the second Poison Identification Report which showed that the

EXHIBIT ___87___

GEORGIA BUREAU OF INVESTIGATION
REGION 8
INVESTIGATIVE SUMMARY

08-0005-01-20

On Thursday, November 5, 2020, at approximately 1:38 p.m., GBI Special Agent KELLY ALDRICH telephonically spoke with GBI Medical Examiner's Office Dr. ANDREW KOOPMEINERS in regard to the second autopsy report done by Dr. ADEL SHAKER for TAMLA HORSFORD. (see attached) It should be noted that SA ALDRICH previously provided a copy of this autopsy and an audio recording with SHAKER that had previously been provided by MICHELLE GRAVES to Dr. KOOPMEINERS and GBI Chief Medical Examiner JONATHAN EISENSTAT.

Dr. KOOPMEINERS stated that he and Dr. EISENSTAT had reviewed the autopsy and did not feel that Dr. SHAKER'S autopsy report was that different from Dr. KOOPMEINERS'S. Dr. KOOPMEINERS stated that he and Dr. SHAKER noted different conclusions. Dr. KOOPMEINERS stated that he noted some that Dr. SHAKER did not, and Dr. SHAKER noted some that Dr. KOOPMEINERS did not. SA ALDRICH asked Dr. KOOPMEINERS if he saw where Dr. SHAKER said that HORSFORD'S wrist injury was postmortem. Dr. KOOPMEINERS stated that he said it could be post or peri mortem, which is in agreement with Dr. KOOPMEINERS findings that it was perimortem. Dr. KOOPMEINERS stated that is why there would have been a small amount of hemorrhaging because it happened at the time of death. Dr. KOOPMEINERS also talked about HORSFORD'S neck injury. Dr. KOOPMEINERS stated that is agreed that HORSFORD'S neck was not broken. Dr. KOOPMEINERS said it was more of crack which was caused from hyperextending of HORSFORD'S neck due to she hit the ground. Dr. KOOPMEINERS stated that would have not been a fatal injury. Dr. KOOPMEINERS stated that the laceration of the heart along with head trauma would have been HORSFORD'S fatal injuries. Dr.

EXHIBIT ___85___

CHAPTER 10
"First Round of Interviews"

The first round of interviews began November 9, 2018, with Jose. Jose was asked to go to the sheriff's office. Keep in mind, Jose had already accessed the file (November 7, 2018) and seen the injuries from the medical examiner and his determination of accident. Jeanne, her aunt, and Nichole were all interviewed together on November 9 at Jeanne's home. The only reason these people were required to give another statement was because of the severe injuries found initially by the medical examiner. It was apparent Tamla had not just fallen at ground level and passed out as Detective Michael Christian suggested to Leander on November 4, 2018. The partygoers were never "interrogated." They were only interviewed at home and together, including the very first statements written and provided to police at the scene. Jeanne, Jose, Jenn, and the aunt all wrote their statements at the dining room table together, while the others stood outside together waiting to be called in one by one at the scene. Those interviewed by the police originally were not all interviewed by the GBI. Many who were interviewed by the GBI were never mentioned in the original police investigation. For example, Gary was never mentioned anywhere in the county investigation and was never listed on the timeline or witness list. Jose said he was not there, but Gary and the aunt both put Gary there.

The interviews the county performed lasted from five to forty-five minutes and took up to three weeks for Detectives Sexton and Mike Christian to complete.

The interviews stretched through November 20, 2018, and Tom was the last one interviewed. He only wrote a single sentence at the scene but gave a fifteen-minute account of every detail, down to when he went to urinate. Jose accessed the case files from November 7–28 while all these interviews were being conducted.

Jeanne was allowed to interrupt her aunt's interview three times, including once to offer donuts and gift cards to the police right after the aunt mentioned Tom and Stacy leaving in the early morning hours, which was contrary to the story Jeanne, Stacy, and Tom gave the police. There was no seriousness or protocol whatsoever in this case.

Jeanne's Interview, November 9, 2018

Mike Christian began the interview by bringing up the gift cards Jeanne bought and how he couldn't keep them but appreciated the gesture. Jeanne said, "I guess it would not look good to give gift cards before the case was closed." The aunt made the police cookies as well. Mike Christian complained about all the people he had to "talk to today." Jeanne joked and said, "I am going to have to start charging you all rent." Mike responded with, "Get out of my head." Mike Christian had the audacity to make fun of Tamla's boys screaming and crying at the scene, which could be heard on the body cam. Mike texted a woman about the boys "going apeshit." The "apeshit" was Tamla's boys screaming "My mom did everything for me," which could be heard on the body cam. That was who Tamla Horsford was—an incredible mom. That is why she was still in touch with her family while at the party unlike anybody else. In fact, Paula was rushing Tamla off the phone for a meaningless card game. The heinous acts by Christian were found in the open record file of his peace officers standard of training (POST) investigation, as well as in the

September 29, 2021, issue of *Rolling Stone* magazine. I was provided with the texts by the girlfriend he sent them to, who reached out to me on Facebook messenger. As a result of the POST investigation, Christian lost his ability to be a police officer and his pension but was allowed to resign.

Jeanne immediately told Mike Christian that Tamla brought a bottle of Tequila as a gift, but when she smelled it, she threw up in her mouth and told Tamla she did not drink Tequila. At the scene on the body cam, Jeanne told the police that Tamla brought the bottle for herself and drank the entire thing. In fact, Tamla did not bring anything for herself to drink—only Jeanne's gift. The written statement Jeanne provided at the scene also said Tamla drank "her" entire bottle of Tequila and said nothing about it being a gift.

Jeanne and Jose both told police in their interviews that Tamla and Jeanne had an exchange of words, because Tamla smoked pot at her house and Jose was in "law enforcement."

However, Tamla had a joint behind her ear in the kitchen during the Happy Birthday song, when everyone was present. Jose was standing just to the right from Tamla. Everyone there knew Tamla had a joint. Jeanne told the police in her interview that no one smoked pot at her house on Halloween because the kids were there. Jeanne told Kelly Aldrich, Investigator, two years later in her interview that Tamla, Dianne, Stacy, and others smoked pot at her house on Halloween while everyone's kids were present. It appears Jeanne couldn't keep her stories straight and wanted to appear as the southern belle. Jeanne told Mike Christian she did not smoke marijuana and "did not know if Tamla was the only one who smoked marijuana, but she was the only one who smoked cigarettes." This was contrary to the statement Bridgett told police: Stacy also smoked cigarettes. Tom also said Marcy smoked cigarettes. These people never mentioned anything about taking Bridgett's pills to the county investigators. They told a different account of Halloween. We also know the confrontation about Tamla smoking weed at the party was a lie because they all knew Tamla had weed.

Jeanne's aunt lived with her and her kids and admitted to smoking pot with Tamla. Jeanne accused her of smoking with Tamla on Halloween too. In his interview in 2020, Jeanne's ex-husband told Kelly Aldrich from the GBI that he'd had a problem with Jeanne's personal decisions and who she brought around his kids. Jose even mentioned to the GBI that Jeanne's ex did not like him.

Jeanne told Mike Christian she was not drunk but knew "none of us could drive." She explained how her party was a sleepover, yet everyone was gone before dawn except Tamla, who they refused to allow to leave. Jeanne told the police at the scene "everybody" was drinking heavily. However, in court on January 9, 2019, she testified under oath that Nichole did not drink.

Jeanne told Mike Christian that Paula went upstairs. Marcy and Jenn went to bed on the main level. She, Stacy, Bridgett, Jose, Tamla, and Tom all stayed in the living room on the main level until 1:30 a.m. This was contrary to what Jose told the police about how he saw Tamla alone in the kitchen at 1:00 a.m. Jose said he went to basement to get his phone charger at 1:30 a.m.

Jeanne told Officer Waldrop on the body camera at the scene that Jose got water and that was why the garage door opened multiple times between 1:32 a.m. and 1:40 a.m. Jose had no idea what Jeanne was talking about, as heard on the body camera when she questioned him about getting water. Two years later Jeanne told GBI Agent K. Aldrich that she and Jose were having sex just after 1:30 a.m. and he returned "quicker than expected" from getting his phone charger. This was never mentioned to the county police in their investigation. It seemed Jeanne was making an excuse for Jose's absence. Those door times mysteriously never made it into the case file, and there was also no mention of him getting water in the county investigation. I found this body cam footage from the county in the GBI file.

Jeanne specifically told the 911 dispatcher that "Everyone went to bed, and one stayed on the deck drinking." Jenn told the police she was up calling and texting her husband all night, who did not respond until 6:30 a.m. The first-floor bedroom Jenn slept in had a window that was on the deck and stretched the height of the wall, yet no one heard Tamla fall off the balcony or pondered why multiple doors in the house were opening and closing from 1:32 a.m. to 1:57 a.m. Jeanne said Tamla went outside to smoke and never came back in. The door to the garage was left open at 1:40 a.m. and was never shut, but that was not mentioned in the county investigation either. I found it by examining a screenshot taken by the police.

Three months later February 20, 2019, Marcy told the police she did not set an alarm and just woke up. That was until Detective Tyler Sexton prompted her in a call on February 20, 2019, when he reminded her about setting an alarm to go to work for her second day at the Coach outlet. Marcy had the same memory loss when she spoke to Agent K. Aldrich and denied the alarm or getting a formal invite to the sleepover party. Fortunately, the evite that was sent out was in the GBI file and showed Marcy's reply and invite. Marcy had trouble remembering if she'd had to turn the TV down in the living room when she left. She gave the police and the GBI two different accounts of that as well. On one account she recalled the TV being loud and having to turn it down. In another interview, the TV was not loud at all.

Two years later, Marcy said she'd left at 5:00 a.m., which throws off all the door times and the times of everyone's departure. K. Aldrich tried to cover for her by saying it was the time change, but the door notification was 4:10 a.m., not 5:00 a.m. Bridgett texted her husband at 1:47 a.m., not 2:47 a.m., because phones update automatically. Kelly Aldrich confirmed Bridgett and Gary's text messages coincide with the 1:47 a.m. front door opening.

Jeanne tried to tell Mike Christian her alarm batteries were dead, and she did not know how to change them. Jeanne told the GBI that there was a charger she could not find because her "demented" aunt lost it. Jose also mentioned he helped look for the charger. A simple internet search online will show you how to change Arlo batteries. There is no mention of a charger. Oddly enough, when Jose was questioned about the alarm system later, he said he didn't know anything about a charger. Jose told the GBI he had the same alarm system at his house. The batteries worked from August through November 1, after the last email about batteries needing to be charged. Furthermore, Jose installed Jeanne's alarm system, and he has the same one at his home.

Why did the notifications stop after the 4:10 a.m. opening and closing of the front door again? Had someone disabled the door notifications at that time? Jose told the GBI, Jeanne's alarm system that sent the notifications to the phone was completely separate than the Arlo cameras. No camera or notifications of everyone leaving were provided for police. Sarah and Nichole said they left at 10:30 p.m., but police did not request any proof. Two years later, Nichole produced a phone call around 10:30 p.m. that proved nothing. Sarah provided a Life360 app history which could have been any driver in the home. In addition, the car did not travel straight to Sarah's house as she claimed. Tom and Stacy claimed to have left at 8:30 a.m. and/or the "early morning hours" per the aunt. Paula claimed she left at 7:45 a.m. Jose and Tom claimed to "get ice" at 10:30 p.m., but none of this activity was recorded. No one's arrival time, not one door notification from the basement door—none of these times were collected by police. Why?

Jeanne told Detective Christian that "Jose and Tom were not supposed to be there, and that Jose was not really drinking." She said both men were not feeling well and that is why they came to her house. Tom said he did not want to be at the house with a bunch of college girls when she spoke to police. Two years later, Jeanne told Aldrich with the GBI that Jose and Tom had a "cooler full of beer in the basement." Tom told Kelly Aldrich, Investigator, that he'd had four Crown Royal and Cokes. There was no mention of beer. Furthermore, Jose told Mike that he had been bugging Jeanne all week to find out who was coming to the party and that he and Tom did not want to spend money going out, so they would stay in the basement. Jeanne was adamant because it was "burned in her brain" that both Tamla's arms were behind her back, but they were not. Jose also told the police that both arms were behind her back, but they were not. Jeanne told Mike Christian she stood in the gravel after she followed Jose downstairs to the basement "so she could see." Jeanne did not see the fracture on Tamla's wrist when she was standing in the gravel. She told the police that Jose told her about "the cut" he'd described, which was a compound fracture. Jeanne would have been standing over Tamla's body if she were in the gravel. If she'd tried to see, it was because the body was "out in the yard" like the body imprint and crime scene pictures showed. To date, no one has determined how Tamla's arm was moved, not even two years later in the GBI interviews. Jeanne told Mike Christian, Detective, that she remembered Jose telling her it was "personal" for him because he saw her "wedding ring when he was down there and both hands were behind her like that." This was contrary to what she'd just told Christian in her previous statement, when she said she'd followed Jose down to see Tamla. So, when did he go down alone? The aunt woke up, saw Tamla, prayed, and washed her face before going to get Jose. But they did not answer her, so she ran back down to the basement and looked out the window again. Then she finally contacted Jose. Why were Jeanne and Jose the only ones who mentioned the arms were both at her side? The aunt was the first to see Tamla. Jenn also saw her when she looked over the deck. Neither of them described Tamla's arms by her sides.

Jeanne told Detectives Christian and Sexton November 9, 2018, that Tamla was fine, she was not drunk when she went to bed, and that Tamla mentioned going home because she was fine. But Tom and Stacy REFUSED to let her leave! On November 5, 2018, at Jeanne's house, it was Jose who would not let her leave, according to Jeanne. It's interesting that Nichole was there on November 5 and had to do her interview with Jeanne at Jeanne's house November 9.

Jeanne told the GBI about her phone call to Bridgett, which occurred at 9:00 a.m. on November 4, 2018. Jeanne called Bridgett and stated, "She's dead!" How would Bridgett have any idea who Jeanne was talking about unless Bridgett knew something happened specifically to Tamla and was waiting for her demise. Bridgett never asked who Jeanne was talking about. At 9:00 a.m. 911 was just being called and the aunt had laid eyes on Tamla. How did they know she was dead? Everyone at that party knew Tamla was injured prior to their departure, and no one bothered to get her medical help. Instead, the individuals involved went home and went to bed with no empathy or conscience whatsoever. Sarah was the one on the stand on January 9, 2019, who told the judge she left before "it went down." Nichole told Detective Christian she did not know what "they did" after she left. The aunt said she turned on her thunderstorm music because it was so loud upstairs and she "didn't hear anything that went on down here." That is an interesting statement since no one mentioned anything "going on" in the basement and no photos were ever taken of the basement by police or the GBI.

Jeanne called Dianne and I "heifers" in her interview because we made mention that Tamla would never attend a party all night and have not taken pictures. Tamla was on her phone throughout the evening with her husband at 9:23 p.m. and her stepdaughter at 12:32 a.m. Jeanne forgot that she told us on November 5, 2018, at her home, that Tamla took pictures. Yet no photos from that night were on her phone.

83

Jeanne went on to tell Detective Mike Christian that we'd posted as Tamla on her Facebook page, and he requested she send him everything from Facebook. By November 9, 2018, the police had already started their attack and collaboration with Jeanne and the others using Facebook to attempt a stalking charge against me.

Jeanne asked Mike Christian if he'd "got the neighbor's video camera." Mike replied, "We have been playing doorbell tag." Two years later, the GBI interviewed the neighbors, and no one was asked by police about cameras, including the neighbor to the right of Jeanne whom my friend spoke to and who had a Ring doorbell camera. When I spoke to Andy Kalin on November 8, 2018, he too told me that "he" was going to get the shoes and the cameras. Neither were turned up by police.

The neighbor with the Ring camera next door to Jeanne mentioned Jeanne's Expedition disappearing. Other neighbors called the police, asking about details and were told there were none to share.

Three months after this interview, Tamla's father was told the "camera police thought the neighbor had, had been a light." It was clear Jeanne knew her neighbors had cameras, or she would not have inquired about their whereabouts. In fact, she told one neighbor her own camera caught Tamla fall face-first and not stop herself, according to the neighbor's interview with the GBI in 2020. Jeanne later denied this statement in her interview with the GBI.

One of these neighbors even told the GBI that they gave Jeanne Chick-fil-A gift cards for Tamla's husband and boys because their son was in Tamla's youngest boy's Pre-K class. However, Leander and the boys never received the gift cards. The neighbor mistakenly thought that being Tamla's friend, Jeanne would have given the cards to the family.

Jose Barrera Interview, November 9, 2018

Jose was the one who produced all the "scenarios" of how Tamla died, including suicide.

As mentioned previously, Jose Barrera was allowed to "run the show" at the scene secondary to his positions in the county, which resulted in many connections within the district attorney's office and sheriff's office, which were also mentioned in the body cam by Mike Christian himself. One officer at the scene can be heard telling the others that they were at Jose's house. Officer Spriggs, who was at the scene, also wrote in his scene report that he knew Jose.

Jose told Mike at the very start of his interview about the trip he and Tom made to the store to get ice at halftime, even though they had a cooler full of it in the basement, and the aunt had ice in the basement, according to her statement. Neither agency bothered to get a receipt, ask which car was used, or who drove. Why did they need ice when Nichole and Sarah were supposed to have left at halftime? Jose had beer; Sarah had red wine before she left along with Jenn, Tamla was taking tequila shots, and Bridgett was drinking Smirnoff Ice wine coolers out of the bottle, as seen in photos.

Who needed all the ice? There was a bottle of Pedialyte photographed in the kitchen no one would claim. Who needed Pedialyte, and why would you not admit to buying and/or drinking it? Detective Christian does not check to see if there was a fridge, a cooler in the basement where men were said to be drinking, the neighbor's Ring camera to verify this ice trip, Jeanne's door notifications that would have shown this trip. Nothing was done the way a normal crime scene investigation should go because the scene was treated as an "accident" because everyone at the scene "trusted" Jose Barrera.

Paula, Tom, and Stacy all left within a few minutes of each other, yet all said no one was awake when they left. Jenn was up calling her husband in the kitchen at the same time these people left, yet no one saw each other.

Jose never mentioned anything to Detective Christian about the video of Tamla and the girls dancing he took that Bridgett mentioned to police. The video was never included in the case file or available by public record request.

During Jose's GBI interview, when they asked for his phone to perform a search warrant, he responded with, "My lawyer advised me not to." Consequently, the GBI got a search warrant and there was nothing on his phone from 2018. GBI Detective Glasco told Jose not to wipe his phone clean before they got the phone because they have technology to tell if this was done. Jose later told Glasco, "He would do his best" not to delete anything when Glasco told Jose, not to delete anything, he was trying to help Jose. Jose told Mike it was "pitched to him" that Tom did not want to be at his house because something was going on, which was contrary to Jeanne's statement to Mike that the "men weren't supposed to be there and were not feeling well." Jose told Mike he "didn't want to spend money going out." Jose did not ever give an exact time of arrival. He just said that it was about kickoff time. No one can remember what Jose was drinking either, not even Tom, who was with him all night.

Detective Christian referred to Tom as Michael instead of Tom, and Jose did not correct him. Mike was listed as being there in Jeanne's initial statement at the scene because it was in the initial report from Sergeant Corey Miller. Mike was unreachable all night. Jenn was texting but got no response until 6:30 a.m.

Jose told Detective Christian that he and Tom stayed upstairs after they came up from the basement during halftime to eat. Tom told Detective Christian that the guys went back down to the basement after halftime to continue to watch football. Gary told Mike Christian that Jose was in the kitchen when he arrived between 7:30 p.m. and 8:00 p.m., and they spent time together there during his twenty minutes at the party.

Jose had a video on the phone police did get from 11:26 p.m. of when Tamla was trying to talk to Jenn, who was visibly falling-down drunk. You could hear a man say, "That makes three of us" at the end of the video while he was filming Tamla from across the room. Jose told Mike he'd turned on the movie *Shrek* for Marcy and Jenn when he put them to bed around 1:00 a.m. When Marcy was interviewed the first time on November 14, 2018, she told Detective Christian that when she woke up the TV was very loud, so she turned it off before she left. Marcy told Detective Sexton over the phone on February 20, 2019, which was the day they closed the case, that the TV was not loud. It was just on, and she grabbed her bag and left. Marcy also forgot she set an alarm on November 20 as well. She said she "just woke up."

Jose went on to tell Mike there were twelve to fifteen people at the party, which would include Gary and Mike, whom he'd said were not there. Mike, Tom, Jose, Gary, Marcy, Jeanne, the aunt, Nichole, Sarah, Bridgett, Tamla, Stacy, Paula, and Jenn make fourteen.

Jose as well as Jeanne and the other women all describe Jenn as being the "most intoxicated" and "wasted" person there, but she was put to bed by Jose, and Marcy. She was tucked in with the TV turned on for her. So, what about Tamla? If she was so intoxicated, why did no one take care of her to prevent the negligence that resulted in her death? Jenn could be seen falling and dancing in a corner by herself in videos from that night which Channel 2 aired in Atlanta. Tamla was standing on one foot trying to have a conversation with that drunken idiot. She was never photographed intoxicated or with a drink in her hand.

On November 9, 2018, Jenn told Detective Christian when she was interviewed that she was on the phone with her husband at 7:32 a.m. when the aunt went tearing past her to get Jose. However, Mike said he did not talk to his wife until 8:00 or 8:30 a.m., and she'd just called to casually mention she was up. There was nothing about her trying to contact him all night. If Jenn was up all-night texting her husband, then how did she not hear Tamla fall off the deck that was right outside her room?

Jose said he'd stayed on the phone with the dispatcher until Sergeant Corey Miller, the first officer on scene, got there and walked him onto the back deck. Corey Miller was not the officer dispatched; Officer Waldrop was. How and why did Corey go to Waldrop's call and cancel the ambulance without contacting the body, per his report?

In the 911 audio, Jose told the dispatcher to have Corey come around to the back gate because she was lying "out in the yard," then says, "under the deck," which are two vastly separate places. Jose also told 911 he had to put his shoes on to go check on Tamla for them, but I thought Jose already was with Tamla when Jeanne called? He had already been outside because he went on the deck and picked up evidence off the floor because he was OCD. Jose also told 911 only four people had left that were there the night before. Yet, as mentioned before, in this interview he said twelve to fifteen people were there and only three, including himself, were at the scene. Mike asked Jose directly, "What he thought happened to her?" Jose explained how he had to "come up off his heels significantly to lean over the railing." Tamla was not as tall as Jose. So how exactly did she get over the railing by herself? Jose said it was "inexplicable as to why she would be sitting on it." Mike asked if he had ever seen her sit on it and he said no. Then Jose went into the possibility of Tamla "standing on a propane tank to light her cigarette and fell." None of Jose's "theories" explain the cuts, lacerations, and abrasions all over her arms, legs, face, or the broken bones.

Jose denied ever telling Investigator Andy Kalin he moved Tamla's arm when he checked her pulse, per Andy Kalin's conversation with the GBI in 2020. Jose never told Mike Christian he checked Tamla's pulse before declaring her dead to everyone at the scene, which resulted in her ambulance being cancelled en route.

J ose nor anyone else at the scene ever turned Tamla over to see if she was breathing or if CPR could be attempted? Jose just told everyone she "was dead," per Jeanne's conversation with Bridgett at 9:00 a.m. and the body cam. Jose told Mike Christian that he, Tom Tamla, Jeanne, and someone else (he couldn't remember who) were out on the deck "trying to get the firepit lit."

In his November 19, 2018, interview Tom also said his wife rode to the party with someone but couldn't remember who. Jose told Detective Christian "There was a small group of us out on the deck, but in no way was the deck the hang out area or focal point of the party." Bridgett told Detective Christian and Detective Sexton in the transcribed interviews from November 14, 2018, that Tamla never went on the deck alone. Detective Christian asked Jose if he knew of anyone who went out on the deck with Tamla to smoke. He said, "Not that I know of."

Jose mentioned that he'd asked Tom about the propane tank. According to Jose, Tom slid the tank over against the railing because the tank was empty and not a firepit issue. Christian joked and asked Jose if he threw Tamla over the railing. Jose replied, "No, no I did not!"!

As mentioned previously, Jose told police that Gary was not at the party. This was contrary to Gary's interview with Detective Tyler Sexton the day they closed the case. Tyler told Gary that he'd realized Gary had bever been interviewed. That conversation was found only on audio and not in the transcribed statements. Bridgett was so "freaked out" she had to have Gary at the scene to be interviewed by police. With all the medicatons Bridgett was prescribed, what caused her to be so "freaked out"? Bridgett did not complete her GBI interview alone either, Mommy and Daddy were there with her crying and explaining how she was on four Xanax. Detective Christian said she "jumped out of her skin" when her husband touched her. Why did the detectives not interview Gary while he was there? Sheriff Ron Freeman told the family in a recording how he'd personally reviewed this case.

The death certificate claimed Tamla died at 10:47 a.m. The GBI photographer, Jimmy Brown, started taking pictures at 10:10 a.m., consistent with death at 10:47 a.m. Jimmy Brown was also responsible for the autopsy photos that should have been taken but were not, which Dr. Koopmeiners claimed was a result of "miscommunication." Photos are standard procedure in every autopsy. No miscommunication about that, especially when it was the same photographer who saw that Tamla was alive or had just passed when he rolled her over to photograph her.

Jose told Detective Christian that he thought Bridgett was the last with Tamla because she left at 1:47 a.m., but Jose said he saw Tamla alone in the kitchen at 1:00 a.m. to the 911 dispatcher. In one of six interviews the GBI did with Jose, he said he saw Tamla eating in the kitchen at the island. From the basement door going upstairs to the bedroom, it was impossible for Tamla to be seen in the kitchen at the island. Bridgett also told the police Tamla was eating gumbo in the kitchen.

On November 14, 2018, Bridgett told Mike Christian and Tyler Sexton that Tamla walked her out the door and kissed all over her so her DNA will be all over Tamla's jammies. Was Jose waiting for Bridgett to leave and came upstairs when Tamla was "alone" in the kitchen?

Gary, who is Bridgett's husband, told Tyler Sexton "No one" was with his wife at the door when he picked her up. The front door was all glass. GBI, K. Aldrich even mentioned that fact during her interview with Gary. Police ignored that discrepancy when they spoke to Gary because they were closing the case in a few hours anyway.

The Aunt, Interviewed November 9, 2018

Mike Christian started the interview with, the aunt, with, "We have talked a couple times before, but we are going to get it on the record this time." The same was mentioned in Jose's interview: "Mike, you and I talked about that before." So, we can assume before any investigation had started, Mike Christian had been prepping these people prior to recording them.

The aunt told police she had not turned her clock back from the time change because "she did not know how" (The time changed that evening at 2:00 a.m.). The aunt also told police she was able to synchronize her Bose speaker to thunderstorm music with her phone, which she used to drown out the noise "upstairs." She followed with "I didn't hear a single thing that went on down here, I went to sleep right away." So, this sixty-five-year-old woman could not set a digital clock but figured out how to use her smart phone to play music through her speaker. In the early morning hours, the aunt got up to turn down the music, because she thought it would awaken others upstairs.

According to the aunt, she went to take a bath at 10:30 p.m. when the guys went to get ice, even though Jeanne had a fridge in the garage, the basement, and according to her GBI interview, a fourth in her bedroom. The aunt could be seen in the birthday video, which was also supposed to be at 10:30 p.m., just before Nichole and Sarah left.

The aunt said that she and Jeanne woke up Jenn when they went running to see Tamla in the yard. This was contrary to Jenn's interview on November 19, 2018, when she said she was up calling her husband when the aunt went running up the stairs without so much as a hello at 7:32 a.m. She'd thought the aunt was not "a morning person."

The aunt specifically said, "Tam did not seem drunk at all," like everyone else who was interviewed. The aunt said Tamla and Marcy had a conversation about not wanting to change their Florida driver's licenses to Georgia because they got discounts at Disney. The aunt admitted to smoking pot with Tamla and Stacy at the party and speaking to Tamla about how she made a breakfast casserole for her family for the morning and cooked dinner before she left. The aunt then went into the story of how she tripped and fell over the metal garden border (Mike Christian told Leander Horsford his wife tripped over when she died) when she'd had a dog for a brief time. She used to trip over it when she would go out to walk the dog. Amazing that a brittle sixty-five-year-old woman survived multiple trips over the same metal border Tamla tripped over and died. You would think Jeanne would have done something about the border if her aunt fell over it before it took a life.

Nichole's Interview November 9, 2018, at Jeanne's Residence

Nichole claimed to have left at 10:30 p.m. with Sarah to get to a "puppy" at home, and she and Sarah spoke the entire way home on the phone. Jeanne told the police it was childcare the women left for, but there were no door notifications to indicate this departure. Jeanne even testified under oath on January 9, 2019, that Nichole and Sarah rode together to the party, but we know that was perjury per Nichole's and Sarah's interviews. Bridgett told the police the girls left for puppies, but Nichole gave several different departure times. According to Facebook, neither had puppies. Nichole got a dog in March 2018. Tamla died November 4, 2018. There was never any mention of a dog by Sarah in either of her interviews. She told police in a second statement that she left at 10:30 p.m. with Sarah. Nichole also told Mike Christian, Detective, in this interview that she was present for Tamla's Facetime call with her stepdaughter, which was at 12:32 a.m.

Kelly Aldrich, GBI Investigator, requested Sarah's Life360 app history to verify she left the party at 10:30 p.m. and went right home. The picture provided did not verify she left at 10:30 p.m., the vehicle did not go straight to Sarah's house, and there was no way to verify this was even Sarah's vehicle. Sarah admitted to having two glasses of wine. Why would a local teacher drink and drive?

Nichole said her and Sarah both went to bed when they got home. How does she know what Sarah did at her own home? Nichole passed Tamla's bottle of Tequila around the room for everyone to "smell" while Tamla was out on the porch smoking a cigarette according to her police statement. Nichole told police the party was to be a small intimate gathering of Jeanne's closest friends. They did not want to go out and deal with a bunch of drunks. Tamla was hardly treated as one of Jeanne's closest friends. Jeanne along with the rest of her friends could not say enough terrible things about Tamla.

Nichole claimed she did not know if Tamla smoked weed but was standing directly across from Tamla in the happy birthday video in the kitchen and Tamla had a joint behind her ear. She did not recall anyone doing shots while she was there either, which was contrary to both Jeanne's statement to police in her November 9 interview and at the scene on the body cam. Jeanne was heard telling the police that Tamla came in swinging the bottle of Tequila and doing Fireball shots.

Bridgett Interviewed at Work, November 14, 2018

The first thing Bridgett described to Detective Christian was how "Tamla came hopping in on one foot to take off her boots." These were the same boots Investigator Kalin said were not evidence and that Stacy had snuck back into Tamla's house on November 12, 2018. Even Stacy's husband told the police he recalled seeing Tamla's boots when he left.

Investigator Kalin told me he was getting the boots on November 8, 2018, as mentioned previously, but when I told him Stacy brought the shoes back weeks later, they became "not evidence." Tamla did not go barefoot to this party, so why were her boots not kept as evidence like her outfit, bra, panties, etc.?

Bridgett said Stacy went to bed by herself, but later said with Tom. So, was she by herself or with her husband? Bridgett also said Stacy and Marcy went to bed, then corrected herself and said Marcy and Jenn went to bed at the same time. Jeanne said all these people were in the living room at 1:30 a.m. in her interview and that Paula went upstairs to bed after Jenn and Marcy. According to the death certificate, Tamla died at 1:47 a.m. There was no way everyone was fast asleep and heard nothing if Tamla fell off the deck, especially if she was stumbling around or standing up on the propane tank. You would have heard it tip over if she'd tripped and fell from it as Jose indicated. Tom told the police in his interview on November 20, 2018, that he was up still at 1:37 a.m. because he looked at the clock. Mind you, Tom wrote one sentence on the statement at the scene. Three weeks later he told a fifteen-minute story and recalled time specific details.

Bridgett immediately told Mike Christian and Tyler Sextons, Detectives, that she did not put anything in Tamla's drink when they questioned her about the Xanax. Why would you say that when no one has even brought that up, or the fact that she said her DNA would-be all-over Tamla's jammies? There were no pictures of the basement taken and there were no door notifications to verify when the doors opened or closed. The aunt made the basement a focal point of the story because she said she was walking past the door when she saw Tamla. Pictures should have been taken to show where the coffee maker was, trash can, etc. to verify the story and give a synopsis/description of the scene for the investigation.

Bridgett said she was working all night and could be seen on her laptop, a laptop that was never taken as evidence or examined by the GBI or police.

Bridgett told Detectives Christian and Sexton she never let Tamla go out alone to smoke. Someone was always with her. She told them that Stacy smoked too. That was only heard in the audio conversation, but it was not transcribed into statements in the file. Bridgett then repeated Jose's story about the propane tank and said, "I don't know what would possess her to step up on it." Again, Jose was the leader of all the stories and scenarios given about the partygoers to the police to establish a story. It was the same way in court on January 9, 2019. Everyone who took the stand that day gave the exact same story that was well-rehearsed with their attorney.

Bridgett said Tamla was not drunk and it would have taken a lot to "knock her on her ass." Tamla would have had alcohol poisoning and thrown up if that were the case. She said Tamla was not "sloppy and disoriented like Jenn."

Bridgett and Stacy did not tell the police in the first investigation that Bridgett had on a necklace with Xanax at the party. Stacy and Bridgett waited two years and told the GBI, but they denied that anyone gave Tamla Xanax. Bridgett said that she needed her meds and that she would not give out her meds if she did not know how the person would react. Bridgett, Jeanne, and Stacy lied to the

GBI about taking Bridgett's medications and meeting around town to get it. These women were caught lying multiple times to the GBI, and Agent Aldrich made a point to tell them not to lie about the drugs because that meant they were lying about other things. Unfortunately, Agent Aldrich and DA Penny Penn just let it go.

Bridgett made a point to tell Detective Christian that "no one was leaving, no one was driving drunk," but they all did, and they would not let Tamla leave. In fact, Bridgett was one of the ones who'd said she would not let Tamla leave even though she did not seem intoxicated. Bridgett also made the comment, "It wasn't like intention, none whatsoever."

November 14, 2018, Marcy Interviewed at Her Home

Marcy started off her interview telling Detective Christian about how Jose put *Shrek* on the TV for her, and she and Jenn watched it just "a little tiny bit, just a little bit." She was another one who alluded to not hearing or seeing anything because they went right to sleep.

Just two days after Tamla's passing, Jeanne's real birthday arrived on November 6. Marcy posted a picture with Tamla in it wishing an "incredibly Happy Birthday to Jeanne" and said, love you bunches. Jeanne can be seen sporting the historically racist hand signal in the photo.

Marcy said she was on her way to work when she got the call that Tamla was dead, but the Coach outlet did not open until 12:00 p.m. on Sunday and she was notified at 9:00 a.m., the same time Bridgett said she was called by Jeanne who'd said, "She's dead." In another interview, Marcy told police she had to be at work at 10:30 a.m. Either way, officers at the scene could be heard telling Marcy she was more than fine, because his wife is her boss.

Marcy said Tamla was talking to someone at the table while they were playing cards, and she kept telling Tamla to take her turn and play her card. Marcy then said she had to tell Tamla to pay attention and that she "was pretty tired. I wasn't that tired. I mean I was tired, but I wasn't like not able to function." This woman made no sense. What does being tired have to do with telling Tamla to hurry up and play a game?

Marcy told Detective Christian about how she and Tamla "were out on the deck for fifteen minutes" and talked about how they both have boys named Gaven, both were Libras, and they were from Florida. Marcy's excuse for being on the deck with Tamla was because she was "hot." Tom told the GBI that Marcy smoked. Stacy told Mike Christian, Detective, on November 19 in her interview that Tamla and Marcy were on the deck for an extended period.

Marcy said she had nothing to do with Tamla smoking weed and was not part of it when Christian asked her about Tamla going on the deck to smoke. Marcy was the one with her arm around Tamla, singing Happy Birthday in the kitchen with the joint behind her ear.

Marcy said they all did a Fireball shot at some point in the evening. Jeanne told the police at the scene that Tamla came in and immediately started taking Fireball shots and Tequila to catch up to everyone else, as heard on the body cam. Paula said Tamla never took a shot of Fireball. She took a shot of Tequila when everyone else did a Fireball shot because she did not like it. Marcy told Detective Christian she took a shot of Tamla's Tequila and that only a "quarter of it had been drank. Over half the bottle was left." Stacy also confirmed that Marcy took shots from Tamla's bottle.

Marcy said when she left, she grabbed her purse off a chair in the kitchen. She looked in the living room and saw the TV was still on loud. She saw the TV was on loud? When she left, the front door was unlocked. I thought Tamla locked the front door behind Bridgett leaving, which she would have done, according to Bridgett's statement. Marcy then told Detective Christian that the back door was not open when she grabbed her purse of the chair in the kitchen.

Paula's Interview November 14, 2018, at Her Home

Paula told detectives she went to bed about 1:30 a.m. and left at 7:00, 7:30, or 7:45 a.m. She could not recall the exact time, but she was the only one awake. Paula said she was the first one to bed (again another allusion to being asleep and not hearing anything). Everyone else indicated Jenn and Marcy were the first to bed because Jenn was so drunk. Paula reinterated , as did everyone else, at the party, that Jenn was the only one at the party "to be concerned about." She was tipsy.

Paula and Jose both told the police Tom was out on the deck with Tamla trying to get the firepit lit and everyone else had trickled in. Jeanne said she smelled gas, so she went back inside, which is what every good homeowner does!

Paula told Detective Christian that Jose and Jeanne came up about 1:40 a.m. to talk to her before they went to bed. She then said she texted Stacy at 1:45 a.m. but "she did not respond, so she must have already been asleep." Christian never requested those texts from Paula to Stacy, nor did the GBI to collaborate that story. Stacy was not asleep. She had just gone upstairs, according to Jeanne and Tom in his interview on November 20, 2018. They said Stacy, Jose, Tom, Tamla, and Bridgett were all downstairs just before Bridgett left at 1:47 a.m.

Paula told Mike Christian, Detective, that Tamla smoked weed on her own and no one knew about it until the next day. As mentioned before, the joint was behind her ear and not at all hidden from anyone.

Paula told Detective Christian that she texted Dianne about Tamla and that she thought she might have "tripped and fell," but Paula sent Dianne a text that said "At 1:57 a.m. we all went to bed and Tamla went out on the back deck tripped and fell face-first." This was like the story Christian gave Leander at his home: that she walked down the stairs and then fell and died. Two minutes after that text, Jeanne texted Dianne, (our friend who was also friends with Jeanne), and said "Tamla wandered outside for a cigarette and died."

Detective Christian and Paula discussed Jeanne's mom offering to pay for the funeral and to fly Tamla's daughter and boyfriend down. Christian went on to say, "I don't think anyone killed this woman."

Sarah's Interview, November 14, 2018 (Lasted Only Five Minutes)s

The first thing Sarah told Detective Christian was "There was drinking. Not a lot, very minimal." This was contrary to everyone else's statement from the party. Sarah admitted to having at least two glasses of wine and then suggested she left after cake at 10:34 p.m., according to her Life360 app. The county never bothered to get the history or location from Sarah or Nichole to verify that these two left at 10:34 p.m. Two years later, Agent Aldrich got the app history, but there was no way to determine if SC left at 10:34 p.m. It showed a car that drove to other streets and stopped somewhere for 30–40 minutes then went to another street in the neighborhood that was not Sarah's Street. All drivers can be seen on the app, so there's no way to verify it was Sarah and not her husband or kids.

Sarah said she never saw Tamla take anything out and drink it while she was there. Sarah said the party was extremely low-key and Tom and Jose were the only guys there. Bridgett told the GBI that Tamla was drinking straight from the bottle at one point even though no one else ever said that. Not sure what party Sarah was at to not have seen anyone drinking? The pictures were not consistent with the allegations of Tamla acting so inebriated.

Stacy's Interview November 16, 2018

S tacy started off her first statement with, "I sent out the invitations and it was a "sleepover so no one had to drink and drive!"

Stacy told Mike Christian and Tyler Sexton, Detectives, that Tamla brought the Tequila and "wanted to share." She failed to mention it was Jeanne's gift and immediately started to demoralize Tamla. Stacy told detectives that Tamla smoked weed but never mentioned she also smoked until the latter part of her interview. Stacy mentioned her sister worked for DFCS (Division of Family and Children Services) and asked Detective Christian if he knew her. The conversation continued about what she was having (she was pregnant), and how the detective knew her. All this happened while he was supposed to be figuring out what happened to Tamla, not making friends.

S tacy told Detective Christian that her husband and Jose stayed in the basement, and at halftime they came up to eat and played *Cards Against Humanity* before they retired to bed at 1:30 a.m. At the scene, Stacy wrote that her and Tamla and her husband all went to bed at 1:30 a.m. Stacy was the only one to indicate Tamla made it to bed. On November 20, 2018, Tom, who is Stacy's husband, told detectives he and Jose went back down to the basement to watch football after halftime. Gary said Jose was up in the kitchen when he arrived and hung out with him in the kitchen between 7:30 p.m. and 8:00 p.m., not in the basement. Tom did not arrive until after Tamla at about 8:45 p.m. You will read this in his interview later.

Stacy said she was "adamant" Tamla was not to drive home, and Tom also told her not to drive. Stacy told detectives that the weekend before, she did not want Tamla to drive home but she did from the Halloween party. According to everyone else at the party, Tamla was fine. She was not stumbling, not slurring her speech, etc.

Detective Christian asked Stacy if she'd heard Tamla come to bed since Stacy and her husband were staying in the room next to Tamla's. Stacy said she didn't hear anything because she passed out because she was so tired. Stacy wrote in her statement at the scene that Tamla went to bed at 1:30 a.m. when she and her husband went to bed. Stacy told Detective Christian in this interview that Tamla told her she was going to smoke and then was going to bed, which was contrary to her written statement on November 4.

Stacy told Detective Sexton that "the aunt smoked pot too" and that Marcy took a shot from the bottle and there was "a lot gone." Marcy said there was only a quarter of the bottle gone and that barely any at all had been drunk when she was with Tamla. Stacy told Sexton that Tamla "aggravated her" because she said Stacy made "wimpy drinks." Stacy was the only one who told the GBI Bridgett had a necklace with Xanax in it at the party, and Stacy admitted to making Tamla drinks even though several said Tamla only did shots. The aunt said Tamla was drinking water and Tequila, and Stacy said she was drinking Sprite or Mountain Dew with Tequila. Tamla was never pictured with a drink in her hand in any video or photo, unlike the others. Tamla never drank soda, nor did she mix her Tequila with it. There was never any mention in the police investigation of Bridgett having Xanax on her at the party. The GBI requested the bottle be tested two years later and it was negative. Everyone at the party had access to the bottle Tamla was drinking, according to interviews.

Stacy went on and on to Christian about how Tamla had "so much to drink the week before at the football game." Stacy said she drank too, but Tamla had one four-pack of little wine bottles equivalent to a bottle of wine. Stacy said she had four vodka drinks and two shots. I am quite sure that is equivalent to a bottle of wine if not more, along with the weed she admitted to smoking. Wine is approximately 13% alcohol, Vodka is 30–80 proof straight alcohol. Stacy told detectives she and Tom got up about 8:00 or 8:30 a.m., but her husband said they left at 8:00 a.m. The husband said he got up to urinate at 7:30 a.m. then woke his wife up about 20 minutes later. They grabbed the Crock-Pot and left. Two years later, the neighbor said they left at 9:00 a.m. Crock-Pot in hand—the same time police were called.

Stacy made a Freudian slip and said, "I came downstairs, I mean "we" came downstairs. Stacy had to go home and shower and was doing so when Tom got the call that they needed to go back to Jeanne's. Stacy expressed disbelief over how Tamla could have died. She did not think she would have been "vomiting and fell leaning over." Stacy told Detective Sexton she was "acting like normal, laughing and stuff." Stacy even admitted to the police in this interview that Jose told them she may have "stood on the propane tank and fell." This was a clear "collaboration" story and contrary to the "tripping over the garden border" synopsis I was shown on November 5, 2018, and what Christian told the husband November 4, 2018.

Stacy said she was anti-smoking, and Bridgett said Stacy was a social smoker. Tom told the GBI that Marcy was smoking cigarettes. Two separate brands of cigarettes were photographed at the scene, but they were tossed out and not kept for DNA evidence. Detective Christian told the family in a recorded conversation that the cigarette butts were just not something they would keep. Why? It was evidence, especially when the ashtray had already been tampered with along with the scene by Jose moving the unlit cigarette and lighter he said he'd found before police arrived. The police report from the scene said the cigarette butts were on the porch ledge, so Jose moved the cigarettes, again altering the scene. Possibly to fabricate the story she fell off while smoking he came up with?

Mike's Interview, November 19, 2019

Upon arrival on scene on Sunday morning, November 4, 2018, Mike's first statement was "It is a beautiful morning, isn't it?" This was recorded on the body cam footage that was released in the open record file from the GBI investigation.

Mike mentioned not liking the bullhorn Tamla used to "cheer" her boys on at the football games during his interview with police. Whenever Tamla's boys would score or make a great play, Tamla would holler "Can't stop greatness!" Mike told the police that he'd heard from his wife, Jenn, at 8:00 a.m. or 8:30 a.m. Mike told the police the nature of his wife's call was just that she was up. His wife said she was up all night texting him with no response until 6:30 a.m. Mike denied knowing Tamla or her husband. He only knew she was the one with the bullhorn. This man was included in the five from the party who applied for magistrate arrest warrants that claimed stalking and harassment, which were denied in court January 9, 2019. The applications as well as the show cause hearing were both denied and dismissed.

Mike was included in the witness and timeline report and the list of people invited in the initial police report from the scene provided by Jeanne. Mike was not included in the evite thread. Mike denied being at the party both to the police and in court.

Jenn's Interview, November 19, 2018

Jenn was a cheer coach and blamed me for losing her coaching job. Jenn was the one who started spreading the story that "Tamla was so drunk she could not lift her head up to breathe and had dirt in her nose" in the morning. We had a mutual friend named Tina who called me on the afternoon of November 4 and told me this story she'd heard from Jenn. Jenn never mentioned anything about seeing dirt in Tamla's nose to the police, and no one ever rolled her over so that would have been impossible. Furthermore, Jenn only looked over the deck and saw Tamla according to this interview because the "two men there in the morning would not let the women go see." There was a text about this, which meant Tom and Stacy were still there in the morning before police were called. This was also confirmed by neighbor.

Jenn's story about her time calling her husband and the nature of the texts she sent him were inconsistent with what he told police. Jenn refused to be interviewed by the GBI. She told the GBI agents she knew her answers would be the same, and that she did not need to answer questions again. Jenn avoided her phone being searched by refusing to let the GBI interview her.

Jenn told the police her husband "dropped her off," but then she said, "we stayed awhile, drinking, chatting." Jenn spent the night and said, "I knew I wasn't leaving." There was a video from Jose's phone at 11:26 p.m. with Tamla talking to Jenn in the kitchen, and you hear, "That makes three of us." There were two videos Jose took of Tamla at the party. Only one could be found open record. Makes you wonder why Jose was so interested in Tamla and if the two men sitting with Jose were also as interested in doing something?

Jenn talked about when "everyone did a shot or almost everyone did a shot" and did not mention Tamla. Jenn admitted to drinking a lot because "she knew she wasn't leaving." Why did she text her husband all night trying to get him to get her? How many husbands turn off their phones and/or ignore texts/calls from their wife all night?

Jenn said when she woke up "no one was awake." She then said Jeanne, Jose, and the aunt came "scuffling" down the stairs with panicked looks on their faces. Jenn said she put her shoes on and looked over the deck and saw Tamla. Jeanne told the GBI when she saw Jenn, she already had her shoes on waiting for her husband to pick her up.

Jenn told the police her husband was en route to get her while all the above was happening, and this was all before 9:00 a.m. The police were not called until 9:00 a.m. Jenn told the police that her husband said the police officer on scene told him he could leave if he did not want to be there, so he left. Mike was interviewed twice by the police and was included in the list of witnesses at the party and in the investigation.

Jenn said she and Marcy "laid on the bed/went to sleep." She had all her clothes on except her shoes, and started to stir at 7:32 a.m.

Jenn said her husband was on his way by 8:00 a.m., but he said he did not even hear from his wife until 8:00-8:30 a.m. Jenn told Detective Christian that Tamla was found between 8:45-8:50 a.m.

Jenn told the police that Jose looked at her while running down the stairs and turned and went "down the basement stairs." Jose said the aunt took him to the back deck, and on the 911 call Jose told the dispatcher for the arriving officer to come around the back through the gate. Jose told the police in his interview that he took the officer to the back deck through the house to see Tamla. Jenn told the police that she was on the phone with her husband when the aunt and Jose came running down the stairs at 7:32 a.m. Detective Christian asked for screenshots of Jenn's texts with her husband, but they were never in the case file. They quashed my motion to get the text messages during my defamation lawsuit on the grounds that texts between spouses are "privileged." The same month the case was reopened, Jenn filed for divorce and is already remarried. Jeanne is already remarried as well and not to Jose. These women wasted no time starting new lives yet crying they had ruined reputations.

Jenn originally said the police officer told her husband to leave. Then, in the same interview she told Detective Christian she asked her husband to come in the house between 9:04-9:15 a.m. She then said the police officer told him to stay in the car.

Jenn and Jeanne were the only two to corroborate the story of the back door being left open in the morning. Jose went out the door when he picked up the cigarette and lighter on the deck and never mentioned the back door being opened.

Tom's Interview, November 20, 2018

Tom wrote only one short sentence at the scene but gave a fifteen-minute interview to police sixteen days later. Tom even recalled urinating at 7:30 a.m. and looking at the clock at 1:37 a.m. when he and his wife went to bed.

Tom said his wife left their house at 6:00 p.m. to head to Jeanne's house for the party, and she rode with "somebody else" but he couldn't remember whom. This was the third person who'd referenced "somebody else" but he couldn't remember whom. According to Tom, he and his wife rode separately, and he drove "her car."

Tom went on to say he woke his wife up at 8:00 a.m. and they left, which was contrary to the neighbor and Tina's message. Tom made the comment that he left with the Crock-Pot, which corroborated the neighbor's story that a couple left in an Audi at 9:00 a.m. with a Crock Pot. Stacy had an Audi and Tom said he drove his wife's car.

Tom told the police he'd had a couple of shots and two mixed drinks. He told the GBI he'd had two shots and four mixed drinks. Jeanne told the GBI that the guys were drinking a cooler of beer in the basement.

Tom said no one was awake when they left between 8:00 a.m. and 8:30 a.m. at the same time Jenn was calling her husband and thirty minutes after the aunt, Jose, and Jeanne went running through the house. Paula had just left sometime between 7:00 a.m. and 7:45 a.m. She could not recall exactly.

Tom told the police that when they went to get ice "they did not get anything" because his wife wanted ginger beer and they did not have any.

Tom spoke highly of Tamla and said for the past "year" she, Tom, and his wife had gotten close because their son was close with one of Tamla's boys and they played several sports together. Stacy said she had only hung out with Tamla for one month prior to the party.

Gary's Interview (Audio Only), February 20, 2019

The day they closed the case, Detective Sexton called Gary and said he'd realized he was never questioned. The interview with Gary was never entered in the case file and his name was never included in the witness list even though he was at the party. Jose specifically told Mike Christian Gary was NOT at the party. Gary said his wife had not worked for the past several years and he was surprised she had gone back to work for the past year. According to Gary, his wife could not keep a job. Bridgett told the police she was a "nanny" for the past nine years and was "working" while on her laptop at the party.

Mike Christian said Gary came as moral support for his wife, never that Gary was at the party or that he missed the opportunity to interview Gary at the scene. Gary told Tyler Sexton he came in, saw Tamla, and stayed about fifteen to twenty minutes.

Tamla did not arrive until 8:34 p.m. and Gary and Bridgett arrived between 7:30 p.m. and 8:00 p.m., so Gary could not have seen Tamla. The aunt told the police in her interview that Gary came in with his wife and stayed.

Gary told Detective Sexton and Agent Aldrich no one was at the door when he picked his wife up. Bridgett said Tamla walked her outside the door and this was a glass door, no mistaking if someone was there or not, especially at night with lights on.

Gary said he would send the call log of when his wife called him to get her as well as the text when he said he was there. Gary said his wife came out "almost immediately," and according to text it was 1:45 a.m. The front door did not open until 1:47 a.m. The screenshots never made it in the police file, but the GBI put them in their file. Detective Sexton told Gary there was no hurry to get the screenshots to him, considering it was the day they closed the case and their first time interviewing Gary. It clearly was not going to affect the outcome of the investigative results, and it was appalling the police did such a thorough investigation, yet just realized the day they closed the case they'd never spoken to a witness. When Gary spoke to Detective Sexton he could not recall if it was daylight when he dropped his wife off. When he spoke to Agent Aldrich two years later, he thought it was 2:00-3:00 p.m. in the afternoon. Bridgett called Gary, her husband, around 12:30 a.m., which was during the card game. The video provided via Jeanne's phone showed Bridgett was fine and drinking on the couch across the room.

Bridgett's Second Interview, (Audio Only), February 20, 2019

On February 20, 2019, Bridgett and Marcy were interviewed a second time hours before they announced case closed. Tamla's family was notified of the press conference about the case by a news station reporter from Channel 2 WSB-TV, Atlanta, not the police. They were turned away when they arrived at the sheriff's office to attend. Meanwhile, Investigator Kalin and Detective Sexton both told the witnesses they spoke to this day that they were closing the case and no charges were being filed. The people involved at the party were all kept abreast of everything going on with the investigation while the family was kept in the dark the entire time and then chastised by Sexton. You could hear it during the interviews with Tamla's father, like he was bothering them trying to find out how his daughter died.

Bridgett spoke of how she took her "medicine" and became "best friends" with Detective Sexton and Investigator Kalin when they came to interview her initially at her job. Bridget told them how she "cannot tell a lie when she takes her Xanax." Bridget said she did not put anything in Tamla's drink, nor did she give her any upon request because she needed her medication.

Bridgett told Agent Aldrich that Tamla straddled her and grabbed her boobs, and Tamla had no boundaries. Bridgett had had too much and wanted to go home. This was not mentioned in her interview on November 14, 2018, during the sheriff's office investigation. She only said Tamla was trying to get her to be social at the party.

Bridgett referenced not trusting people, and Investigator Kalin reminded her about "the list" he'd provided her that she'd used when "Cumming police pulled her over" and he had "Jason" escort her home. Kalin said, "You can trust me, right"? All this during an "open" investigation these people were involved in.

Bridgett told Kalin how she threw away the lighter, cigarette, and ashtray off the firepit when they were released back into the house after a two-hour crime scene investigation. I thought Jose threw these items away, which he specified to the police at the scene and in his interview on November 9, 2018, when he "cleaned up" before the police arrived. Detective Christian told the family that Jose threw the items away and they only photographed them but did not need the cigarette butts as evidence. There were two assorted brands of cigarettes and several cigarette butts all outside the ashtray. The lighter was on table, which was where Bridgett said Tamla sat and smoked. Tamla was not sitting on the railing or even standing near the railing to smoke.

Bridgett told the detectives she knew what marijuana smelled like because Jeanne's son had seizures and took marijuana drops. No prescriptions were ever checked at the home by the police or the GBI. Tyler Sexton tried to tell

Bridgett that the Xanax in Tamla's system could have been remnants from days prior. Tamla had no access to Xanax prior to the party and it was not found in her liver, so it was not from days prior, but police ignored that. The police never provided an exact amount of Xanax found in Tamla's body. Tyler Sexton said, "It was a small amount." Even after Tamla's family and both friends (one being me) were interviewed and told the police Tamla did not have or take Xanax, the detectives just ignored all of us, and to date NO ONE has said where the Xanax came from in Tamla's system.

Marcy's Second Interview (Audio Only), February 20, 2019

Marcy told Detective Sexton she just woke up at 4:00 a.m. She wanted to get home because she had to work her second day at the Coach store. Marcy never mentioned waking to an alarm in her statement on November 14 with the detectives. It was only in the written statement at the scene. Marcy said she got the call that Tamla had passed at 9:00 a.m. I am still confused how if Jeanne was on the phone with 911 at 9:00 a.m. When did she call these people?

It is not until the end of the phone conversation that she said, "I mean I set an alarm, but I woke before it went off," after Sexton mentioned an alarm. Marcy said when she left, the TV was on, but was not loud or anything. In her interview on November 14, 2018, she said the TV was "really loud" and she looked in the living room before she left.

The story since November 4, 2018, was Marcy left out the front door at 4:10 a.m., that door notification was last one recorded and entered into evidence. Marcy made the comment "Is it a crime to get up early?" Marcy asked Detective Sexton for details about the case, and Sexton said they were closing the case and it was done.

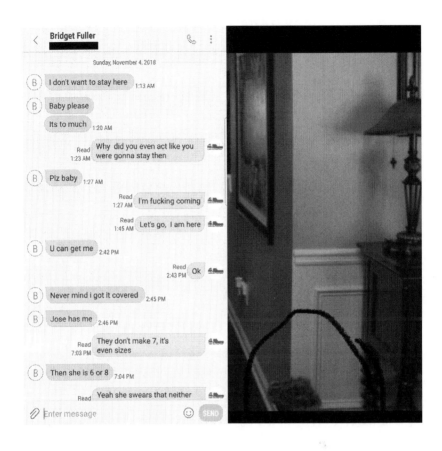

Bridget Fuller

Sunday, November 4, 2018

(B) I don't want to stay here 1:13 AM

(B) Baby please

Its to much 1:20 AM

Read Why did you even act like you
1:23 AM were gonna stay then

(B) Plz baby 1:27 AM

Read I'm fucking coming
1:27 AM

Read Let's go, I am here
1:45 AM

(B) U can get me 2:42 PM

Read Ok
2:43 PM

(B) Never mind i got it covered 2:45 PM

(B) Jose has me 2:46 PM

Read They don't make 7, it's
7:03 PM even sizes

(B) Then she is 6 or 8 7:04 PM

Read Yeah she swears that neither

Enter message

FULLER: YOU KNOW AND IT'S MORE GROWN UP PEOPLE THAT I DON'T TRUST, IT'S NOT SO MUCH CHILDREN. BUT UM, I WAS THERE FIRST, TAM GOT IN LATE, SHE CAME HOPPING ALONG INTO THE FRONT DOOR, TRYING TO TAKE HER BOOTS OFF TO BE CONSIDERATE

CHRISTIAN: UM HUM.

STACY was asked what kind of vehicle TAMLA drove. STACY stated that TAMLA drove a Ford SUV, and that the police drove it from MEYERS' residence. STACY stated that police left TAMLA'S boots so she took them to LEANDER'S residence. LEANDER was distraught when STACY arrived. STACY stated that she had found the boots in MEYER'S dining room, she believed. STACY did not believe that TAMLA wore the boots while she was at MEYERS' residence. SA ALDRICH asked STACY about TAMLA'S relationship with LEANDER. STACY stated that TAMLA loved her husband, and never said anything bad about him.

THOMAS stated they did not hear anything during the night. THOMAS got up around 6:50 a.m. to use the bathroom and then woke STACY up approximately fifteen to twenty minutes later. THOMAS did not recall STACY getting up during the night. THOMAS and STACY got dressed, got their stuff together, went downstairs. THOMAS remembered seeing TAMLA'S boots and belongings. STACY stated that she was glad TAMLA had stayed the night since she had waffled on going home. No one else was up at that time of the morning, the TV was off, and THOMAS did not notice if the back door was open or closed. THOMAS also was not aware if the front door was locked or unlocked and stated he could not remember which door they left the house through. The SMITH'S left in STACY'S white Audi A4 and went home.

THOMAS did not know TAMLA to be suicidal. THOMAS stated TAMLA had different groups of friends and was very social. THOMAS stated that he did not take Xanax and

On November 4, 2018 at approximately 0900 hours, I was dispatched to 4450 Woodlet Court reference to a deceased person located. Once on scene, I went to the back yard and observed a black female face down in the backyard of the residence. She did appear to be deceased. I immediately went inside to gather information from those at the residence. While I was doing this, Crime Scene, the Coronor's Office, and the other appropriate authorities were being notified of the incident and to respond.

CHRISTIAN: RIGHT.

MEYERS: SO THEY STAYED UP HERE AND THEN UM MY AUNT ALWAYS GOES OUTSIDE TO MAKE, TO SEE THE WEATHER BECAUSE SHE'S STILL ADJUSTING TO, IT'S SAVED NOW, ADJUSTING TO GEORGIA WEATHER SO ACCORDING TO HER SHE WENT OUTSIDE SAW TAM, CAME INSIDE WASHED HER FACE AND PRAYED BECAUSE I GUESS SHE THOUGHT SHE WAS SEEING THINGS AND WENT BACK OUT THERE AND SAW TAM. SHE SAID SHE CAME

The following morning, November 4, 2018, LOMBARDI woke up and went to get coffee in the room near the basement door. LOMBARDI went to the window to look outside and saw HORSFORD'S fuzzy dalmatian pajamas. HORSFORD was on her stomach

BARRERA: I HAVE NO CLUE. UM WHEN I WAS ON THE PHONE WITH NINE ONE ONE AND I CHECKED I'D GONE BACK INSIDE THE HOUSE AND I STAYED ON THE PHONE WITH THEM UNTIL COREY MILLER GOT THERE. I WALKED HIM THROUGH, OUT ON THE BACK DECK AND OBVIOUSLY SHOWED HIM WHAT WE SAW AND HE TOLD ME TO STAY UPSTAIRS LIKE UP ON THE BACK DECK AND THAT'S THE LAST TIME I EVER SAW HER.

CHRISTIAN: AND SO WHO, WHO TOLD YOU THIS?

FULLER: UM JOSE HAD MADE A COMMENT THAT THERE WAS AND I DID PICK THE LIGHTERS UP, I THINK WHAT HAPPENED WAS, WHEN HE FIRST WALKED OUT HE DIDN'T REALIZE THERE WAS ANY BAD THINGS GOING ON SO HE JUST PICKED UP THE CIGARETTE AND LIGHTER OFF THE WOOD AND PUT IT UP ON THE FIREPLACE AND THEN PROCEEDED TO THE EDGE AND SAW THERE WAS A GAS, SORRY, A GAS PROPANE TANK SITTING THERE. WHAT WOULD HAVE POSSESSED HER TO USE THAT AS A STEPSTOOL, I HAVE NO IDEA.

CHRISTIAN: OK, WELL LET ME REDIRECT YOU BECAUSE

FULLER: I'M GETTING OFF TOPIC?

CHRISTIAN: I NEED WHAT YOU KNOW, WHAT YOU DID, NOT WHAT YOU HEARD FROM OTHER PEOPLE.

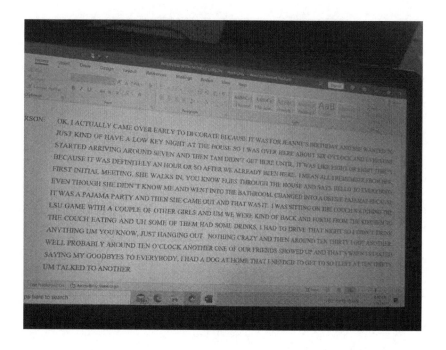

KSON: OK, I ACTUALLY CAME OVER EARLY TO DECORATE BECAUSE IT WAS FOR JEANNE'S BIRTHDAY AND WE WANTED TO JUST KIND OF HAVE A LOW KEY NIGHT AT THE HOUSE. SO I WAS OVER HERE ABOUT SIX O'CLOCK AND EVERYONE STARTED ARRIVING AROUND SEVEN AND THEN TAM DIDN'T GET HERE UNTIL, IT WAS LIKE EIGHT OR EIGHT THIRTY BECAUSE IT WAS DEFINITELY AN HOUR OR SO AFTER WE ALREADY BEEN HERE. I MEAN ALL I REMEMBER FROM HER FIRST INITIAL MEETING, SHE WALKS IN, YOU KNOW FLIES THROUGH THE HOUSE AND SAYS HELLO TO EVERYBODY. EVEN THOUGH SHE DIDN'T KNOW ME AND WENT INTO THE BATHROOM, CHANGED INTO A ONESIE PAJAMAS BECAUSE IT WAS A PAJAMA PARTY AND THEN SHE CAME OUT AND THAT WAS IT. I WAS SITTING ON THE COUCH WATCHING THE LSU GAME WITH A COUPLE OF OTHER GIRLS AND UM WE WERE KIND OF BACK AND FORTH FROM THE KITCHEN TO THE COUCH EATING AND UH SOME OF THEM HAD SOME DRINKS, I HAD TO DRIVE THAT NIGHT SO I DIDN'T DRINK ANYTHING UM YOU KNOW, JUST HANGING OUT. NOTHING CRAZY AND THEN AROUND TEN THIRTY I GOT ANOTHER. WELL PROBABLY AROUND TEN O'CLOCK ANOTHER ONE OF OUR FRIENDS SHOWED UP AND THAT'S WHEN I STARTED SAYING MY GOODBYES TO EVERYBODY. I HAD A DOG AT HOME THAT I NEEDED TO GET TO SO I LEFT AT TEN THIRTY UM TALKED TO ANOTHER

FULLER: DON'T PUSH IT ON ME, I HAVE NOTHING TO SAY ABOUT WHAT YOU DO. BUT I HAVE MY LINES AND JUST AS HAPPY AS COULD BE. AND THEN PEOPLE STARTED LEAVING, NICHOLE LEFT, SHE HAD TO GO TAKE CARE OF HER PUPPY. SARAH LEFT, SAME OLD DEAL, TAKE CARE OF HER PUPPY. STACEY AND TOM STAYED, THEY WENT UP AND I THINK THEY STAYED IN REESE'S ROOM AND UM PAULA WENT UP AND STAYED IN EMMA'S ROOM.

Jeanne told me Nicole and Sarah had left around 2230 hours due to childcare issues. Bridgette left at 0147 hours, and Marcy left at 0410 hours. All other parties stayed the night and left the morning of the 4th to her knowledge.

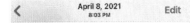

Posts

📷 **Photos**

████████ **Renée** updated her ···
cover photo.
4d · 🌐

███████ I wanted to
comment on your Easter
picture. Beautiful. Those
dogs look exactly like my
brother's. So cute. How
old are they?

9h   Like   Reply

  ████████ **Renée**
  Jenny Rosa thank you.
  One of the dogs is 3 and
  the other is almost 5
  months.

  Apr 4, 2021 · 🌐

My Baby Girl 😊 👯 💜 (2)   12:32 AM
FaceTime Video

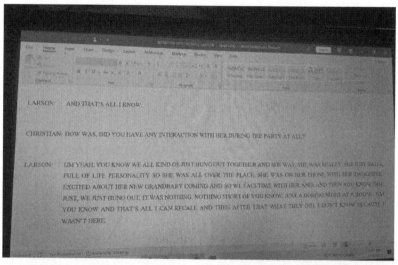

LARSON: AND THAT'S ALL I KNOW.

CHRISTIAN: HOW WAS, DID YOU HAVE ANY INTERACTION WITH HER DURING THE PARTY AT ALL?

LARSON: UM YEAH, YOU KNOW WE ALL KIND OF JUST HUNG OUT TOGETHER AND SHE WAS, SHE WAS REALLY, SHE JUST HAD A FULL OF LIFE PERSONALITY SO SHE WAS ALL OVER THE PLACE, SHE WAS ON HER PHONE WITH HER DAUGHTER EXCITED ABOUT HER NEW GRANDBABY COMING AND SO WE FACETIME WITH HER AND, AND THEN YOU KNOW SHE JUST, WE JUST HUNG OUT, IT WAS NOTHING, NOTHING SHORT OF YOU KNOW, JUST A BORING NIGHT AT A HOUSE, YOU YOU KNOW AND THAT'S ALL I CAN RECALL AND THEN AFTER THAT WHAT THEY DID, I DON'T KNOW BECAUSE I WASN'T HERE.

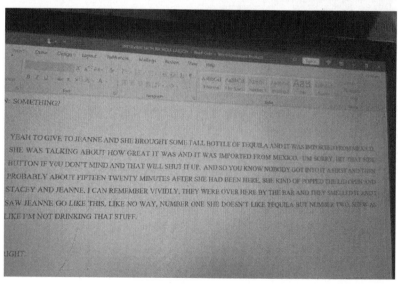

N: SOMETHING?

YEAH TO GIVE TO JEANNE AND SHE BROUGHT SOME TALL BOTTLE OF TEQUILA AND IT WAS IMPORTED FROM MEXICO. SHE WAS TALKING ABOUT HOW GREAT IT WAS AND IT WAS IMPORTED FROM MEXICO. UM SORRY, HIT THAT SIDE BUTTON IF YOU DON'T MIND AND THAT WILL SHUT IT UP. AND SO YOU KNOW NOBODY GOT INTO IT A FIRST AND THEN PROBABLY ABOUT FIFTEEN TWENTY MINUTES AFTER SHE HAD BEEN HERE, SHE KIND OF POPPED THE LID OPEN AND STACEY AND JEANNE, I CAN REMEMBER VIVIDLY, THEY WERE OVER HERE BY THE BAR AND THEY SMELLED IT AND I SAW JEANNE GO LIKE THIS, LIKE NO WAY, NUMBER ONE SHE DOESN'T LIKE TEQUILA BUT NUMBER TWO, SHE'S AS LIKE I'M NOT DRINKING THAT STUFF.

IGHT.

MICHELLE GRAVES

CASE NUMBER: 2018-11 0777

Name: Jeanne Meyers   Employer:
Address: Address:
City: State: City: State:
Zip   Phone: Zip: Phone:
DOB: 73 Sex: F Place of Birth: Email
Race: W   Height: 5'1 Weight: 130 Hair: Blonde   Eyes: Blue

DESCRIBE IN DETAIL AND IN YOUR OWN WORDS, THE EVENTS OF THE INCIDENT OR ACCIDENT:

People started to arrive for my birthday girls night 11/3 sleepover. We had drinks and food. Most got here at 7-7am arrive. Everyone 18-30 we were watching the ISU game and drinking and socializing. Most were drinking heavily. We played a card game that ended around 1. Many of us went to bed by 1:30, approximately woken up at 8:50am by my aunt Madeline Lombardi to tell me that Pam was faced down in the backyard & not moving. I immediately called 911.

BARRERA: UH I MEAN, SHE KNOCKED ON THE DOOR, I NEED JOSE, OK, I'M WORRIED ABOUT ONE OF YOUR FRIENDS, I WAS LIKE OK, SHE WENT OUT OF THE ROOM, GOT DRESSED AND JEANNE WAS LIKE DO I NEED MY PHONE, I SAID GRAB IT JUST IN CASE, WENT DOWN AND I MEAN I JUST MADE MY WAY ALL THE WAY DOWN

SEXTON: OK.

BARRERA: AND UH

SEXTON: WHERE DID SHE TAKE YOU TO?

BARRERA: UH BACK DECK.

SEXTON: OK.

BARRERA: SO WENT OUT ON THE BACK DECK, SAW HER LAYING THERE, WENT DOWN TO CHECK ON HER AND THEN TOLD JEANNE THAT, I THINK SHE WAS ALREADY ON THE PHONE WITH NINE ONE ONE.

At approximately 1:00 or 2:00 a.m., everyone started getting ready for bed. BARRERA showed HARDIN and MORRELL where they would be sleeping on the main level of the house. THOMAS and STACY had already gone to bed by that time. THOMAS and STACY were sleeping on the top floor. SEALS also slept in a bed on the top floor.

BARRERA went to the basement to get a phone charger. BARRERA came up the stairs to the main floor and saw HORSFORD standing in the kitchen. BARRERA did not see anyone else with her. BARRERA continued upstairs to go to sleep with MEYERS on the top floor.

The morning of November 4, 2018, BARRERA was sleeping with MEYERS in MEYERS' room. LOMBARDI knocked on the door and said she needed BARRERA. BARRERA followed LOMBARDI to the main level of the house and walked on the back porch and saw HORSFORD lying in the backyard facedown.

BARRERA went down the steps and tapped on the back of HORSFORD'S leg. HORSFORD did not respond. BARRERA found HORSFORD'S body to be stiff when he tapped her. BARRERA knew she was dead and did not try to resuscitate.

As BARRERA was walking out onto the deck, he saw a cigarette lying on the deck. BARRERA picked the cigarette up and laid it on a table. BARRERA did this before he knew what LOMBARDI was trying to show him. BARRERA could not clearly recall if the item he picked up was a cigarette, a lighter, or both.

117

MORRELL: I STARTED TO STIR, I THINK I WISH I KNEW WHEN I TEXT MIKE, BUT IT WAS BETWEEN SEVEN THIRTY AND EIGHT BECAUSE BY ABOUT

CHRISTIAN: IS ON YOUR PHONE?

MORRELL: WELL, IT MIGHT BE ACTUALLY BECAUSE I DON'T USUALLY DELETE HIS TEXT SO LET ME GET THAT GOING. UM BY EIGHT O'CLOCK I HAD HIM IN GEAR TO COME AND GET ME.

CHRISTIAN: OK.

MORRELL: SO IT WAS PROBABLY SEVEN THIRTY OR SO, SEVEN FORTY-FIVE. I'LL GO BACK, I'LL WORK ON GETTING BACK TO IT.

CHRISTIAN: OK. AND SO YOU SAW MADELINE OR MADELINE AND

MORRELL: SHE CAME TEARING THROUGH THE KITCHEN AND I SAID GOOD MORNING AND SHE WAS LIKE, HI, KIND OF A WEIRD HI AND I WAS LIKE, THINKING NOT A MORNING PERSON,

CHRISTIAN: UM HUM.

MORRELL: I STILL DIDN'T HAVE ANY IDEA. UM AND THAT'S ABOUT WHEN JOSE

CHRISTIAN: RIGHT.

MORRELL: CAME STORMING DOWN THE STAIRS AND I SAID WHAT'S GOING ON AND HE JUST LOOKED AT ME, TURNED AND WENT DOWN THE BASEMENT STAIRS I BELIEVE TO GO OUTSIDE AND JEANNE CAME DOWN BEHIND HIM AND THAT'S WHEN SHE SAID TAM'S NOT MOVING. I WENT TO GT MY SHOES ON, THEY WERE BY THE FRONT DOOR, SO I DON'T KNOW WHAT JEANNE WAS DOING. I DON'T KNOW IF SHE WENT DOWN STAIRS AND CAME BACK UP OR IF SHE STAYED UPSTAIRS AND WAS JUST CALLING NINE ONE, ONE, I'M KIND OF

HARDIN: AND THEN AFTER THAT, WE DIDN'T EVEN FINISH THE GAME, EVERYBODY WAS TOO DISTRACTED TAKING AND JUST HANGING OUT OR WHATEVER, SO ME AND JEN GOT UP, JEN MORELL UM I'D SAY AROUND TWELVE THIRTY, TWELVE FORTY-FIVE, I MADE HER GET UP AND HAD JOSE PUT IN A MOVIE, WE WATCHED SHREK FOR A LITTLE TINY BIT, JUST A LITTLE BIT AND THEN WE WENT TO SLEEP. BUT NY THE TIME WE WERE IN THE BEDROOM, YOU COULD STILL HEAR PEOPLE OUT IN THE LIVING ROOM TALKING AND THERE WAS A TV ON OUT THERE AS WELL TOO. UM JEANNE TRIED TO LIKE ENCOURAGE PEOPLE TO GO TO BED BECAUSE SHE WAS TIRED AND WANTED TO GO TO BED TOO. SO SHE PROBABLY I DON'T KNOW, SHE WENT UPSTAIRS ABOUT THE SAME TIME AS ME AND JEN WENT AND LAID DOWN. BUT I KNOW SHE HAD PICKED UP LIKE THE LIVING ROOM AND PUT ALL THE PILLOWS ON THE COUCH ALL NICE AND NEAT BEFORE SHE WENT TO BED, WHICH WAS KIND OF TELLING US ALL HEY GUYS I'M TIRED.

At approximately 1:15 a.m. SEALS went to bed upstairs. SEALS believed the last she saw HORSFORD, she was in the kitchen. Approximately twenty minutes after going upstairs SEALS saw MEYERS and BARRERA. MEYERS and BARRERA told SEALS goodnight and went into their room to go to sleep.

SEALS recalled the time changed that evening. Between 7:45 and 8:00 a.m. SEALS woke up and left the residence to return to her home. SEALS walked out the front door. SEALS did not recall seeing anyone and did not see anything suspicious. SEALS could not recall if the doors were locked or unlocked. SEALS did recall seeing what

MORRELL: SO, THE NEXT MORNING WHEN I GOT UP, THERE WAS NO ONE AWAKE AND I HAD NO IDEA WHO WAS IN THE GUEST BED OR WHO WASN'T. SO AS IT TURNS OUT, IT WAS UM MYSELF, JEANNE, JOSE AND JEANNE'S AUNT MADELINE AND SCUFFLING DOWN THE STAIRS UM PANIC LOOKS ON JOSE AND JEANNE'S FACE, I SAID WHAT'S GOING ON, SHE SAID TAM'S IN THE BACKYARD NOT MOVING. UM AS SOON AS I COULD GET MY SHOES ON I WENT OUT ON THE DECK AND LOOKED OVER BECAUSE I THOUGHT THAT CAN'T BE, SHE'S PROBABLY JUST PASSED OUT, BUT WHEN I SAW HER I THOUGHT THAT DOESN'T LOOK GOOD AT ALL. SHE YOU KNOW, SOMETHING IS WRONG, DEFINITELY WRONG AND THEN IT ALL HAPPENED REALLY QUICKLY, I MEAN, SHE HAD CALLED NINE ONE, ONE, MY HUSBAND WAS ENROUTE TO GET ME, THIS IS ALL BEFORE NINE O'CLOCK IN THE MORNING AND HE GOT THERE AND WE BASICALLY, THE COPS CAME RIGHT AS HE'S PULLING UP, THEY COME RIGHT BEHIND HIM AND KIND OF SAID LOOK, IF YOU DON'T WANT TO BE HERE HER HOURS YOU MIGHT JUST WANT TO GO UM SO HE DID AND I WAS TEXTING HIM AND THEN WE WERE KIND OF SHUFFLED INTO THE DINING ROOM

SEALS: WHEN I GOT UP UM JUST BECAUSE I WAS BEING QUIET GETTING OUT THE DOOR YOU KNOW, I WAS LIKE DON'T WAKE ANYBODY UP AND I HAD ALL ME STUFF IN REECE'S ROOM, LIKE MY BAG, CELLPHONE AND EVERYTHING WAS WITH ME.

SEXTON: YEAH.

SEALS: SO I GRABBED MY STUFF AND I JUST WENT (INAUDIBLE) DOOR.

SEXTON: AND THAT WAS ABOUT WHAT TIME?

SEALS: I THINK IT LIKE SEVEN, SEVEN THIRTY OR SEVEN FORTY-FIVE. I CAN'T EXACTLY RECALL.

SEXTON: WAS ANYBODY ELSE UP MOVING AROUND?

SEALS: NOBODY ELSE WAS UP AND I DO RECALL LIKE WHEN I, WHEN I CAME DOWN THE STAIRS I REMEMBER SEEING UM STACY AND TAM'S PHONE ON THE THING.

upstairs around the same time. FULLER was cleaning and heating up some gumbo. HORSFORD started to eat the gumbo and said she was going to smoke a cigarette and then come upstairs. After they got upstairs BARRERA went back down to the basement to get his phone charger and came right back. MEYERS stated that she felt

LOMBARDI: SO UM I DIDN'T START THE COFFEE, I, I GOT ON MY KNEES AND I SAID A PRAYER AND THEN I RAN UPSTAIRS AND I KNOCKED ON THE DOOR AND I THOUGHT I HEARD WATER RUNNING AND I THOUGHT MAYBE IT WAS JEANNE TAKING A SHOWER SO I WENT DOWNSTAIRS BECAUSE I WAS LIKE THINKING I SHOULDN'T WAKE UP, MAYBE SHE'S UP, SO I WENT DOWNSTAIRS AND I LOOKED OUT THE WINDOW AGAIN AND IT WAS JUST LIKE I COULDN'T BELIEVE MY EYES, I WAS SAYING INSIDE MY HEAD, SHE'S NOT MOVING, SHE'S NOT MOVING. SO THEN I WENT AND KNOCKED ON THE DOOR LOUDER.

SEXTON: YOU NEVER WENT OUT THERE?

LOMBARDI: UM UM.

SEXTON: YOU JUST LOOKED THE WINDOW, RIGHT?

LOMBARDI: NO, NO.

SEXTON: ALL RIGHT.

LOMBARDI: AND THAT'S WHEN I TOLD JOSE THAT UH I KNOCKED ON THE DOOR AND JEANNE SAID COME IN AND HE WAS SITTING UP IN BED AND I SAID JOSE AND I LOOKED AT JEANNE AND I SAID I JUST WANT TO TALK TO JOSE, I WASN'T HIM TO COME DOWNSTAIRS WITH ME AND JEANNE SAID, WHY WHAT'S WRONG AND I SAID UM YOU'RE FRIEND, YOUR FRIEND FROM THE ISLANDS IS LAYING IN THE BACK YARD AND SHE'S NOT MOVING.

CHRISTIAN: UM HUM.

LOMBARDI: AND THEN THAT'S WHEN JOSE WENT OUT AND JEANNE WENT OUT RIGHT BEHIND HIM, I DON'T EVEN KNOW WHICH DOOR THEY WENT OUT OF. I CAME BACK IN HERE AND I, I GUESS WE WOKE UP JEN BECAUSE WE WERE TALKING YOU KNOW AND SHE

Name (Last, First, Middle) Juvenile	Case #
HORSFORD, TAMLA	2018-110177
NARRATIVE CONTINUED	

Madeline was the first person to discover Tamla's body. She had gone to the backyard to see what the temperature outside was and noticed Tamla laying face down in the back yard. She watched her for a moment to see if she was moving and immediately became concerned. She went to Jeanne at her bedroom and told her of the situation. Dispatch was immediately notified.

CONVERSATION WITH MADELINE LOMBARDI:
On Tuesday, November 6th, 2018 at approximately 1630 hours and while at   , I spoke with Madeline Lombardi a second time.
Madeline stated she had gone to bed before any of the partygoers. She said that she had gotten up the next morning about 0830 and had looked outside before going for coffee. Madeline said that is when she saw Tamla laying in the back yard. Madeline said she went immediately upstairs and knocked on Jeanne's door asking for Jose.
Madeline said she took Jose to the back deck and showed him Tamla laying in the yard.

Since we were out of ice, I went downstairs in the basements to get a tray of ice in the mini-fridge. I gave ice to Tam & Marcy then filled the tray & put it in the freezer in the kitchen. I went to take a bath in the basement, I never went back upstairs. Jeanne came to the basement and brought my cellphone. I woke up around 9 am. I went to my fridge in the basement to make coffee. I gazed out the door to see what kind of morning it was. I don't remember if I opened the back door. I saw Tam laying face down in the grass. I thought she was asleep, then her position startled my mind. I ran to my bathroom and said a prayer.

SEARCH FOR THE TRUTH

MEYERS met HORSFORD in August or September of 2018. MEYERS got to know her from their boys playing football every Saturday. The weekend prior to HORSFORD'S death, HORSFORD came to MEYERS' house to carve pumpkins for Halloween. HORSFORD brought her three middle boys with her. HORSFORD was invited because MEYERS' son asked if HORSFORD'S son could come to the party.

MEYERS said there were a lot of people at the Halloween party, and she could not remember exactly who. MEYERS did recall that HORSFORD and her sons, STACY SMITH and her two children, BRIDGET FULLER, DIANE GICCOA and her son, JOSE BARRERA, MADELINE LOMBARDI, and MEYERS' four children were at the party. People were drinking at the Halloween party, but not heavily. During the party MEYERS caught HORSFORD, GICCOA, and LOMBARDI smoking marijuana on the patio. MEYERS told them not to smoke marijuana because it could affect BARRERA'S job. MEYERS stated that HORSFORD and GICCOA knew each other from their kids going to elementary school, but it was HORSFORD'S first time meeting LOMBARDI.

MEYERS also opened the door to the balcony when she noticed that STACY, HORSFORD, and LOMBARDI were smoking marijuana. MEYERS told HORSFORD that she told her last weekend that she could not smoke marijuana with BARRERA there. HORSFORD made a joke that she forgot.

During the party LOMBARDI and HORSFORD would go outside frequently, and STACY went out to spend time with HORSFORD a couple of times. LAWSON was not sure what they were doing outside on the balcony, and she never went out there. LAWSON did recall MEYERS going out at one point and telling HORSFORD she could not be smoking marijuana because of BARRERA'S job.

At halftime in the football game THOMAS and BARRERA went upstairs and the girls sang happy birthday to MEYERS. THOMAS used PAULA SEALS' cell phone to video tape them singing happy birthday. THOMAS stated that he stayed upstairs for a little while and then went back downstairs. While THOMAS was upstairs, he noticed that FULLER was working, but was still being included. Everyone was having a good time.

SMITH: WE TALKED, WE LAUGHED, WE DANCED, WELL SOME DANCED AND UM I MEAN THEY APPARENTLY TAM WENT OUTSIDE AND HAD SMOKED POT AND THEN WE ALL I MEAN WE PLAYED CARDS TO HUMANITY, WE PLAYED, I THINK THAT WAS IT REALLY, THE GAME.

CHRISTIAN: UM HUM.

SMITH: UM WE LAUGHED, WE GIGGLED, WE WERE GIRLS.

CHRISTIAN: YEAH.

SMITH: THE GUYS, MY HUSBAND CAME AND JOSE WAS HERE AND MY HUSBAND CAME BECAUSE, EARLIER THAT DAY I HAD MY SISTER'S UM, UM BABY REVEAL PARTY

CHRISTIAN: UM HUM.

SMITH: YOU PROBABLY KNOW HER, SHE USED TO WORK AT DFACS, JAMIE (INAUDIBLE)

CHRISTIAN: YEAH.

SMITH: SHE YEAH,

CHRISTIAN: BOY OR GIRL?

SMITH: IT'S A BOY AND SO I HAD HER REVEAL PARTY SO I WAS ACTUALLY KIND OF TIRED.

CHRISTIAN: UM HUM.

SMITH: SO I WASN'T QUITE IN THE PARTING MOOD,

CHRISTIAN: YEAH.

SMITH: SO WE UM I HAD PROBABLY FOUR DRINKS AND BETWEEN THE HOURS OF PROBABLY SIX AND ONE THIRTY, I DID HAVE TWO SHOTS OF THE FIREBALL TOO AND WE PLAYED CARDS OF HUMANITY AND WE LAUGHED AND GIGGLED AND LAUGHED AND SO MY HUSBAND WANTED TO STAY WITH US BECAUSE HE DIDN'T WANT TO STAY AT THE HOUSE

MICHELLE GRAVES

GBI TOXICOLOGY REPORT:
On January 7th, 2019 the GBI Toxicology Report for Tamla Horsford was downloaded from the GBI DOFS Website.
This report was authored by Skye Mullarkey, a Forensic Toxicologist with the GBI. This report shows Tamla to have a trace amount of Alprazolam in her system.
THC was not tested for. Anecdotally, it was understood that Tamla had smoked marijuana at the party and a small amount of marijuana and rolling papers were found in her purse.
A call was placed to Skye Mullarkey. She replied that testing had showed THC present but that was not a test normally conducted post mortem. I requested that a test for the amount of THC be conducted. She replied she would get with her supervisor and run the appropriate test.
A copy of the Toxicology Report has been added to the case file.

THAT TAM SMOKED WEED EARLY AT THE PARTY AND HAD YOU HEARD THAT, IT SOUNDS LIKE YOU MAY HAVE CAME IN AFTER THAT.

SEALS: I DID NOT KNOW THAT UNTIL THE NEXT DAY.

CHRISTIAN: OK, THAT WAS SOMETHING THAT YOU HEARD?

SEALS: YES, RIGHT AND I, BUT THAT WAS NEVER SEEN AND EVIDENTIALLY SHE DID IT ON HER OWN.

EYERS came outside and told TAMLA to put it away because it would get BARRERA trouble. STACY believed that TAMLA put it away, but could not be sure because she ent inside and did not go back out. STACY stated that it was not a secret that TAMLA noked marijuana because she talked about it and even said she did not hide it from er kids. After STACY had gone back inside everyone came in and they sang happy rthday to MEYERS and had cake.

On 01/24/19 I checked the GBI website for any updated crime lab reports on this case. I found that the additional toxicology report was completed. It revealed that Tamala's blood was positive for THC. I placed a copy of the report in Christian's case file. [01/24/2019 14:27, TRSEXTON, 122, FCSO]

On 01/24/19 I spoke with Kurt StJour over the phone and updated him on the status of the case. I spoke with Kurt for approximately 30 minutes. I informed him I would contact him as soon as we had any new information. I called the GBI and spoke with Dr. Koopmeiners. He stated that he should have the autopsy completed soon and advised he would do his best to have it done sometime next week.

MEYERS: BECAUSE I SAID OH SPEAK OF THE DEVIL, CAN'T TALK NOW, I SAID YOU HAVE LOST YOUR MIND, I LIVE HER BECAUSE I USED TO TEASE HER, I'M LIKE YOU'RE THE FEMALE BOB MARLEY AND I SAID, YOU'RE LOST YOUR MIND, JOSE IS DOWN THERE AND HE WOULD NOT BE OK BECAUSE HE'S IN LAW ENFORCEMENT AND DON'T GET ME IN A FIGHT OVER THIS DUMB STUFF, I ACTUALLY THINK I SAID THIS DUMB SHIT BECAUSE I'M LIKE DON'T DO THIS AND SHE SAID, OH MY GOD I REMEMBER YOU TOLD ME THAT LAST WEEKEND.

SAID, DO YOU KNOW THAT ANYONE ELSE AT THE PARTY SMOKE CIGARETTES?

SMITH: I DON'T KNOW, I DON'T KNOW IF MARCY SMOKED, I DID, I DID TAKE ONE HIT OFF OF IT, I DID.

BARRERA did not know of anyone having marijuana at the party. BARRERA also did not know of anyone having prescription pills at the party. BARRERA was unaware that HORSFORD had drugs on her until after her death.

HARDIN did not see HORSFORD smoke marijuana, but remembered her making a comment that BARRERA had said "don't bring that shit around here". HARDIN was also not aware of HORSFORD taking any Xanax. HARDIN did not take Xanax, and was not aware of anyone else having any Xanax at the party. HARDIN was aware that BRIDGET FULLER, who was at the party, had severe anxiety, but was not sure if FULLER had Xanax.

SEALS was unaware of any illegal drugs or prescription pills at the party.

121

HARDIN: SMILING, HAVING FUN, UM SHE DIDN'T SEEM BELLIGERENT OR ANYTHING LIKE THAT REALLY BUT I MEAN I, THAT WAS LIKE MID WAY THROUGH THE NIGHT AND THEN WHEN THEY WERE PLAYING CARDS, SHE WAS TALKING WITH SOMEBODY LIKE AT THE TABLE, LIKE WE HAD TO KEEP TELLING HER, HEY PLAY YOUR CARD, LET'S GO

CHRISTIAN: RIGHT.

HARDIN: PAY ATTENTION GUYS, BUT I MEAN THEY STILL DIDN'T SEEM OR SHE DIDN'T SEEM LIKE SHE WAS LIKE OUT OF IT REALLY BUT I MEAN I WAS, I WAS PRETTY TIRED, I WASN'T THAT TIRED I MEAN I WAS TIRED BUT I WASN'T LIKE NOT ABLE TO LIKE FUNCTION IN MY SURROUNDINGS OR ANYTHING LIKE THAT.

SEXTON: OR ANY KIND OF ARGUMENT OR

LOMBARDI: NO, IN FACT ONCE I PUT THAT, THAT THUNDERSTORM ON THE BOSE SPEAKER I DIDN'T HERE A SINGLE THING GOING ON DOWN HERE, I WENT TO SLEEP RIGHT AWAY.

LOMBARDI: AND BECAUSE IT WAS THE BOSE SPEAKER AND I DIDN'T WANT TO HEAR WHEN THEIR UPSTAIRS, ESPECIALLY WHEN THE KIDS ARE AT HOME, THEY'RE REALLY LOUD AND THEY'RE THUMPING ON THE FLOOR AND EVERYTHING AND IT'S LIKE OH MY GOD, I CAN'T GO TO SLEEP WITH ALL THE NOISE SO I PUT THAT ON AND THEN AFTER THAT I NEVER GOT UP A SINGLE TIME, BUT UH I TURNED THE MUSIC DOWN, I DON'T KNOW SOMETIME I GUESS DURING THE EARLY MORNING HOURS BECAUSE I FELT LIKE OH MY GOD I GOT THIS SO LOUD UM MAYBE I'M KEEPING OTHER PEOPLE AWAKE SO I TURNED THE MUSIC DOWN.

CHRISTIAN: UM HUM.

LOMBARDI: AND THEN AROUND EIGHT THIRTY I STARTED LOOKING AT THE CLOCK THINKING YOU KNOW WHAT, IT'S TIME TO GET UP AND I THINK I LINGERED IN BED FOR PROBABLY CLOSE TO FIFTEEN MINUTES

CHRISTIAN: DID YOU SET YOUR CLOCK BACK THE NIGHT BEFORE?

LOMBARDI: NO.

CHRISTIAN: OK.

LOMBARDI: BUT MY CLOCK WAS ALREADY FROM THE LAST TIME I CAME.

CHRISTIAN: SO IT NEVER UNSET?

LOMBARDI: FROM, FROM THE LAST DAY LIGHT SAVINGS TIME

CHRISTIAN: YEAH.

LOMBARDI: BECAUSE I DIDN'T KNOW HOW TO DO IT.

SMITH: AND SO I WAS VERY ADAMANT ABOUT HER NOT DRIVING HOME AND SO TOM HAD TOLD HER YOU KNOW, HE'S, DO NOT DRIVE, SO WHEN I GOT UP THE NEXT MORNING I WAS SO PROUD OF HER BECAUSE I SAW HER PHONE AND I SAW HER STUFF THERE BECAUSE I WAS TERRIFIED THAT SHE WOULD DRIVE.

CHRISTIAN: RIGHT.

SMITH: AND

SEXTON: DID YOU EVER HEAR HER COME UPSTAIRS, YOU SAID SHE WAS GOING TO SLEEP IN THE BEDROOM UP THERE NEAR YOU GUYS BUT

SMITH: YEAH, NO I PASSED OUT, I WAS SO TIRED.

CHRISTIAN: UM HUM.

LOMBARDI: AND SHE TOOK MY ICE AND THEN AFTER THAT I WENT DOWNSTAIRS AND WHILE THE GUYS WERE GONE, I TOOK A BATH AND UM I THINK I TURNED ON THE TV FOR A LITTLE WHILE AND I STARTED TO GET TIRED SO I SYNCED MY PHONE UP WITH THE BOSE SPEAKER DOWNSTAIRS FOR AN APP THAT'S NATURE NOISES AND I PUT ON THUNDERSTORM.

CHRISTIAN: UM HUM.

SEXTON: WHO SHOWED UP AT TEN?

LAWSON: UH THAT WAS PAULA, PAULA SEALS SHOWED UP, PRETTY LATE, IT WAS SOMEWHERE AROUND NINE FORTY-FIVE, TEN. UM AND THEN YOU KNOW I GUESS HER DAUGHTER HAD A GAME THAT NIGHT AND SHE COULDN'T GET HER BEFORE. SO I LEFT AND TALKED TO ANOTHER GIRL THAT LEFT AT THE SAME TIME I DID, SARAH ON THE WAY HOME JUST TO MAKE SURE SHE GOT HOME OK AND BOTH OF US WENT TO BED AND THEN UM I GOT UP EARLY THE NEXT MORNING. WENT TO THE GYM, CAME OUT OF THE GYM AND I GOT, I HAD JUST GOTTEN HOME AND I GOT A CALL SAYING THAT WE HAD TO COME BACK BECAUSE THEY HAD FOUND TAM IN THE BACKYARD.

CHRISTIAN: RIGHT.

LAWSON: AND THAT'S ALL I KNOW.

CHRISTIAN: HOW WAS, DID YOU HAVE ANY INTERACTION WITH HER DURING THE PARTY AT ALL?

LAWSON: UM YEAH, YOU KNOW WE ALL KIND OF JUST HUNG OUT TOGETHER AND SHE WAS, SHE WAS REALLY, SHE JUST HAD A FULL OF LIFE PERSONALITY SO SHE WAS ALL OVER THE PLACE, SHE WAS ON HER PHONE WITH HER DAUGHTER, EXCITED ABOUT HER NEW GRANDBABY COMING AND SO WE FACETIME WITH HER AND, AND THEN YOU KNOW, SHE JUST, WE JUST HUNG OUT, IT WAS NOTHING, NOTHING SHORT OF YOU KNOW, JUST A BORING NIGHT AT A HOUSE. UM YOU KNOW AND THAT'S ALL I CAN RECALL AND THEN AFTER THAT WHAT THEY DID, I DON'T KNOW BECAUSE I WASN'T HERE.

122

SEXTON: HOW INTOXICATED WAS SHE?

BARRERA: UM I THINK IT WAS UNTIL THAT NEXT MORNING WHEN SOMEBODY ASKED HOW MUCH SHE HAD TO DRINK AND LOOKED OVER AT THE BOTTLE OF TEQUILA SHE HAD BROUGHT

SEXTON: RIGHT.

BARRERA: UM BUT AS FAR AS MANNERISMS THAT WHOLE NIGHT, BY ALL ACCOUNTS, FINE.

SEXTON: NO ISSUES WITH ANYBODY?

LAWSON: NO AND THAT'S WHY WE DID WHAT WE DID, WE WANTED TO HAVE SOMETHING HERE WHERE YOU DON'T GO TO A BAR AND THERE'S NOT DRUNK PEOPLE EVERYWHERE THAT CAN CAUSE PROBLEMS AND PEOPLE AREN'T DRIVING AND DRINKING AND SO WE JUST CAME HERE WITH A FEW SELECT FRIENDS BECAUSE OF THAT. WE JUST WANTED TO HAVE A LOW KEY NIGHT.

CASE NUMBER: 2018110177

Name: Paula V. Seals   Employer:
Address: Address:
City: State: City: State:
Zip: Phone: Zip: Phone:
DOB: 172   Sex: F   Place of Birth: Email
Race: W   Height: 5'4"   Weight: 155   Hair: Blonde   Eyes: Blue

DESCRIBE, IN DETAIL AND IN YOUR OWN WORDS, THE EVENTS OF THE INCIDENT OR ACCIDENT:

I Arrived around approximately 4:30 p.m. everyone had already eaten. We were just having drinks in the kitchen. Girl talk and then we played cards for about an hour - (maybe closer after midnight) Tami seemed happy, spoke about her kids didn't seem too intoxicated.

I went to bed around 1:30 am and left this morning around 7:45 am.

FORSYTH COUNTY SHERIFF'S OFFICE
STATEMENT FORM

CASE NUMBER: 2018110177

Name: Nichole Lawson   Employer:
Address: Address:
City: State: City: State:
Zip: Phone: Zip: Phone:
DOB: 79   Sex: F   Place of Birth: Email
Race: White   Height: 5'5   Weight: 140   Hair: Blonde   Eyes: Brown

DESCRIBE, IN DETAIL AND IN YOUR OWN WORDS, THE EVENTS OF THE INCIDENT OR ACCIDENT:

We were here having a birthday party for a friend. We watched football and played games. I left at 10:30 p.m. on 11-3-18. She was absolutely fine when I left.

SEXTON: OK. HOW WAS, I DON'T KNOW, HER LEVEL OF INTOXICATION OR APPEAR DID SHE SEEM LIKE SHE WAS REALLY DRUNK OR NOT AT ALL OR

LOMBARDI: UM KNOW SHE DIDN'T SEEM REALLY DRUNK AT ALL BECAUSE UM THERE WAS ANOTHER GIRL HERE, I BELIEVE HER NAME MIGHT BE MARGIE OR MOLLY OR SOMETHING THAT STARTS WITH A M AND BOTH OF THEM WERE FROM FLORIDA AND THEY WERE HAVING A DISCUSSION WHILE I WENT AND GOT THE ICE AND I CAME BACK AND I LISTENED TO THE DISCUSSION, THEY WERE HAVING A DISCUSSION ABOUT BOTH BEING FROM FLORIDA AND THAT THEY DIDN'T WANT TO CHANGE THEIR FLORIDA DRIVERS LICENSE BECAUSE THEY LOVED DISNEY WORLD BECAUSE THEY GOT A HUGE DISCOUNT BY BEING A FLORIDA RESIDENT AND UH I TOLD THEM THAT MY DAUGHTER WORKED AN EIGHT MONTH INTERNSHIP IN DISNEY WORLD AND WE WENT FOUR TIMES THAT YEARS AND IT'S LIKE WERE DISNEY ADDICTS TOO.

during the party. FULLER stated that she would not have left HORSFORD alone if she thought that HORSFORD was not okay. When GARY arrived at MEYERS' residence, HORSFORD walked FULLER to the door, hugged her and told FULLER that she was going to smoke. FULLER stated that she arrived home around 2:00 a.m. and went to sleep.

During the night HARDIN sat out on the back porch with HORSFORD, and stated that other people were out there at the time. HORSFORD told HARDIN she was from Florida and that her parents were from the Caribbean. HORSFORD was smoking, and went outside several times that HARDIN noticed. HARDIN was not aware of anyone else smoking. HARDIN observed HORSFORD drinking tequila from Mexico. HARDIN did not see anyone else drink the tequila, but HARDIN did have a sip of it from a Dixie cup. HARDIN did not remember if she touched the tequila bottle, but did not think that she did. HARDIN stated that HORSFORD was happy, bubbly, and glad she was out of the house without her kids. HORSFORD did not seem intoxicated, but did appear "tipsy". HARDIN stated she was not really paying attention to everyone.

At approximately 9:30 p.m., SEALS arrived at MEYERS' residence located in Cumming, Forsyth County, Georgia. Everyone had been watching the Alabama vs. LSU football game. When SEALS arrived, everyone sang happy birthday to MEYERS and drank a round of shots.

COCKERHAM: LIKE I REMEMBER HER SPECIFICALLY SAYING, I'M COMING HERE LATE TONIGHT BECAUSE I HAD TO MAKE MY BOYS DINNER, GET EVERYTHING CLEANED UP MADE THEM A BREAKFAST CASSEROLE.

CHRISTIAN: UM HUM.

COCKERHAM: AND THEN SHE SHOWED US A BOTTLE OF HER TEQUILA

CHRISTIAN: RIGHT.

COCKERHAM: THAT SHE BROUGHT FROM MEXICO AND IT WAS A TALL BOTTLE WITH PICTURES ALL OVER IT, THAT'S WHAT I REMEMBER.

CHRISTIAN: DO YOU REMEMBER WHAT COLOR?

COCKERHAM: BLUE MAYBE?

CHRISTIAN: OK.

COCKERHAM: UM I NEVER SAW HER GET ANYTHING OUT AND START DRINKING IT WHILE I WAS THERE.

SMITH: THERE WAS A LOT GONE OUT OF THAT BOTTLE. I KNOW THAT I, I KNOW MARCY TOOK A SHOT WITH HER UM BUT OTHER THAN THAT I REALLY DON'T KNOW AND I DID MAKE TAM ONE DRINK AND I DID MAKE HER A DRINK UM BUT SHE MADE FUN OF ME BECAUSE I PUT SPRITE IN IT.

HARDEN: AND IN ORDER TO LIKE BE CLASSIFIED A CERTAIN (INAUDIBLE) OR SOMETHING, IT HAS TO HAVE A SPECIAL SEAL WHERE IT'S ACTUALLY PRODUCED AND MADE AND THIS TEQUILA HAD THIS SPECIAL SEAL ON IT AND SHE'S LIKE OH YOU KNOW ALL ABOUT IT, LIKE SHE GOT EXCITED THAT I LIKE KNEW WHAT THAT SEAL MEANT BUT SHE'S LIKE THIS IS A REALLY GOOD BOTTLE OF TEQUILA, IT'S AMAZING, LIKE THE BEST THEY EVER MADE, SO SHE WAS LIKE REALLY EXCITED ABOUT IT. BUT I MEAN AT THAT POINT I WANT TO SAY MAYBE THIS MUCH WAS GONE OUT OF IT.

CHRISTIAN: OK.

HARDIN: LIKE MAYBE, MAYBE A QUARTER OF IT.

CHRISTIAN: OK.

HARDIN: NOT EVEN HALF OF THE BOTTLE HAD BEEN DRINKED OR DRANK.

MEYERS: LIKE I SAID, TAM GOT HERE AT EIGHT THIRTY, SHE BROUGHT A BOTTLE OF TEQUILA AS MY GIFT AND SAID IT WAS TEQUILA FROM MEXICO AND I SAID THANK YOU BUT I DON'T DRINK TEQUILA AND SHE SAID NO, YOU DON'T UNDERSTAND, IT'S GOOD AND SHE OPENED IT AND I SMELLED IT AND I THREW UP IN MY MOUTH AND SAID NO. SO SHE OFFERED IT TO OTHER PEOPLE.

LAWSON: YEAH TO GIVE TO JEANNE AND SHE BROUGHT SOME TALL BOTTLE OF TEQUILA AND IT WAS IMPORTED FROM MEXICO, SHE WAS TALKING ABOUT HOW GREAT IT WAS AND IT WAS IMPORTED FROM MEXICO. UM SORRY, HIT THAT SIDE BUTTON IF YOU DON'T MIND AND THAT WILL SHUT IT UP. AND SO YOU KNOW NOBODY GOT INTO IT A FIRST AND THEN PROBABLY ABOUT FIFTEEN TWENTY MINUTES AFTER SHE HAD BEEN HERE, SHE KIND OF POPPED THE LID OPEN AND STACEY AND JEANNE, I CAN REMEMBER VIVIDLY, THEY WERE OVER HERE BY THE BAR AND THEY SMELLED IT AND I SAW JEANNE GO LIKE THIS, LIKE NO WAY, NUMBER ONE SHE DOESN'T LIKE TEQUILA BUT NUMBER TWO, SHEW AS LIKE I'M NOT DRINKING THAT STUFF.

CHRISTIAN: RIGHT.

LAWSON: AND THEN THE SAME WITH STACEY AND THEN ALL OF US WERE SITTING ON THE COUCH AND TAM WAS ON THE BACK PORCH SMOKING AT THE TIME AND I WAS SITTING ON THE COUCH RIGHT HERE AND THEY ALL SAID SMELL THIS STUFF, YOU GOT TO SMELL THIS, IT'S AWFUL AND EVERYONE OF US SMELLED IT AND WE'RE LIKE I DON'T WANT ANYTHING TO DO WITH THAT YOU KNOW. AND THEN THAT WAS IT, I DIDN'T SEE HER MAKE A DRINK BUT I WASN'T PAYING ATTENTION SO.

LAWSON recalled that HORSFORD showed up with a blue bottle of tequila from Mexico and asked if everyone wanted to try a shot. HORSFORD went around the room letting everyone smell the tequila and everybody declined taking a shot. LAWSON stated that the tequila smelled very strong. LAWSON was not sure if anyone did a shot at some point during the night or not. LAWSON also did not remember if she touched the bottle. LAWSON stated that she may have touched the bottle when HORSFORD asked her to smell it. HORSFORD did not seem intoxicated during the night and was vibrant and happy. LAWSON stated that HORSFORD was the same all night just as she was when she arrived at the party. LAWSON and COCKERHAM left the party at approximately 10:30 p.m. LAWSON gets up early and was waiting at the party for PAULA SEALS to arrive so they could sing happy birthday to MEYERS. SEALS arrived around 10:00 p.m., they all sang happy birthday, and LAWSON and COCKERHAM left. Everyone else that had arrived at the party were still there when

---

During the party LAWSON was not drinking alcohol, and MEYERS believed that SARAH COCKERHAM maybe had one glass of wine. MEYERS advised that LAWSON and COCKERHAM had to leave early. Everyone else at the party was drinking alcohol. MEYERS, STACY, and SEALS had blueberry vodka and ginger beer, and BRIDGET FULLER had a malt beverage. MEYERS recalled JENNIFER MORRELL got drunk quickly but was not sure what MORRELL was drinking. MARCY HARDIN was drinking wine and HORSFORD was drinking tequila. No one was falling down drunk even later in the night. MEYERS said that everyone seemed good. HORSFORD had brought MEYERS the bottle of tequila for her birthday, but MEYERS opened it, smelled it, and said no thank you because it smelled so strong. MEYERS stated that she did touch the tequila bottle when she opened it. At one point in the evening everyone did a shot for MEYERS' birthday. MEYERS stated that everyone had Fireball except for HORSFORD, who took a shot of her tequila.

MEYERS: ABOUT ONE THIRTY WE ALL STARTED GOING, WELL PROBABLY AT ONE WE WERE TRYING TO PUT JEN (INAUDIBLE) TO BE BECAUSE SHE WAS WASTED.

CHRISTIAN: OK.

HARDIN: SMILING, HAVING FUN, UM SHE DIDN'T SEEM BELLIGERENT OR ANYTHING LIKE THAT REALLY BUT I MEAN I, THAT WAS LIKE MID WAY THROUGH THE NIGHT AND THEN WHEN THEY WERE PLAYING CARDS, SHE WAS TALKING WITH SOMEBODY LIKE AT THE TABLE, LIKE WE HAD TO KEEP TELLING HER, HEY PLAY YOUR CARD, LET'S GO

CHRISTIAN: RIGHT.

HARDIN: PAY ATTENTION GUYS, BUT I MEAN THEY STILL DIDN'T SEEM OR SHE DIDN'T SEEM LIKE SHE WAS LIKE OUT OF IT REALLY BUT I MEAN I WAS, I WAS PRETTY TIRED, I WASN'T THAT TIRED I MEAN I WAS TIRED BUT I WASN'T LIKE NOT ABLE TO LIKE FUNCTION IN MY SURROUNDINGS OR ANYTHING LIKE THAT.

SEXTON: OR ANY KIND OF ARGUMENT OR

LOMBARDI: NO, IN FACT ONCE I PUT THAT, THAT THUNDERSTORM ON THE BOSE SPEAKER I DIDN'T HERE A SINGLE THING GOING ON DOWN HERE, I WENT TO SLEEP RIGHT AWAY.

LOMBARDI: AND BECAUSE IT WAS THE BOSE SPEAKER AND I DIDN'T WANT TO HEAR WHEN THEIR UPSTAIRS, ESPECIALLY WHEN THE KIDS ARE AT HOME, THEY'RE REALLY LOUD AND THEY'RE THUMPING ON THE FLOOR AND EVERYTHING AND IT'S LIKE OH MY GOD, I CAN'T GO TO SLEEP WITH ALL THE NOISE SO I PUT THAT ON AND THEN AFTER THAT I NEVER GOT UP A SINGLE TIME. BUT UH I TURNED THE MUSIC DOWN, I DON'T KNOW SOMETIME I GUESS DURING THE EARLY MORNING HOURS BECAUSE I FELT LIKE OH MY GOD I GOT THIS SO LOUD UM MAYBE I'M KEEPING OTHER PEOPLE AWAKE SO I TURNED THE MUSIC DOWN.

CHRISTIAN: UM HUM.

LOMBARDI: AND THEN AROUND EIGHT THIRTY I STARTED LOOKING AT THE CLOCK THINKING YOU KNOW WHAT, IT'S TIME TO GET UP AND I THINK I LINGERED IN BED FOR PROBABLY CLOSE TO FIFTEEN MINUTES

CHRISTIAN: DID YOU SET YOUR CLOCK BACK THE NIGHT BEFORE?

LOMBARDI: NO.

CHRISTIAN: OK.

LOMBARDI: BUT MY CLOCK WAS ALREADY FROM THE LAST TIME I CAME.

CHRISTIAN: SO IT NEVER UNSET?

LOMBARDI: FROM, FROM THE LAST DAY LIGHT SAVINGS TIME

CHRISTIAN: YEAH.

LOMBARDI: BECAUSE I DIDN'T KNOW HOW TO DO IT.

SMITH: AND SO I WAS VERY ADAMANT ABOUT HER NOT DRIVING HOME AND SO TOM HAD TOLD HER YOU KNOW, HE'S, DO NOT DRIVE, SO WHEN I GOT UP THE NEXT MORNING I WAS SO PROUD OF HER BECAUSE I SAW HER PHONE AND I SAW HER STUFF THERE BECAUSE I WAS TERRIFIED THAT SHE WOULD DRIVE.

CHRISTIAN: RIGHT.

SMITH: AND

SEXTON: DID YOU EVER HEAR HER COME UPSTAIRS, YOU SAID SHE WAS GOING TO SLEEP IN THE BEDROOM UP THERE NEAR YOU GUYS BUT

SMITH: YEAH, NO I PASSED OUT, I WAS SO TIRED.

CHRISTIAN: UM HUM.

LOMBARDI: AND SHE TOOK MY ICE AND THEN AFTER THAT I WENT DOWNSTAIRS AND WHILE THE GUYS WERE GONE, I TOOK A BATH AND UM I THINK I TURNED ON THE TV FOR A LITTLE WHILE AND I STARTED TO GET TIRED SO I SYNCED MY PHONE UP WITH THE BOSE SPEAKER DOWNSTAIRS FOR AN APP THAT'S NATURE NOISES AND I PUT ON THUNDERSTORM.

CHRISTIAN: UM HUM.

SEXTON: WHO SHOWED UP AT TEN?

LAWSON: UH THAT WAS PAULA, PAULA SEALS SHOWED UP, PRETTY LATE, IT WAS SOMEWHERE AROUND NINE FORTY-FIVE, TEN. UM AND THEN YOU KNOW I GUESS HER DAUGHTER HAD A GAME THAT NIGHT AND SHE COULDN'T GET HER BEFORE. SO I LEFT AND TALKED TO ANOTHER GIRL THAT LEFT AT THE SAME TIME I DID, SARAH ON THE WAY HOME JUST TO MAKE SURE SHE GOT HOME OK AND BOTH OF US WENT TO BED AND THEN UM I GOT UP EARLY THE NEXT MORNING, WENT TO THE GYM, CAME OUT OF THE GYM AND I GOT, I HAD JUST GOTTEN HOME AND I GOT A CALL SAYING THAT WE HAD TO COME BACK BECAUSE THEY HAD FOUND TAM IN THE BACKYARD.

CHRISTIAN: RIGHT.

LAWSON: AND THAT'S ALL I KNOW.

CHRISTIAN: HOW WAS, DID YOU HAVE ANY INTERACTION WITH HER DURING THE PARTY AT ALL?

LAWSON: UM YEAH, YOU KNOW WE ALL KIND OF JUST HUNG OUT TOGETHER AND SHE WAS, SHE WAS REALLY, SHE JUST HAD A FULL OF LIFE PERSONALITY SO SHE WAS ALL OVER THE PLACE, SHE WAS ON HER PHONE WITH HER DAUGHTER, EXCITED ABOUT HER NEW GRANDBABY COMING AND SO WE FACETIME WITH HER AND, AND THEN YOU KNOW, SHE JUST, WE JUST HUNG OUT, IT WAS NOTHING, YOU KNOW, SHORT OF YOU KNOW, JUST A BORING NIGHT AT A HOUSE. UM YOU KNOW AND THAT'S ALL I CAN RECALL AND THEN AFTER THAT WHAT THEY DID, I DON'T KNOW BECAUSE I WASN'T HERE.

SEXTON: SO SHE HAD ACTUALLY SAID, YOU HEARD HER SAY SOMETHING ABOUT GOING OUTSIDE RIGHT BEFORE YALL WENT TO BED?

SMITH: YEAH, SHE TOLD ME SHE WAS GOING OUTSIDE TO SMOKE BEFORE SE WENT TO BED.

SEXTON: OK.

SMITH: AND I SAID OK WELL GO OUTSIDE AND GOTO BED. I'M NOT A SMOKER.

CASE NUMBER: 2018 H0177

Name: Stacy Smith   Employer:

Address: Address:

City: State: City: State:

Zip: Phone: Zip: Phone:

DOB: -78   Sex: F   Place of Birth: Email

Race: White   Height: 5'3   Weight: 145   Hair: Blond   Eyes: Brown

DESCRIBE, IN DETAIL AND IN YOUR OWN WORDS, THE EVENTS OF THE INCIDENT OR ACCIDENT:

Tam was going to bed last night about 1:30. My husband and I told her good night and went to bed. My husband and I left this morning at 8:30 am.

BARRERA: TRUTHFULLY JEN WAS THE MOST INTOXICATED THERE AND SHE WAS BEING FUNNY SO I TOOK A PICTURE AND THAT WOULD SHOW LIKE ELEVEN TWENTY-SIX. SO YEAH AS FAR AS UM EVERYBODY GOING TO BED

BARRERA had taken a video of MORRELL dancing during the party. BARRERA advised MORRELL was the most intoxicated person at the party. BARRERA advised he had some drinks but was not intoxicated. BARRERA didn't drink too much because he wasn't feeling well. HORSFORD was not stumbling or slurring her words and was not acting super intoxicated.

MEYERS: SHE FELT GOOD, SHE MADE THE COMMENT SHE WAS JUST GOING TO GO AHEAD AND GO HOME AND I SAID, NO AND SHE SAID I'M FINE AND THEN THAT'S WHEN TOM AND STACEY SMITH WERE LIKE ABSOLUTELY NOT. PROMISE US YOU WON'T DRIVE BECAUSE SHE WASN'T STUMBLING AND THAT'S WHY WE'RE SO CONFUSED, SHE WASN'T STUMBLING, SHE WAS HER SAME OLD HAPPY, HUG ON MY SELF OF WE'RE GOING TO HAVE A GOOD TIME.

FULLER: JEN CANNOT HANDLE HER LIQUOR AND THEN SHE GOES THROUGH THAT WHOLE MODE, I GOT TO EAT WORMS, NOBODY LIKES ME. I'M LIKE SHUT IT OR I'M GOING TO TAKE A BOTTLE OF WATER AND SCREW IT UP IN YOUR BRAIN AND CLEAN IT OUT FOR YOU. SO YEAH I MEAN I'M JUST AND I, I DON'T GENERALLY TRYING TO PASS BEING UGLY.

The night of MEYERS' party LAWSON did not see any marijuana and only heard MEYERS say something about it. LAWSON did not take Xanax but was aware that BRIDGET FULLER was prescribed Xanax. LAWSON could not see FULLER giving her Xanax to HORSFORD or anyone because she really needed it. LAWSON added that overall, it was a boring night and nothing odd happened while she was there. LAWSON also stated that she did not know HORSFORD but that HORSFORD seemed "lovely". HORSFORD did not seem intoxicated, but LAWSON was also not paying attention to how much HORSFORD was drinking either. LAWSON did not take any

At approximately midnight everyone started figuring out what bedrooms they were going to use. FULLER texted GARY to tell him to come pick her up. Prior to FULLER leaving, STACY SMITH and THOMAS, MEYERS and BARRERA and PAULA SEALS all went upstairs to their respective bedrooms. JENNIFER MORRELL and MARCY HARDIN went to bed in a room on the main floor. FULLER stated that if she was going to stay the night, she was going to sleep in the living room but decided she did not want to stay the night. After everyone went to bed it was just FULLER and HORSFORD. FULLER was cleaning up while she waited for GARY. HORSFORD did not seem intoxicated like MORRELL. FULLER stated that MORRELL was very intoxicated

SA ALDRICH asked FULLER who all she knew at the party. FULLER stated that she had met MORRELL and HORSFORD at the Halloween party. FULLER stated that MORRELL was drunk and obnoxious both nights. FULLER met COCKERHAM and HARDIN the night of the birthday party. FULLER knew STACY SMITH, LAWSON, SEALS, and LOMBARDI previously through MEYERS.

THOMAS stated that during the party he observed that MORRELL was pretty intoxicated at the end of the night, and that TAMLA seemed intoxicated but not as much as MORRELL. MORRELL was slurring, stumbling and loud. TAMLA had quite a bit to drink but wasn't stumbling or slurring to the best of THOMAS' memory. THOMAS stated that TAMLA had a higher tolerance than the other girls, and seemed more discreet about her intoxication.

CHRISTIAN: WHO WAS THE TIPSY ONE?

SEALS: UM JENNIFER MORRELL.

CHRISTIAN: UM HUM.

SEALS: LIKE I MEAN THAT WAS ONLY ONE LIKE TO BE CONCERNED ABOUT ANYBODY.

FORSYTH COUNTY SHERIFF'S OFFICE
STATEMENT FORM

CASE NUMBER: 2018110177

Name: Marcu Hardin   Employer:

Address: Address:

City: State: City: State:

Zip: Phone: Zip: Phone:

DOB: 185 Sex: F   Place of Birth: Email

Race: White   Height: 5'4   Weight: 159   Hair: Blonde   Eyes: Blue

DESCRIBE, IN DETAIL AND IN YOUR OWN WORDS, THE EVENTS OF THE INCIDENT OR ACCIDENT:

We all cam here for Jeanne Birthday this was the
First time i have ever met Tam. Around 12:30-12:45 Everyone
Started to lay Down to go to bed. Jose put Shrek the
Movie on for me and jennifer Morrell and we layed
Down. at last time i seen Tam was around 12:30-12:45
When woke up to go home the TV was not pretty Loud
and Everything look Clean and normal This was around
4:15 i had Set my Alram because i have to work
on Sunday I Left at 4:10 am

HARDIN: SO I JUST WENT AND GRABBED IT AND I, I KIND OF LOOKED OVER IN THE LIVING ROOM CAUSE THE TV WAS STILL ON WHEN I LEFT TOO AND IT WAS REALLY LOUD.

CHRISTIAN: DO YOU REMEMBER WHEN YOU LEFT, WAS THE FRONT DOOR LOCKED OR UNLOCKED?

HARDIN and MORRELL were two of the first to go to bed. They went to sleep on the main floor around 11:00 p.m. Neither HARDIN nor MORRELL got up during the night. HARDIN had set an alarm for approximately 5:00 a.m. the next morning. When HARDIN got up, the TV and lights were still on. HARDIN stated that the door to the balcony appeared to be closed. HARDIN got her purse and left the residence shortly after getting up. MORRELL was still in bed when HARDIN left.

MEYERS: OR IF, IF I JUST KNOW IT HADN'T CLOSED BECAUSE THEN THE NEXT THING THAT SHOWS UM AS REGISTERING WITH THE SECURITY SYSTEM WAS THE FRONT DOOR OPENED AT FOUR TEN AND THAT WAS MARCY LEAVING BECAUSE I KNEW SHE SET AN ALARM BECAUSE SHE HAD TO WORK

HARDIN: AND THAT WAS THE LAST, THAT WAS IT, WE WENT TO SLEEP. I GOT UP UM ABOUT FOUR O'CLOCK IN THE MORNING BECAUSE I HAD TO GO TO WORK THE NEXT DAY AND THEN I'M JUST USED TO WAKING UP EARLY BECAUSE I WORK DURING THE DAY AS WELL.

SEALS recalled HORSFORD facetiming her daughter who was pregnant and lived in Texas. HORSFORD also facetimed her husband LEANDER. HORSFORD appeared

PALLERINO: UM BOY, IT WAS, SHE TEXTED ME EIGHT, EIGHT THIRTY, SOMETHING LIKE THAT.

CHRISTIAN: OK.

PALLERINO: JUST THAT SHE WAS UP AND YOU KNOW. AND THEN WE DECIDED THAT SINCE I HAD SUCH TOUGH, VIA TEXT, NO SENSE TRYING TO GET UBER AND WAITING AN HOUR.

CHRISTIAN: RIGHT.

PALLERINO: I'LL JUST COME AND PICK YOU UP.

CHRISTIAN: ALL RIGHT.

SEVERAL SCREEN SHOTS. I SAID MARCY JUST LEFT BECAUSE SHE COULD DRIVE.

CHRISTIAN: UM HUM.

MORRELL: IN DOWNSTAIRS BEDROOM (INAUDIBLE) HE SAID OH BOY, SO HE MUST HAVE NOT SEEN THOSE UNTIL SIX THIRTY.

CHRISTIAN: OK, SO YALL HAD ACTUALLY BEEN TEXTING THROUGH THE NIGHT?

MORRELL: WELL I DON'T THINK HE SAW THIS, I MEAN HE WAS ASLEEP.

CHRISTIAN: OK.

MORRELL: AND I THINK HE, THAT'S WHEN HE SAW IT AT SIX THIRTY.

MORRELL: I SAID EIGHT FORTY-EIGHT, SO THIS STILL HAD NOT HAPPENED OR WE DIDN'T KNOW YET, I SAID SHOULD I WALK OUT AND HE SAID EIGHT FIFTY-ONE, NOT YET AND NINE AM HE SAID TO COME OUT, I'M HERE. NINE O-TWO I SAID HANG ON, JUST COME IN. I GOT, SO IT MUST HAVE BEEN RIGHT THEN THAT LIKE ALL THIS, WITHIN FIVE MINUTES.

CASE NUMBER: 2018 1/0177

Name: Michael Pallerino   Employer:

Address: Address:

City: State: City: State:

Zip: Phone: Zip: Phone:

DOB: 63 Sex: M Place of Birth   Email

Race: Caucasian Height: 6'2" Weight: 218 Hair: Grey/Bn Eyes: Brown

DESCRIBE, DETAIL AND IN YOUR OWN WORDS, THE EVENTS OF THE INCIDENT OR ACCIDENT:

Came to pick up my wife this morning at 9:01 AM. She asked me to hold on as there was an ambulance to the police and fire department had already been called so I moved my vehicle up the street. I only had to see the doorway at front entrance

---

MORRELL: SO HER AUNT IS THE ONE WHO KIND OF SAW HER FIRST. OK, HERE IT IS...OK, EIGHT THIRTY, OK SEVEN, SEVEN THIRTY-TWO. , SO I'M LETTING HIM KNOW THE ADDRESS AND HE SAID I WILL, I WILL WAZE IT, EIGHT THIRTY I SAID ARE YOU CLOSE, HE SAID ON THE WAY. I SAID WHAT'S THE ETA, HE SAID FIFTEEN MINUTES.

CHRISTIAN: OK.

MORRELL: AND THAT'S WHEN I SAID COME IN AND HE SAID THEY WANT ME TO STAY IN THE CAR SO THE COP HAD PULLED UP BETWEEN NINE O-FOUR AND NINE FIFTEEN.

CHRISTIAN: SO WHAT TIME DID MADELINE, THE WHOLE THING WITH TAM, WHAT TIME DID, WHAT TIME DID THEY FIND HER BODY? CAN YOU KIND OF ESTIMATE THAT?

MORRELL: YEAH, LET'S SEE, ALL RIGHT SO I SAID WHAT'S THE ETA, I SAID SHOULD I WALK OUT, THAT WAS AT EIGHT FORTY-EIGHT. HE SAID NOT YET, EIGHT FIFTY-ONE HE SAID NOT YET, SO I'M THINKING IT MUST HAVE BEEN SOMETIME BETWEEN EIGHT FORTY-FIVE AND EIGHT FIFTY?

COCKERHAM: UM I HAD TWO GLASSES OF WINE THAT NIGHT AND THEN WE DID BIRTHDAY CAKE.

CHRISTIAN: OK.

COCKERHAM: WE SANG HAPPY BIRTHDAY, ATE BUNDT CAKE AND AT TEN THIRTY I LEFT.

SMITH: AND I PUT A LITTLE BIT OF TEQUILA, I WAS MAKING IT THE WAY I WOULD DRINK IT AND I PUT A LITTLE BIT OF TEQUILA AND I PUT SPRITE IT IN

CHRISTIAN: YEAH.

SMITH: AND APPARENTLY SHE HAD BEEN DRINKING TEQUILA AND WATER.

CHRISTIAN: OK.

SMITH: AND SO SHE WAS AGGRAVATING ME. SHE WAS LIKE OH YOU MAKE WIMPY DRINKS AND SO

SEXTON: SO YOU DON'T KNOW ANYBODY THAT WAS DRINKING OUT OF THAT TEQUILA BOTTLE OTHER THAN HER?

SMITH: THE ONLY ONE THAT I KNOW OF IS MARCY TOOK A SHOT OF IT. ALL I KNOW IS ONE, ALL I SAW HER DO IS ONE AND I WASN'T REALLY PAYING ATTENTION

All the girls at the party were drinking. STACY had three or four blueberry vodka and ginger beers. JENNIFER MORRELL was drinking wine, and STACY was not sure what everyone else was drinking. STACY went out on the porch with TAMLA a few times while TAMLA was smoking. STACY stated that a lot of the girls were in and out on the back porch. At one point STACY got THOMAS to come upstairs to try to light the firepit on the back porch, but both propane tanks were empty. THOMAS moved one of the empty propane tanks next to railing. STACY only saw TAMLA smoking while she was outside. During the night TAMLA got marijuana out, and STACY took a hit of it.

When THOMAS arrived, STACY, MEYERS, MADELINE LOMBARDI, SARAH COCKERHAM, NICOLE LAWSON, BRIDGET FULLER, BARRERA and possibly JENNIFER MORRELL were already at the residence. THOMAS and BARRERA hung out in the basement of the residence, had a few drinks, and watched football. THOMAS stated he had approximately four Crown and cokes. THOMAS was not sure what BARRERA was drinking, but stated that BARRERA did not seem intoxicated. THOMAS said that neither he nor BARRERA are big drinkers, and he had never seen BARRERA drunk in the fifteen to twenty times they have hung out.

Humanity with everyone. BARRERA and THOMAS had been drinking beer, but MEYERS was not sure how much because they had a cooler that they were using in the basement.

SMITH: THAT WAS OUR LAST FOOTBALL GAME SO UM, HOLD ON I CAN PROBABLY TELL YOU, UM LET ME LOOK AT TEAM SNAP, THAT WOULD HAVE BEEN OUT LAST FOOTBALL GAME. SINE WE HAD THAT LAST, HALLOWEEN AND LET ME LOOK AT THE CALENDAR, TEAM SNAP IS ALREADY GONE. I'M SORRY, UM IT HAD TO BE SO IT WAS THE THIRD, TWENTY-SEVENTH. THAT WAS THE TWENTY-SEVENTH.

SEXTON: SATURDAY THE TWENTY-SEVENTH OF OCTOBER?

SMITH: YES, AND THEN ON HALLOWEEN WE ALSO HUNG OUT AND WE ALL WENT TRICK OR TREATING.

SEXTON: UM HUM.

SMITH: AND WE HAD A BLAST AND UM THERE WAS DRINKING INVOLVED. US GIRLS DRINKING, HUSBANDS BEING RESPONSIBLE AND

CHRISTIAN: GIRLS GONE WILD.

SMITH: YES, AND SO IT WASN'T, HALLOWEEN WASN'T TOO CRAZY BUT IT WAS FUN.
CHRISTIAN: YEAH.

SMITH: AND WE WENT TRICK OR TREATING AND WE ALL HAD A BLAST AND ATE SOME FOOD AND EVERYONE GOT HOME SAFE. AND THEN HER AND I AND THEN WE HUNG OUT AT UM WE WENT TO THE FALCON'S MOM

BARRERA: GARY WHO WAS NOT AT THE PARTY, I THINK HE PICKED HER UP, I THINK THEY MIGHT HAVE SOME SORT OF A TIME STAMP AS TO HEY I'M HERE

CHRISTIAN: UM HUM.

BARRERA: HEY COME OUTSIDE BUT UM

SEXTON: IS SHE THE ONE THAT LEFT AT WHAT TIME?

CHRISTIAN: NO, UH

BARRERA: I THINK BASED OFF THE DOOR ALERT ON JEANNE'S PHONE, LIKE FORTY-(INAUDIBLE).

SEXTON: OK, RIGHT YEAH.

BARRERA: THAT'S WHAT TIME IT SHOWS THE FRONT DOOR OPENING AND FROM WHAT I KNOW, BRIDGETT IS BEATING HERSELF UP SAYING I COULD HAVE STAYED, I COULD HAVE THIS.

The following weekend FULLER had been invited to MEYERS' birthday party. FULLER met MEYERS through work. FULLER'S husband, GARY FULLER, dropped her off and came inside for just a few minutes to say hello to everyone. BRIDGET was dropped off because no one was supposed to go anywhere so they could drink and be safe. HORSFORD was the last to arrive to the party and arrived approximately thirty minutes after FULLER. HORSFORD brought a bottle of tequila with her. FULLER stated that

GARY did not know HORSFORD. On November 3, 2018, GARY dropped off his wife, BRIDGET FULLER at JEANNE MEYERS' residence. GARY went into MEYERS' for approximately fifteen to twenty minutes. GARY observed all of the girls at the party and stated that HORSFORD was there. GARY could tell that HORSFORD had a few drinks and was having a good time. GARY was sure that he introduced himself to HORSFORD. JOSE BARRERA was in the kitchen while GARY was there. GARY knew BARRERA through MEYERS. GARY did not see anything that caused him any concern while he was there.

COCKERHAM: AND THEN WHEN WE DID THE BIRTHDAY CAKE THEY CAME UPSTAIRS BUT THEN THAT'S WHEN I LEFT, WAS SHORTLY AFTER THAT.

CHRISTIAN: ALL RIGHT, WHO WERE THE GUYS?

COCKERHAM: UM TOM AND JOSE.

CHRISTIAN: OK.

COCKERHAM: IT WAS VERY LOW KEY.

LOMBARDI: THE NEXT PERSON ARRIVED WAS UM I CAN'T REMEMBER HER NAME, BRIDGETT AND HER HUSBAND.

CHRISTIAN: OK.

LOMBARDI: OK. SO BRIDGETT AND HER HUSBAND GOT HER UM THE GIRLS WERE ALREADY ON THE COUCH AND THEY WERE SAYING BRIDGETT COME SIT DOWN AND UH TAM WAS GOING TO TAKE A PICTURE OF EVERYBODY ON THE SOFA AND SHE WASN'T IN THE PICTURE AND I SAID NO, GO SIT DOWN OVER THERE I'M GOING TO TAKE THE PICTURE SO THEN I TOOK A PICTURE OF EVERYBODY. I MADE GUMBO THAT DAY SO UH I KEPT TELLING THEM HEY YOU GOT TO EAT SOME OF THIS GUMBO AND THEN UH WE SAT DOWN AND WE WATCHED THE GAME. I WATCHED TILL HALF TIME.

GARY was expecting BRIDGET to stay the night at MEYERS. BRIDGET texted GARY to come pick her up. GARY said that that was typical of BRIDGET, and he was expecting her to want to come home. GARY did not believe that he still had the text messages on his phone. GARY got a new phone approximately six months ago. BRIDGET stated that she wanted GARY to come get her and that she could not stay. When GARY arrived at MEYERS' residence he stayed in his car and texted BRIDGET that he was there. GARY saw BRIDGET come out of the residence, and did not see HORSFORD. GARY could not recall what was said in the car when BRIDGET got in.

FULLER: AT THE ISLAND, SHE WAS NOT STUMBLING, SHE WAS NOT SPLURING EVERYWHERE, SHE WASN'T DROOLING LIKE HAD TO WORRY ABOUT A BIB, NONE OF THAT. I MEAN SHE SEEMED

CHRISTIAN: YEAH.

FULLER: PERFECTLY FINE AND GARY TEXTED ME AND TOLD ME THAT HE WAS THERE, I WAS PUTTING MY SHOES ON, GRABBING MY BAG, HEADING TO THE FRONT DOOR. SHE WALKED ME TO THE FRONT DOOR, SHE GAVE ME A BIG LOVING HUGS AND SHE EVEN GAVE ME A

FULLER: SO, I LEFT. SHE WALKED ME TO THE DOOR, GAVE ME KISSES SO MY DNA WILL BE ALL OVER THEM JAMMIES BECAUSE THE WOMAN, I DON'T KNOW WHY, BUT SHE JUST FELT THE NEED THAT SHE NEEDED TO KISS ME AND HUG ME AND WE (INAUDIBLE) SOCIALLY AWKWARD PERSON, SHE THOUGHT IT WOULD BE FUN TO WHILE I WAS SITTING THERE MINDING MY OWN BUSINESS, AND I WAS WORKING AT THIS PARTY MIND YOU.

BARRERA: BECAUSE SHE WILL BE A LITTLE (INAUDIBLE)

CHRISTIAN: SHE JUMPED OUT OF HER SKIN THAT MORNING, JUST GARY TOUCHED HER AND I DON'T THINK SHE WAS EXPECTING IT AND SHE

BARRERA: YELLED AND JUMPED?

CHRISTIAN: YEAH.

BARRERA: YEAH SHE'S THE ONE THAT WILL KIND OF BE JUST A MESS, EMOTIONAL MESS.

CHRISTIAN: OK. ALL RIGHT UM OBVIOUSLY WE KNOW AT THIS POINT WE DON'T TALK TO ANYBODY

BARRERA: RIGHT.

CHRISTIAN: ABOUT ANYTHING.

BARRERA: RIGHT.

BARRERA: WHEN I CAME UP FROM THE BASEMENT, SAW TAMELA IN THE KITCHEN JUST GLANCING OVER AND SAW SHE WAS THERE.

CHRISTIAN: WHO WAS SHE WITH?

BARRERA: I JUST SAW HER BY HERSELF.

CHRISTIAN: OK.

BARRERA: BUT FROM THAT, I GUESS THAT VANTAGE POINT FROM COMING UP FROM THE BASEMENT, THERE IS THAT WALL THERE

CHRISTIAN: UM HUM.

BARRERA: SO I JUST KIND OF SAW HER THROUGH HERE, KIND OF WHERE THE STOVE WOULD BE, I CAN'T SEE ANYTHING BACK IN THE KITCHEN AND I JUST WENT UPSTAIRS.

CHRISTIAN: OK, SO YOU WENT TO BED WITHIN ABOUT WHAT TIME?

BARRERA: UM BALLPARK MAYBE ONE THIRTY.

CHRISTIAN: OK. DID YOU SLEEP THROUGH THE NIGHT, DID YOU GET UP?

BARRERA: NOT AT ALL.

FORSYTH COUNTY SHERIFF'S OFFICE
STATEMENT FORM

CASE NUMBER: 2018 0177

Name: BRIDGET FULLER   Employer:
Address: Address:
City: State: City: State:
Zip: Phone: Zip: Phone:
DOB: 79   Sex: F   Place of Birth: Email
Race: W   Height: 5'04   Weight: 180   Hair: BROWN   Eyes: BLUE

DESCRIBE, IN DETAIL AND IN YOUR OWN WORDS, THE EVENTS OF THE INCIDENT OR ACCIDENT:

ARRIVED AT 200P, I BELIEVE TAM ARRIVED AT APROX 900
HAD A FEW DRINKS, PLAYING CARDS AND WATCHING
FOOTBALL
WHEN I WAS LEAVING AT APROX 145 AM SHE WAS
EATING IN THE KITCHEN.
SHE WALKED WITH ME TO THE DOOR AND THATS THE
LAST I SEEN HER

PERSON MAKING STATEMENT SIGNATURE   TODAY'S DATE & TIME
10-4-18

DEPUTY'S SIGNATURE   BADGE #
304

PAGE 1 OF 1

01-00-016 (Revised 04/11)

On Monday, January 4, 2021, at approximately 12:26 p.m., GBI Special Agent KELLY ALDRICH telephonically contacted BRIDGETTE FULLER. SA ALDRICH contacted FULLER in regards to the morning of the death of TAMLA HORSFORD. SA ALDRICH utilized a digital recorder during this phone call (see attached).

SA ALDRICH informed FULLER that at approximately 1:40 a.m. on the morning of HORSFORD's death, November 4, 2018, the garage door was opened at JEANNE MEYERS' residence. SA ALDRICH stated that MEYERS' said she believed that it was FULLER that had gone into the garage.

FULLER stated that did not recall if she went into the garage, but said that it was very possible that she did. FULLER said she had cleaned the kitchen, and if she had gone to the garage it would have been to take the kitchen trash to the can.

MEYERS did not see HORSFORD fall off the balcony. MEYERS did not push HORSFORD off of the balcony. MEYERS did not have anything to do with knowingly causing HORSFORD'S death. MEYERS does not think that anyone at the party would have killed HORSFORD and stated that if she thought one of them did, she would be the first to turn them in. MEYERS stated that she and BARRERA broke up in March 2019 over the backlash of HORSFORD'S death. MEYERS is still friends with BARRERA, and does not think that he would have killed HORSFORD. MEYERS is aware that BARRERA looked up the case file through the Forsyth County Sheriff's Office to see where it was in the process.

MEYERS was not aware where HORSFORD got Xanax from. FULLER gave MEYERS Klonopin when MICHELLE GRAVES started harassing the group of ladies present at the sleepover and also gave her something during her divorce. MEYERS was not sure what FULLER gave her during the divorce but stated it was bluish green. MEYERS did not have any kind of pills accessible in her house except for blood pressure medication, migraine medication, and her son's epilepsy medications. MEYERS did not see anyone give HORSFORD anything, and did not believe that FULLER would give HORSFORD her Xanax because she needs them.

MEYERS' mother paid for HORSFORD'S funeral and for HORSFORD'S family to come to Georgia from Texas. MEYERS and her mother were upset that a stay at home mom with no insurance, who was renting a house had passed away, and they wanted to help. They decided MEYERS' mother could pay for the funeral so that the Go Fund Me

Marie
Yesterday at 10:18 AM · 🌐

Late Saturday night a very tragic incident occurred at my home where we lost of one our dear friends. While the cause of her death is still unknown, please refrain from speculating as to what happened until the medical examiner releases the results. There was no fall from my deck. In order to respect her family please refrain from spreading idle gossip and speculating as to what happened. Now is the time to pull together and support them.

November 11
10:11 PM
Jeanne

It was here at my house. We found her this morning. She wandered outside in the night for a cigarette and she died. The cops know she didn't fall, but don't know until the autopsy comes back.

Jeanne's party....We all went to bed. Tam went outside around 1:57. Walked down back deck ... she tripped and fell face first.... police said could've been alcohol poisoning ... they will do autopsy

there are none. She also said there's a video that shows tam as

fine. Pics n video were sent to Di- anne from someone at the party.

She was fine.

CHAPTER 11
"The Troublemaker"

———

On November 19, 2018, at approximately 2:00 p.m. in the afternoon, I received an email from A. Page, who is Sheriff Ron Freeman's secretary. She told me the police would finally afford me the opportunity of a meeting about Tamla's case. I had made four previous attempts to meet with the police. All were denied. On November 8, 2018, I received a voice mail from Secretary Page telling me she spoke to Investigator Kalin about this case and the case had been "reopened" based on new evidence (I still have the voice mail).

My meeting lasted about an hour and was with Detective Sexton and Heather Wheeler, the victim's advocate for the county (or so she was supposed to be). During this meeting, I went on to explain all the inconsistencies I had heard and seen with my own eyes after our visit to Jeanne's home on November 5, 2018. I told Detective Sexton how I, Dianne, and our neighbors went to Jeanne's invited by Jeanne.

I explained to Detective Sexton how Investigator Kalin told me in our phone conversation on November 8, 2018, that he was going to get Tamla's shoes and check the neighbor's cameras. Yet, the police told the family in February the camera was a light. Stacy brought Tamla's shoes to the house secretly on November 12, 2018, when she signed up to bring the family food. Kalin told me the shoes were not part of the crime scene when I called him and asked why evidence was removed. There is documentation of me questioning the whereabouts of the shoes in the GBI notes as well. During my interview, the police were made aware of every inconsistency and concern I and the family had, and all of it went ignored. I specifically pointed out the text messages Dianne gave me that were sent November 4, 2018, at 2:30 p.m., with two completely different accounts of what happened from Jeanne and Paula. A third story provided by Tina came from Jenn, another partygoer, around the same time. Multiple stories had been told about what happened to Tamla and I wanted this to be addressed. The subject was changed, and he started asking me questions like where Tamla and Leander Horsford, who was Tamla's husband worked, for how long, and what their marriage was like. Detective Sexton even chuckled and said, "Well, that's nice of him," when he asked me why the husband had not been reaching out to the police.

I told him the husband was trying to let the police do their job. Victim's advocate, Wheeler, tried to convince me Tamla died because she couldn't lift her head up from being drunk. "It happens," she said. I said, not to a forty-year-old woman with five kids at home. Maybe if she was eighteen.

Detective Tyler Sexton told me that Tamla fell off the balcony and that she did not die instantly. She may have moved a little and crawled then collapsed. He said there was a lot of misinformation going around. I said Tamla was the responsible one and was the one who always drove. Tamla did not get drunk because she had five boys to get home to.

I brought up the personal relationship that Investigator Kalin told me himself he had with Jose. Jose said they were good friends. He called him by his first name, which we know is true from his statement to the GBI about how Kalin recommended him for the job he held at the time of Tamla's death. Kalin denied this friendship to Agent Aldrich when he was interviewed by his office mate/GBI Agent. Andy actually called Jose twice on his personal cell phone to ask him about the position of the arm and the body, but he did not record the call or document it because he did not think it was important. It is important to know that the GBI agent they had perform this investigation was housed in the sheriff's office, not at the GBI headquarters. Instead of using an unbiased and impartial agent, the sheriff chose to use his friend who sat with all his officers and detectives at the sheriff's office. You could even see pictures all over Facebook of this agent and several sheriff's office employees out drinking. James Dunn, now the state court judge for Forsyth County and previously an ADA, also recommended Jose for the court officer position he held when Tamla died. James acknowledged Jose's previous loss of employment but still said he was a good guy. I would think a person elected to such an important position would be a better "judge" of character (no pun intended).

I told Detective Sexton how Investigator Kalin admitted at 11:00 a.m. on November 8, 2018, in a phone call that he knew Jose touched the body and gave three inconsistent stories. He didn't know why he touched the body. I mentioned everything that did not make sense and I was told "all these questions would be answered by end of investigation." However, three years later that had not happened. Sexton stated in this interview that it would take three months to get the autopsy back and they would use interviews, crime scene evidence, autopsy, etc. to determine if this was an accident. Ironically, the medical examiner decided it was an accidental fall from a balcony on November 7, less than twelve hours after he finished the autopsy.

He said he went to the autopsy and that they did not need the GBI. Tyler said "I" then quickly said "we" went to the GBI when I questioned him about the injuries and attending the autopsy. Sexton said we investigate a lot of "murders." However, Detective Christian and Dr. Koopmeiners, the GBI medical examiner, both told the GBI that no one attended the autopsy. They came after. Ron Freeman told Kurt St. Jour, Tamla's father, someone went to the autopsy when they met on open record on January 31, 2019.

I told Detective Sexton how even Tamla's father noticed in the crime scene photos that there were two brands of different cigarette butts, but they said Tamla was the only smoker. Tom, Stacy, and Bridgett said Marcy and Stacy smoked too. I was asked where I got my information because it was being convoluted according to Sexton. However, I explained the information was coming from the homeowner herself via text and phone calls to Dianne. I went on to tell Sexton how Jeanne's mom texted Dianne and told her we should be "mourning the loss of our dear friend, not trying to play investigator." These people wanted to tell us how to grieve too.

Detective Sexton said they couldn't interrogate people in this case or conduct lie detector tests. When I asked why, he said "You can't just drag people in to be interrogated." It should be known that the partygoers were all "interviewed," not interrogated, in the comfort of their homes and some together, not alone. The GBI handled them the same way—no interrogation inside of a police station. The day before this interview, Jeanne had gone to the sheriff's office demanding the sheriff close the case and arrest me for stalking. She also said that her boyfriend did not access or share anything (contrary to the investigative report and his termination). The police even "instructed" Jeanne to file knowingly false stalking reports and magistrate arrest warrant applications against me. Sheriff Ron Freeman denied phone searches in this case too. He admitted that in open record on January 31, in a meeting with Tamla's father. The sheriff violated my right to privacy by admitting to Tamla's father that Jose accessed my information, as I'd accused him of, and he was subsequently fired for. The sheriff's office reported that Jose lost his job for accessing Tamla's case file, and they lost "trust" in him, but they did not fire him until they found he'd accessed my stuff. Ron Freeman admitted to Tamla's father that he "marched across the street to the judge's office and told the judge Jose had accessed my information and he was subsequently fired" verbatim from Freeman's mouth!

On November 23, 2018, the "attack" began, four short days after I went to police. On November 28, Investigator Kalin called my ex-husband and asked him about my mental health. I have included the picture of the text to confirm this from my ex. On November 29, 2018, Jeanne attempted to file a temporary protective order (TPO) against me for stalking.

One can only assume Investigator Kalin was trying to get something on me to assist with obtaining this TPO (Temporary protective order). Again, this futile attempt was DENIED by the superior court judge. The sheriff tried to use the failed protective order to justify a third officer pulling my background information. Yet, that was a lie because there was no protective order and no reason for the officer to look me up when two others had already done so. I received a threatening letter from Jeanne's attorney December 7th, 2018, to stop me from posting information about the case on my private Facebook. The defamation claims for damages suit came five days after the case was closed.

On November 30, 2018, Jenn, Sarah, Jeanne, Nichole and Mike filed magistrate arrest warrant applications based on stalking. However, Mike did not join the circus until December 10, 2018.

Making knowingly false reports of a crime is against the law, especially when done by a police officer. I was not allowed to press charges against Jose for accessing my personal information, the police for helping file knowingly false statements, or the people from the party filing these erroneous complaints. I had already called the GBI to file a GCIC (Georgia Crime Information Center) query to see who accessed my information even though I presumed it was Jose. I expressed to Sheriff Freeman that I'd contacted the GBI already. He told me

"The GBI is not investigating." I called Kim today (Agent Kim Williams who also was involved in the GBI 2020 investigation) and told her I wanted to see who accessed the information, again halting the GBI from doing their job to protect Jose and the others.

Fortunately, the arrest warrant applications were all denied. However, there was a show cause hearing held on January 9, 2019, at magistrate court with Judge Boles. All twelve people and their spouses/boyfriends came to court that day and brought with them this inept attorney. An attorney whose firm made a $500 donation to the sheriff's campaign—another open record find. Judge Boles explained that if someone was not contacting you directly it was not stalking or harassment. The counsel for these people had five meetings with the sheriff during the case investigation and charged me $1,800 apiece in his affidavit for attorney fees.

Why was Jeanne's attorney meeting with the sheriff during an active investigation? There was no case filed at that point. They even hired a private investigator to follow me days after Tamla's death. The private Investigator they hired, coincidentally, worked for the sheriff's office for fourteen years prior to opening his PI firm.

Prior to the partygoers taking the stand, there was a short mediation that took place in which the mediator was clearly biased and on the side of the partygoers. She tried to tell me I should do what they were asking and settle because she was trying to keep me out of jail. As I proudly walked into the courtroom, I noticed our coroner, Lauren McDonald, in a brown bushy wig sitting with the partygoers in the back of the courtroom. I found this to be very odd but confirmed that the police and everyone else in town were trying to help these people out of a crime. As I began to question each person on the stand who filed a knowingly false warrant for stalking against me, I heard even more inconsistencies. Some even lied under oath, which was of course reported to police but ignored as everything else.

Counsel had to reprimand his client Jeanne before she even took the stand after she stood up and shouted that I was "a hack and unhinged" across the courtroom prior to my questioning. Recently in a comment to a Facebook post Nichole referred to me as "unhinged" and a "psychopath." I asked her why they did not let Tamla leave when she wanted. She said, "We were trying to keep her safe." I said, well, she died. Jeanne stated that Nichole and Sarah left together, but we later read in statements that they left separately and spoke on the phone together the whole way home.

Sarah said she was told I was crazy but could not say from who. The most disturbing comment on the stand was when she said she "left before it went down!" Mike, Jenn's husband at the time, called the court bailiff over and told him to "stop him from looking at me," referring to Tamla's father. This request was not granted. I drafted a lengthy email to the sheriff's office regarding this hearing and what was said by Sarah, Nichole, and Mike. I'd learned to document everything. But, of course, this email was ignored. Tamla's father even brought it up on January 31, 2019. Judge Boles recognized the lies these people were telling and told the court she was sending notes to the sheriff's office since this was an open investigation. The notes never made it to the sheriff's office or into the Tamla's case file. Sheriff Ron Freeman did admit to Tamla's father on January 31, 2019, that they sent someone to the hearing, which explained the coroner, Lauren McDonald, being there in disguise. Kurt St. Jour, Tamla's father, brought up in the same meeting on January 31, 2019, about Sarah saying under oath that she "left before it went down." Ron Freeman denied this was said and tried to convince Kurt, Tamla's father, that he'd heard wrong. After the magistrate court's show cause hearing was dismissed, their final attempt to attack me was the filing of a "claim for damages" lawsuit, claiming defamation and irreparable damage to the reputations. Only half the people at the party joined. Imagine the cost for a moment of representing five clients for the magistrate hearing and now seven clients for a defamation case? Jeanne was on her fourth attorney, including two criminal defense attorneys.

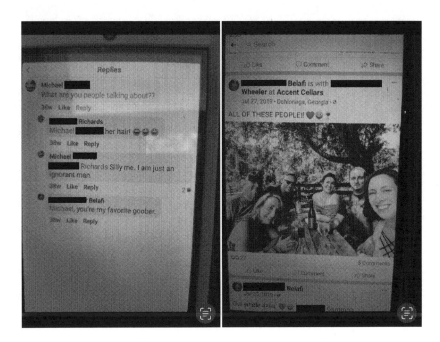

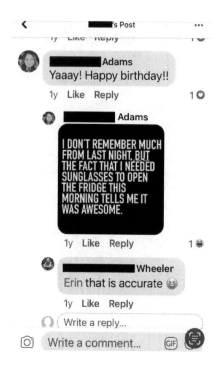

RE: investigation

CJISViolations <CJISViolations@gbi.ga.gov>

Tue 4/23/2019 3:38 PM

To: michelle graves <▆▆▆▆@▆▆▆.com>

Ms. Graves,
The search returned positive results and our Compliance office is in contact with the agency. Please allow up to 30 days for a response.

Denise Hickman

From: michelle graves <▆▆▆▆@▆▆▆.com>
Sent: Thursday, April 11, 2019 9:45 AM
To: CJISViolations <CJISViolations@gbi.ga.gov>
Subject: Re: investigation

> CAUTION: This email originated from outside of the organization. Do not click links or open attachments unless you recognize the sender and know the content is safe.

Still have not revived the info I requested are you still waiting for it?
Michelle

Sent from my iPhone

On Apr 8, 2019, at 10:28 AM, michelle graves <▆▆▆▆@▆▆▆> wrote:

> Thank you
>
> Sent from my iPhone
>
> On Apr 8, 2019, at 9:15 AM, CJISViolations <CJISViolations@gbi.ga.gov> wrote:
>
> > I do not have the search results yet, but will be in touch when they are received.
> >
> > **From:** michelle graves <▆▆▆▆@▆▆▆>
> > **Sent:** Friday, April 5, 2019 4:21 PM
> > **To:** CJISViolations <CJISViolations@gbi.ga.gov>
> > **Subject:** Re: investigation
> >
> > > CAUTION: This email originated from outside of the organization. Do not click links or open attachments unless you recognize the sender and know the content is safe.
> >
> > Have you found it yet because I know the info is there and I know Detective Kailen wrongfully used his position just as his previous employee Jose Barrera did. I guess he taught him well, but Andy should be fired along with his cohort. Is Ron Freeman going to tell you not to tell me the truth as he did with Jose then he said it in a recorded conversation which I have and is why he was fired. I appreciate the effort and know it doesn't take but a click of a button to see who accessed my info.

Exhibit K

https://outlook.live.com/mail/search/id/▆▆▆▆▆▆▆▆▆... 5/22/2019

Case Name:	Graves, Michelle W
Case #:	18061153

LOG OF CONTACT NARRATIVES

Date From:	10/23/2019	**Date To:**	07/29/2020
Person Contacted:	Michelle Wynne Graves (Private Conversation)	**Name of Agency:**	
	▉ Graves (Private Conversation)		
Method:	Announced Face to Face	**Others Contacted:**	Other
Location:	Facility	**Permissions to cross county lines:**	
Purpose:	Case Manager Child Visit	**Type:**	Contact
	CM - Mother Visit		

Discussed/In Reference To:

CONTACT NARRATIVE

CM Stephen Collins arrived at the Forsyth Co CAC. When CM arrived, Det Belafi was present. Mysia Thatcher completed the interview privately with ▉. Before the interview started, Det Belafi stated that she is going to have everything recorded with the interaction with BMO because BMO publicly criticized their department in reference to a girl that had died at a party.

▉ stated the following pertinent information during the interview:
Something happened with BFA.
BFA only yells at her and not at her brother.
BFA and BMO split up when she was 2, and didn't see BFA again until she was 6.
BFA goes to jail a lot.
BFA would make it look like her sister was a horrible person.
Her sister lived with BFA for a couple of months.
Her brother started getting manipulated by BFA and her brother is just stupid and he thinks that BFA is a wonderful person.
Matthew thinks that BFA is a better person than BMO is, but he is not.
She doesn't like BFA. During this past summer, he got custody of them. They were seeing BFA every

Exhibit G1

MICHELLE GRAVES

To: Sexton, Tyler R.
Subject: RE: Warrant Hearing

Judge Boles attempted to record it but the volume is so low you cannot make out what anyone is saying... I have the speakers on my computer maxed out and you still cannot hear anything except a faint whisper now and then.

I will check the settings on our recorder and see if that is the issue.

Sorry.

Connie Griffith | Court Administration Manager
Forsyth County Magistrate Court
1090 Tribble Gap Road | Cumming, Georgia 30040
(770) 781-2211 | (770) 844-7581 *fax*
forsythco.com | Your Community. Your Future.

CASE SUPPLEMENTAL REPORT

Printed: 02/19/2019 08:42

Forsyth County Sheriff's Office

OCA: **2018110177**

THE INFORMATION BELOW IS CONFIDENTIAL - FOR USE BY AUTHORIZED PERSONNEL ONLY

Case Status: ACTIVE/PENDING	**Case Mng Status:** ACTIVE	**Occurred:** 11/04/2018
Offense: DECEASED PERSON		

Investigator: SEXTON, T. R. (B2683)	**Date / Time:**	01/16/2019 08:41:19, Wednesday
Supervisor: KALIN, A. H. (B2637)	**Supervisor Review Date / Time:**	01/17/2019 10:52:50, Thursday
Contact:	**Reference:**	Supplemental Follow-up

On Wednesday, 01/09/19, a warrant hearing was held in Forsyth County Magistrate Court. This case involved alleged stalking with Michelle Graves as the defendant. There were multiple victims that filed for this hearing that were witnesses in the death investigation of Tamala Horsford. I was made aware that the Magistrate Judge did not find probable cause to issue any warrants on the stalking case. I was also made aware that during the hearing Graves questioned multiple people on the stand in regards to the death of Horsford. I inquired about any available transcripts or audio of the hearing. I was informed by Connie Griffith, court administrator, that the hearing was not transcribed. These hearings are not typically transcribed unless specifically requested. She also informed me that they did attempt to audio record the hearing but the audio did not work properly and there was no usable audio available. [01/16/2019 08:49, TRSEXTON, 122, FCSO] [01/16/2019 08:54, TRSEXTON, 122, FCSO]

This letter is in response to a complaint made to your office by Ms. Michelle Graves alleging that a Forsyth County Sheriff's Office employee, Lt. Andy Kalin (CID Division Commander), accessed her information for the purpose of retrieving information on her ex-husband. Ms. Graves states in her complaint that she was not involved in any criminal investigation. Upon receipt of your letter, I authorized an Internal Affairs Inquiry to investigate Ms. Graves' allegations.

During the investigation, there were two driver's license queries initiated through GCIC involving Ms. Graves. The first was on 11/16/18, and this was initiated by Lt. Andy Kalin. On the same date Lt. Kalin also utilize RMS to obtain history on Ms. Graves. The second query took place on 11/29/18, and this was initiated by Cpl. Kevin Mitchell.

Lt. Kalin ran Ms. Graves on GCIC for the following reason:

- Ms. Graves provided emails and allegations as to alleged criminal conduct in an active death investigation (FCSO# 2018-11-0177) where she was not a witness, suspect, or victim, but purported to be a "witness" with facts of the case. Ms. Graves was ultimately interviewed by detectives on 11/19/18, at which time she provided her opinions as to how the deceased died.

Since Ms. Graves interjected herself into an ongoing investigation, Lt. Kalin had a legitimate law enforcement purpose for running her information on both GCIC, as she was also interviewed as part of the investigation.

IN THE SUPERIOR COURT OF FORSYTH COUNTY
STATE OF GEORGIA

JEANNE MEYERS,	)	CIVIL ACTION
	)	FILE NO.: 18CV-2113-3
Petitioner,	)	
	)	
v.	)	
	)	**ORDER**
MICHELLE GRAVES,	)	
	)	
Respondent.	)	

The Court, having received and reviewed Petitioner's *Petition for Stalking Temporary Protective Order ("Petition")*, which Petitioner filed on November 29, 2018, finds and Orders as follows:

The Court has determined that the *Petition* fails to set forth an act of stalking to otherwise support the issuance of an *ex parte* stalking protective order.[1] The statutory definition of "stalking" requires contact or surveillance. The alleged social media statements, while not a direct threat, were apparently "posted" on social media. There is, however, insufficient evidence of improper contact supplied by Petitioner in her verified pleading to support a claim of stalking. Additionally, the Court also finds that issuing an ex parte order prohibiting further social media postings by the Respondent would amount to a prior restraint and invade Respondent's free speech rights. While the postings alleged by the Petitioner may be distasteful, the Court finds that they do not place the Petitioner in reasonable fear for Petitioner's safety.[2]

The Court **DENIES** the Petitioners' request for *ex parte* relief and **DISMISSES** the petition, without prejudice. Should the Respondent post direct threats to the Petitioner's safety or

---

[1] *See* OCGA § 16-5-90.
[2] *See* OCGA § 16-5-90(a)(1).

Page 1 of 2

MAGISTRATE COURT OF FORSYTH COUNTY
APPLICATION FOR ISSUANCE OF CRIMINAL WARRANT

In order to apply for a criminal warrant, you must report your problem to the appropriate law enforcement agency and obtain an incident report on all felony applications before this application will be accepted for review. It is recommended, but not required that you obtain an incident report on misdemeanors before you apply for a warrant. When you have completed this form, return form to the Magistrate Court and sign it under oath. A hearing on this application may be granted after the Judge evaluates and considers the application.

WARNING: False statements made on the application may subject you to criminal & civil liability.

Jeanne Marie Meyers
_____
Full Name   Daytime Phone Number

_____
Street Address   Home Phone Number

Cumming GA 30028
_____
City   State   Zip   Cell Number

I want a warrant for the arrest of the following person:

Michelle Wynne Graves
_____
Full Name   AKA (Alias)

5290 Whisper Point Blvd   678-378-2192
_____
Street Address   Home Phone Number   678-312-6167

Cumming GA 30028   Gwinnett Med. Ctr
_____
City   State   Zip   Employer   Phone

Description: Race W   Sex F   Age 44   Height 5'0   Date of Birth 7/3/1974

SSN _____ Drivers Lic 059473 8 (vehicle) _____ Model _____ Tag _____

15MCR-0743
FIL
Case Filed
1744178

‖‖‖‖‖‖‖‖‖‖‖‖‖

Exhibit "17"

Forsyth County Magistrate Court
FILED IN THIS OFFICE
NOV 3 0 2018

Brachet Fuller

Name. _Jose Barbara_

Addre:

City _Gainesville_   State   Zip

Phone

COMPLAINT AFFIDAVIT

State briefly what happened, in your own words and why this person should be arrested.

I am in fear of my safety. She has been to my home under the guise of being family and questioned me accusingly. She has stated that revenge comes soon. She has stated my name publicly on social media as knowing who killed her fiancé. Most recently stating I won't be home for the holidays with my family.

If property was taken, what was the value? _None_ _____ Was it returned? Yes _N/A_

By signing below, I acknowledge that I have read the court procedure information sheet for issuance of warrants and understand that I am bound by the procedures set forth in said information sheet.

WARNING: False statements made on this application may subject you to criminal and civil penalty.

I do solemnly swear (or affirm) that all information contained in this application for a criminal arrest warrant is true and correct.

Applicant's Signature: _____

Sworn and subscribed before me this _30_ day of _November_, 20 _18_

_____
Clerk/Chief Deputy Clerk/ Deputy Clerk

JG

154

Ms Michelle Ichelle Graves Age 44

FULL BACKGROUND REPORT AVAILABLE »

Current Address

5290 Whisper Point Blvd
Cumming, GA 30028-7028

Phone Numbers

- Wireless
- LandLine/Services
- LandLine/Services

Full Background Report

VIEW FULL BACKGROUND REPORT

Email Addresses

Associated Names

Michelle W Graves

**Court Records:
4 Sources
Found**

I will not use this information to harass anyone whose criminal records are exposed.

**Arrest
Records: 2
Secrets**

< David >

A detective called
me but I never got
his name?? Don't
remember when it
was. I've replaced
my phone since
and have no idea

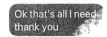
Ok that's all I need
thank you

November 28th

6/28/2019 2:34 PM		BANKS, STUBBS & MCFARLAND LLP Attorneys Fees			Page 5

Slip ID Dates and Time Posting Status Description		Attorney Activity Client Reference	Units DNB Time	Rate Rate Info Bill Status	Slip Value
Seals & J. Morrell					
171642 2/14/2019 Billed Review and edit press release	TIME G:58627	ET RE 3/4/2019 MEYERS JEANNE CIV	0.50 0.00	300.00 T@20	150.00
171685 2/21/2019 Billed Professional fees to William Miller re: investigation	EXP G:58627	VS PROF 3/4/2019 MEYERS JEANNE CIV	1	227.50	227.50
171697 2/18/2019 Billed Draft complaint; case research for jurisdiction	TIME G:58627	ET DR 3/4/2019 MEYERS JEANNE CIV	4.00 0.00	300.00 T@20	1200.00
171698 2/18/2019 Billed Research social media; print pictures	TIME G:58627	BC R 3/4/2019 MEYERS JEANNE CIV	1.00 0.00	125.00 T@20	125.00
171743 2/18/2019 Billed Receipt and review social media posts; revise and edit complaint; meetings w/ clients; meetings w/ sheriff	TIME G:58627	ET RR 3/4/2019 MEYERS JEANNE CIV	6.00 0.00	300.00 T@20	1800.00
171744 2/19/2019 Billed Receipt and review social media posts; revise and edit complaint; meetings w/ clients; meetings w/ sheriff	TIME G:58627	ET RR 3/4/2019 MEYERS JEANNE CIV	6.00 0.00	300.00 T@20	1800.00
171745 2/20/2019 Billed Receipt and review social media posts; revise and edit complaint; meetings w/ clients; meetings w/ sheriff	TIME G:58627	ET RR 3/4/2019 MEYERS JEANNE CIV	6.00 0.00	300.00 T@20	1800.00
171746 2/22/2019 Billed Receipt and review social media posts; revise and edit complaint; meetings w/ clients; meetings w/ sheriff	TIME G:58627	ET RR 3/4/2019 MEYERS JEANNE CIV	6.00 0.00	300.00 T@20	1800.00

MICHELLE GRAVES

CANNE CIV

Case Name:	Graves, Michelle W
Case #:	18119394

LOG OF CONTACT NARRATIVES

Date From: 03/05/2020 **Date To:** 07/29/2020

judge has already ordered such as custody or visitation. CM thanked MGM for showing her around the house that she and BMO own. CM left the house.

Comments:

Contact ID: 65535009

Contacted By:	Bryant, Katelyn	**Date:**	04/01/2020 12:15 PM
Person Contacted:		**Name of Agency:**	
Method:	Telephone Call	**Others Contacted:**	Law Enforcement
Location:		**Permissions to cross county lines:**	
Purpose:	Notification	**Type:**	Contact
Discussed/In Reference To:	Julia L Graves		
	David M Graves		
	Michelle Wynne Graves		

CONTACT NARRATIVE

CM Brynt received a call from GBI Special Agent Aldrich on 04-01-2020 12:15 pm. She stated the following to CM:

· Forsyth county has requested GBI to investigate the allegations that VC Julia was molested by her BFA

BARRERA also looked up MICHELLE GRAVES after she had begun making accusations against BARRERA and the other party members. BARRERA did not know GRAVES and looked her up in the system to see who she was.

At the time of HORSFORD'S death, BARRERA worked for Forsyth County in pre-trial services. In December of 2018, BARRERA looked up the HORSFORD death

investigation over the County system to see if the case had been closed; BARRERA learned that it was still open at that time. BARRERA did this out of "stupid curiosity." BARRERA looked at the case on the County Jail Management System.

CASE SUPPLEMENTAL REPORT

Printed: 02/04/2019 14:28

Forsyth County Sheriff's Office

OCA: 2018120889

THE INFORMATION BELOW IS CONFIDENTIAL - FOR USE BY AUTHORIZED PERSONNEL ONLY

Case Status: UNFOUNDED	Case Mng Status: UNFOUNDED	Occurred: 11/07/2018
Offense: MISCELLANEOUS REPORT		

Investigator: ROE, J. D. (B2448)	Date / Time: 12/28/2018 12:45:38, Friday
Supervisor: KALIN, A. H. (B2637)	Supervisor Review Date / Time: 12/31/2018 13:58:46, Monday
Contact:	Reference: Close Case Status

DETECTIVE ROE sent an emailed request to BRIAN CONVERSE; County IT Department for the purposes of acquiring any emails of JOSE between the dates of November 3, 2018 and December 17, 2018.

On Wednesday, December 19, 2018 DETECTIVE P.T. SIMPSON conducted the analysis of the laptop computer used by JOSE BARRERA. For details see, DETECTIVE SIMPSON's Forensic Report. No information was found in the Forensic Report to support criminal charges of Computer Theft / Trespass.

On Thursday, December 27, 2018 DETECTIVE ROE consulted with supervisory personnel and personnel of the Bell Forsyth Judicial Circuit. Accordingly, this case is designated as unfounded.
[12/28/2018 12:46, JDROE, 104, FCSO]

Investigator Signature   Supervisor Signature

Page 3

F 11

CASE SUPPLEMENTAL REPORT

Printed 02/11/2019 12:49

Forsyth County Sheriff's Office

OCA: 2019020030

THE INFORMATION BELOW IS CONFIDENTIAL - FOR USE BY AUTHORIZED PERSONNEL ONLY

Case Status: ACTIVE/PENDING	Case Mng Status: ACTIVE	Occurred: 02/01/2019
Offense: COMPUTER CRIME, INVASION OF PRIVACY - F		

Investigator: ROE, J. D. (B2448)	Date / Time: 02/07/2019 14:48:05, Thursday
Supervisor: SEXTON, T. R. (B2683)	Supervisor Review Date / Time: 02/07/2019 14:50:59, Thursday
Contact:	Reference: Supplemental Follow-up

either criminal or civil. JOSE denied that the parties worked independent or in any type of conspiracy. When asked direct if anyone had opened accounts or attempted to establish credit lines or make purchases with MICHELLE's PII, JOSE stated, "No".

Upon conclusion of this investigation, DETECTIVE ROE consulted with Supervisory personnel within my chain of command and consulted with the District Attorney's Office. The elements of the crime of § 16-9-93 - Computer Invasion of Privacy in this matter have not been met. JOSE, as does other court personnel, does in fact have authority to access the Forsyth County GA Sheriff's Office, Records Management System (RMS) database through virtue of his position with the county. As part of his job, he and other personnel, have to access RMS as well as the Jail Management System (JMS) to pull incident reports and jail booking information to do their job effectively. While the specific access of the incident reports in question was questionable, given JOSE's involvement in the investigation, it does not rise to the level of criminal prosecution. Accordingly, this case is closed and designated as unfounded.

Investigator Signature   Supervisor Signature

Page 4

F 9

158

CHAPTER 12
"My Credibility"

The police, attorneys, the GBI (Georgia Bureau of Investigation), DFCS (Division of Family and Children Services), the DA (district attorney), and even the guardian *ad litem* assigned to my daughter's case could not restrain from allowing their preference to ride the "good ole boy" train do their job without bias toward me. The guardian and Agent Aldrich both ignored evidence provided by our oldest daughter said during a zoom interview with Aldrich in an abuse case that involved our youngest daughter. Angie wasted time interviewing my ex-husband's new wife, Jessica, who committed a felony computer invasion of privacy against me, changed my username and password in my health insurance account and accessed all my protected health information, from her work computer, on work time, consequently arrested without losing her job or prosecution by Penny Penn, DA. Agent Aldrich hid a police report from the judge and the guardian in my daughter's case that involved a domestic violence incident in which my ex assaulted his wife in front of my son, a minor, and was not arrested, of course. This is the same woman who told Jeanne's attorney in front of me that she would let him know how my daughter's case went in court. Angie told my attorney she was worried I was going to sue her. If you'd done your job without bias per the oath you took as an attorney, you would not have made that comment.

Angie even tried to convince my daughter someone else abused her. The attorney for Jeanne and the guardian *ad litem's* offices are next door to each other and well acquainted with the name "Michelle Graves." Unfortunately for the GBI, DA, DFCS, Angie (the guardian *ad litem*), and the counsel for Jeanne there is one honest judge in Forsyth County who determined I did not lie or make up my daughter's allegations which I was accused of doing to hurt the sheriffs office, proved all those listed above and Detective Sexton wrong! It was amazing to me that no one cared about the well-being of a child but were just trying to get back at me for shouting the truth—the TRUTH about a dead Black woman in Forsyth County.

Thankfully, that day my ex lost visitation of his daughter. I was allowed to move out of state and his child support was raised for a child he cannot see. A lose-lose for my ex and the county, and a win for my daughter and me. I hope Angie enjoyed calling her friend and counsel to tell him the news, "She won"!

I was on to the truth, so instead of doing the right thing and following the evidence, they chose to throw it away and call me crazy. I guess they thought if they tarnished my reputation to discredit me like they did to Tamla to cover up their own wrongdoings, that was okay. Amazing that the police and the GBI pulled my, Tamla's, and Leander's background and no one else at the party. It is quite clear all those at the party had questionable reputations well before I came into the picture. To date, I have not had a chance to grieve my friend because I have been defending the rocket launches from the dirty attorneys and their seven plaintiffs, the GBI, and the DA. Agencies that are supposed to protect the residents of the county. Instead, they knowingly allowed crimes to be committed and put an innocent child in harm's way to protect the reputation of Forsyth County. I have managed to play lawyer for two years, work full-time, obtain Florida and Georgia real estate licenses (including short sale certification), move out of state to protect myself and my family, get a new job, author a book, and fight for my friend by reaching out to anyone and everyone under the sun who could help. All because the police refused to do the damn job my tax dollars paid for. I should not have had to spend thousands of hours and dollars trying to get justice for a deceased woman and uproot my entire family because Forsyth County lacked the integrity, professionalism, and cognitive ability to complete a proper investigation because they couldn't see past COLOR! Not one of the people from the party, the police, or the GBI have spoken the truth about this case, and the DA, Penny Penn, allowed these grave injustices to go on with no accountability or remorse. She should be disbarred and incarcerated for obstructing justice, like the DA in the Ahmaud Arbery case.

An innocent Black woman became the victim of the cult known as Forsyth County. A victim of the brotherhood in blue and good ole boy system. I have had to move to get away from a town being run by nothing but criminals— not just in the town, but employed at the sheriff's office, which is supposed to protect us from these types of predators. Deputy Chief Grady Sandford was Freeman's right-hand man. He ranked just under the sheriff at $124,000 a year. Sergeant Nelson, who was promoted, was featured in the news after having his personal AR-15 stolen out of his unlocked patrol car in his driveway. His significant other also left her weapon in her county car in the driveway unlocked. What is Sergeant Nelson going to do with a personal assault rifle he keeps on him in his county car? What is worse is these criminal officers were all promoted and given $10,000 plus raises, all available for viewing on openpayrolls.com. Sheriff Ron Freeman himself has been the recipient of some hefty raises because of having such a "safe" county, which is why he hides the crimes and calls everything "accident" or "suicide." He does not have to report those, according to his own words at a town hall meeting with James McCoy, the CEO of the Forsyth Chamber. I asked the sheriff directly at the meeting about his stats and what is recorded. All the above information can again be found in open record and/or by Googling the officers who all were pictured on the news and in the newspaper for their crimes.

What is more appalling is these men who committed crimes were all promoted by Sheriff Freeman. Even Investigator Kalin and Sergeant Miller. Investigator Kalin, who helped Jeanne and the others file false magistrate arrest warrants and gave Bridgett a list of police to call in a jam, threatened me and called my ex-husband. Sergeant Miller lacked the mental capacity to check a pulse or assess a human being at a scene he was not dispatched to or in his assigned area. Corey arrived at the same time the dispatched officer, Waldrop arrived. Corey made $70,000 a year in 2019 according to openpayrolls.com and received a promotion since then yet unable to perform his basic duty as an officer of the law.

Along my journey for justice and search for the truth, I met some outstanding people who have also suffered tremendous loss in Forsyth County.

Fortunately, one of these individuals was able to put me in contact with a very well-trained, world-recognized author of several books, and a highly educated retired homicide detective for the New York State Police Department. "Wayne" was able to give me his thoughts and professional opinion on the evidence and/or lack of in Tamla's case based on the photos from the scene, the witness statements, and the audios. He drew the same conclusion. Not only was this sloppy, unprofessional police work but the crime scene screamed foul play. In fact, one of the first things that caught Wayne's attention was that Tamla's left arm was out to the side of her body and in a fist-like position. Who dies like that if they were not defending themselves in some altercation before they passed? The lack of blood at the scene also concerned Wayne. Wayne recently published another book called *Blind Justice* (Gatekeeper Press, 2022) and chapter four is about the following stories and Tamla. The more people know about the corruption in Forsyth County, Georgia, the better.

I met two women who also lost loved ones, both of their cases were determined "suicide" and the same investigators as Tamla's case were involved. Darcy, my new friend and one of the women I met, shared the story of her dear friend "Linda," who was a seventy-year-old woman with an excess of cash, newly married, a devout Catholic, a pickleball player, and on top of the world. Linda was hardly someone who would commit suicide. Statistically, women do not blow their brains out, nor does anyone miss twice at close range. Three bullets were found at the scene of Linda's death. Her husband had his own home in Norcross, Georgia, which investigators never went to looking for evidence. The Amazon Alexas in the home both went missing, and all Linda's journals also disappeared from the scene. The second woman I met lost her son "Kenny" also to suicide even though the evidence was extraordinary in his case as well. Yet, Kenny was denied a proper investigation or an autopsy. Kenny's mother was told if she wanted an autopsy, she would have to pay for it. More disturbing is, on his death certificate it clearly states referred to the medical examiner for an autopsy. I guess our fine sheriff was the one who called the GBI off that case as well. After all, he told me in a recorded conversation that only he and the DA tell the GBI what to do. The pictures in Kenny's case did not correlate with the police report or his determination of death by suicide.

Kenny had bruises all over his body. He was half-dressed and in someone else's shorts. He had branding marks on his body, a visibly broken hand, and was found leaning (not hanging) against a particleboard wood cabinet that

SEARCH FOR THE TRUTH

was a triangular corner piece, which would never have held a grown man's body to hang himself.

The police report stated that there was no forced entry, no sign of a struggle, very few pictures taken at the scene except for what the mother took and provided to me, which were as gut-wrenching as Tamla's photos. It was believed by Kenny's mother that her son's roommate was somehow affiliated with Sheriff Freeman, which makes perfect sense as to why this was a "suicide." Much like Tamla's case, Sheriff Freeman was friends with Stacy, who was best friends with Ms. Deblois, the sheriff's campaign treasurer. Jeanne's ex-husband was friends with Mr. Deblois and the mayor of Cumming, Troy Brumbelow, so the friendships ran deep. If the sheriff prosecuted his friend, that would mean he was associated with criminals. The same reason Jose was protected —because James Dunn ADA, now state court judge, and DA Penny Penn would look bad since they'd hired Jose and he'd worked in the DA's office for the court. It is all about public perception, image, and reputation in Forsyth County.

A town considered to be one of the fastest-growing in the country with no crime and no murders should make everyone wonder. The fact that the sheriff's office and the GBI agents had the audacity to tarnish my good name to cover up a crime against a Black woman to preserve their image and protect their "friends" is sickening. I am not insane. I have never been to a psychiatrist or psychologist. I don't need medication to deal with my life. I was raised to stand up for yourself and deal with whatever life throws at me, not drown my problems in drugs and alcohol. I am a normal law-abiding citizen who minded my own business with no criminal history of any kind, went to church, worked two jobs, took care of my kids financially, owned two homes on my own in this county, paid my taxes, kept my kids in sports, church, Boy Scouts, and mission trips. I volunteered and was attacked, slandered, defamed, and harassed by the police and the GBI because I stood up for a BLACK woman. Racism has been prevalent in Forsyth County since 1912, and it is high time society puts a STOP to the bigotry going on in Cumming, Georgia.

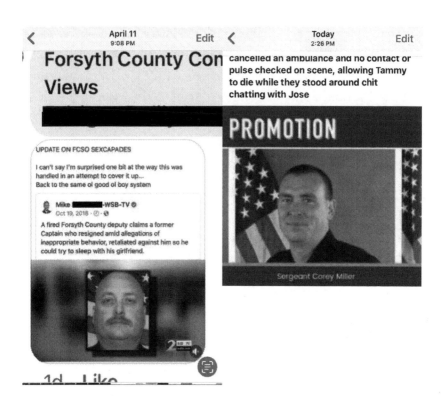

cancelled an ambulance and no contact or
pulse checked on scene, allowing Tammy
to die while they stood around chit
chatting with Jose

Forsyth County Con

Views

UPDATE ON FCSO SEXCAPADES

I can't say I'm surprised one bit at the way this was
handled in an attempt to cover it up...
Back to the same ol good ol boy system

Mike ████████-WSB-TV ✓
Oct 19, 2018 · ⓘ · ❹

A fired Forsyth County deputy claims a former
Captain who resigned amid allegations of
inappropriate behavior, retaliated against him so he
could try to sleep with his girlfriend.

PROMOTION

Sergeant Corey Miller

7/5/22, 5:45 PM   Forsyth County deputy resigns, accused of sending case information to girlfriends

COVID VAX + **BOOSTER**
It's that simpleGA.com

≡   The Atlanta
                   Journal-Constitution   ⟨Ⓘ⟩ Log In

                   Subscribe now and get 6 months for 99¢.

Forsyth County deputy resigns, accused of sending case information to girlfriends

‹ Caption

Salary Records for Michael Christian

CRIME & PUBLIC SAFETY
By Henri Hollis, The Atlanta Journal-Constitution
Jan 8, 2021

Year	Info
2019	$69,843.36 Deputy Sheriff (Corporal)
2018	$61,169.94 Deputy Sheriff (1st Class)

https://www.ajc.com/news/forsyth-county-deputy-resigns-accused-of-sending

Fwd:

Black family
requested report

And of course my first
thought is they did it
to themselves. Because
I am a racist cracker
bastard

Oh he is talking about
them wanting a report
about the mailbox?

Couldn't keep sue the

Sent from my iPhone

2/1/2021   Mail - michelle graves - Outlook

(No subject)

michelle graves <abbey30052@hotmail.com>
Mon 2/1/2021 8:48 PM
To: michelle graves <abbey30052@hotmail.com>

This was what he sent me after
notifying Tams family

M.E.

Well, what kind of slept. Hello sir, I
know we've never met but I'm here
to tell you that your wife and the
mother of your six children is dead.
Oh yes I am happy to report that she
was really really drunk trip landed
face down in the backyard and.
Either through hypothermia,
positional asphyxia, or aspirated on
her own puke, not sure which one. I
know you have fun memories enjoy
corralling these six boys who are now
going ape shit.

MICHELLE GRAVES

(No subject)

michelle graves <abbey30052@hotmail.com>
Mon 2/1/2021 1:24 PM
To: michelle graves <abbey30052@hotmail.com>

7:51 ⚟

🔒 peachcourtfile03.blob.core.windows.net

⌄

20. The reference to an "Order" in the Motions appears to be a reference to the subpoenas directed at Sergeant Garrison and Corporal Christian.

21. The Motions should be denied.

22. The discovery sought in this matter by the Subpoenas appears to be irrelevant to the actual cl...

...s appears to be pursuing ...levance ...

...sing this Court's authority to pursue that g... ...text of a defamation case that ...

...nd its officers are not party to.

24. With regard to the subpoena directed at Corporal Christian, the subpoena is for documents relating to the murder investigation underlying this matter and appears to be premised on the unsupported contention that Corporal Christian has withheld or suppressed evidence that he collected in the course of a homicide investigation. Again, the discovery sought is of questionable relevance to this action and the implication of professional misconduct is abusive and harassing.

169

Forsyth Co. deputy fired after attending event drunk

A criminal investigation is underway.

Forsyth investigator resigns after claims he shared crime scene photos, private info with women he had affairs with

Grady Sanford
Deputy Sheriff,

$124,774.16 $124,774 ⓘ

Forsyth County chief deputy arrested on child porn charges by GBI

Salary Records for
_____ Reeves

Year	Info
2019	$63,212.79 — Deputy Sheriff (1st Class)
2018	$31,716.95 — Deputy Sheriff (1st Class)

October 31, 2018

Via Hand Delivery

Subject: Adverse Action

Mr. Barrera:

The purpose of this Adverse Action letter is to advise you that you will be terminated from employment with the Department of Community Supervision, effective immediately. This dismissal is a result of your failure to adhere to departmental guidelines and expectations.

Specifically, during an official investigation, you made a false statement to investigators.

Your actions violated the following:

DCS Policy 2.301 Professional Standards Investigations

IV.F. Employees shall provide substantive factual answers, which are complete and truthful. Refusal or failure of an employee to cooperate fully with any part of an internal investigation shall be considered insubordination, and may result in disciplinary action up to and including termination.

As a result of your failure to comply, the following adverse action will be taken:

ADVERSE ACTION: Termination of employment effective immediately

---

Good Morning,

Mr. Barrera's termination PA contains his dates of employment. He began employment on 03/06/2017, and his last day worked was 09/15/2017.

Regards,

Judy Turk
Assistant Director, Human Resources
Hall County Government
(770)519-1915-cell
(770)297-2652-office

Salary Records for Andrew Kalin

Year	Info
2019	$80,170.16 — Lieutenant, Deputy Sheriff
2018	$74,043.14 — Lieutenant, Deputy Sheriff
2017	$68,827.91 — Lieutenant, Deputy Sheriff
2016	$25.63/HR — Investigator
2015	$24.89/HR — Investigator

HALL COUNTY

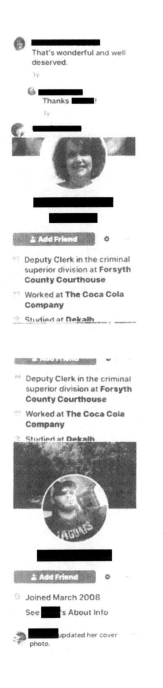

That's wonderful and well deserved.
3y

Thanks ██!
3y

Add Friend

Deputy Clerk in the criminal superior division at **Forsyth County Courthouse**

Worked at **The Coca Cola Company**

Studied at **Dekalb**

Deputy Clerk in the criminal superior division at **Forsyth County Courthouse**

Worked at **The Coca Cola Company**

Studied at **Dekalb**

Add Friend

Joined March 2008

See ██'s About Info

██ updated her cover photo.

1. Lieutenant Shelton was a party to taking photographs of himself and Officer Boughner with statues of black people in an attempt to be humorous that was insulting in nature to several employees of the Brookhaven Police Department when they were sent to numerous people in the department via cellphone.

Huggins sentenced to 10 years probation, has to register as a sex offender

he Forsyth Co... ...e...or Court found former Forsyth County Sheriff's Office deputy Frank Huggins guilty Tuesday on charges of sexual assault

Convicted ex-sheriff's captain arrested again after alleged probation violation

CHAPTER 13
"Claims for Damages"

———

On February 26, 2019, counsel filed an erroneous, devoid-of-any thought "claim for damages" on behalf of only seven of the partygoers, including but limited to, Jeanne, Jose, Nichole, Bridgett Marcy, Stacy and Tom. Since the start of the suit, Jeanne and Jose have withdrawn as a result of their claims being dismissed.

I found out I was being sued the night before by accident. I was looking up court records on the people pursuing me and found this case when I typed in Bridgett's name. I went to the sheriff's office and asked for the filing so they would not need to serve me. They didn't even have the papers ready for service yet. I totally caught them off guard. This lawsuit was a well-orchestrated and well-calculated last attempt to "shut me up" and/or "intimidate me" into no longer posting information about the case on "my" private Facebook page.

From day one, not a single show of empathy or remorse was exhibited by anyone from the party. At the first court hearing the partygoers initiated in magistrate court, they were all incredibly angry on the stand. The most outstanding show of apathy thus far was the picture Jeanne, Stacy, and Nichole posing with Dunkin' Donut masks on at their daughters' cheer competition. Mocking Jeanne bribing police at the scene with Dunkin gift cards and donuts interrupting the aunt's interview with the police. Detective Christian tried to say he could not accept the cards, but according to one of Detective Christian's former girlfriends, he did accept the gift cards and had them in his desk when he was forced to resign.

The seven individuals who sued me claimed that their reputations had been irreparably damaged, and they had lost out financially because of my Facebook posts on "my" private, personal Facebook page only my friends can see. I soon learned after requesting the case file from Tamla's case through open record (Freedom of Information Act) that Detective Christian told Jeanne in her interview on November 9, 2018, to look at my Facebook page and "send him everything she got."

I soon learned that people I thought where my friends were helping Jeanne and the others by sending them screenshots of my posts. I quickly deleted many friends from my Facebook page who I learned were mutual friends with the plaintiffs. I did not know any of these women previously, and in a small town like we were in in North Forsyth, people knew each other through sports, kids, neighborhoods, etc. I had to be careful because I did not know who these women knew who I also knew.

I found a letter titled "Points to Sheriff Freeman" in the GBI file of Tamla's case that Jeanne gave to Sheriff Freeman December 18, 2018, just the day before I found out Jose gave everyone my driver's license number. I found out about the driver's license number after picking up copies of the magistrate arrest warrant applications that were denied by five people from the party. Jeanne even demanded I be arrested and demanded protection from me because I was crazy. Five days later, Detective Christian helped her, and four others file knowingly false police reports against me on November 23, 2018, including Jose of all people. Officer Haff and Investigator Kalin "instructed" Jeanne and the others to go to the magistrate court, which they did. I found where Jeanne ran my background info on People Search, all the while she claimed I was stalking her.

I attempted to retain an attorney during the defamation case, but not a single attorney from Atlanta to Cumming would touch this case or represent me. The superior court judges of Forsyth County "all" RECUSED themselves from this "DEFAMATION" case. Why would all three judges recuse themselves from a simple defamation case that resulted from the death of a Black woman, unless they had no faith in their sheriff's office and the fact that they know the history of their county and did not want to be involved?

Throughout the lawsuit that lasted two years, an enormous amount of evidence surfaced and became known, which further confirmed to me and Tamla's family that everyone involved in this case had lied. As this case progressed, five judges recused themselves—a huge red flag to me and many others who began following this case. Judge Harris, a retired senior judge from an outside county, was appointed to this case. After eighteen months and several court hearings, Judge Harris recused himself from this case, but not before dismissing the claims based on my first amendment right the freedom of speech and the denial of two motions for reconsideration. Judge Harris was kind enough to award the plaintiff's counsel $9,000 in attorney fees they said it cost them to defend their clients against me, which was unrepresented. Fees that included meetings with the sheriff during the investigation, removing pictures from phones, the hiring of the private investigator, and even a subpoena for my job, which had zero to do with this case. All fees were incurred before there was ever a lawsuit and while Tamla's investigation was underway. Judge Harris also denied my counterclaim, even though there was clear evidence these people were stalking, harassing, and filing false claims of crimes against me.

Counsel Bexley even went as far as to collaborate with my ex-husband's new wife, who went into my minor son's phone and took a picture of Tamla's private autopsy that the family paid for. I had sent it to my son accidently and he forgot to delete it. If they did nothing wrong, why did they need to see the private autopsy? The same woman, Jessica, who gave Bexley the autopsy is the one who accessed my health insurance, changed my password and username to access my protected health information, and walked thanks to our DA and her sidekick, ADA Scalia. According to Penny Penn and ADA Scalia, the Georgia statute for felony computer invasion of privacy does not apply to "stepmoms" in the state of Georgia, and they did not like my behavior. I made sure to record this conversation from April 26, 2021, at exactly 10:00 a.m. The State Bar of Georgia saw nothing wrong with ADA Scalia and DA Penn not prosecuting a felon who committed a computer invasion of privacy, which she finally admitted to after lying to the police during the first six months of the investigation. She was eventually arrested but not prosecuted. Mind you, she was told to drive to the police station to give herself up. That way her car could be picked up at the station and not left at her work, where she committed the crime on her work computer.

My ex headbutted his wife in the face and knocked her to the ground in front of our minor son. He then told her he would destroy everything in the house. This report was withheld from the court during the hearing of the abuse allegations my ex was on trial for against our youngest daughter. If that was not bad enough, the sheriff's office did not even arrest my ex for endangering a child, or his wife or for making terroristic threats, because of course, he was friends with the police.

Agent Aldrich was investigating my custody/abuse case with my ex at the same time she was doing Tamla's. As a result of the friendship Forsyth had with my ex, they did not want to find him guilty of abuse, so they passed it to the GBI, Kelly Aldrich! The sheriff's office recused themselves from the investigation into my ex because they said there was a "lack of trust" on my part. Detective Sexton accused me of using my daughter's allegation to hurt the sheriff's office, calling my innocent child a "liar." That is how narcissistic, arrogant, and self-loathing the officers in Forsyth County are. Thankfully, the highest Superior court judge found I did not "make up" anything and my daughter's allegations were warranted after five different doctors and psychologists testified to such. The judge even wrote it in the order that I had nothing to do with these allegations my daughter accused her father of. Agent Aldrich admitted to the partygoers she interviewed that everything else she was working on was on the "back burner." The first paragraph of her statement to DFCS was probably no charges and accused me of lying over custody against my ex and I was using this. Agent Aldrich was so consumed with her own agenda that she did not do her due diligence and instead allowed herself to be influenced by her friends in the sheriff's office by accusing me of starting a Facebook group to defame the police (also wrong) and I proved that in court. As a result of Agent Aldrich's hatred toward me, my daughter was forced to tell her story over and over to multiple doctors to determine her credibility and to find her story was credible and not made up. In the end, Aldrich blamed my daughter's abuse on a deceased ex-boyfriend from 2011 even after my child identified her father, who had clear history of domestic violence. The county has a habit of blaming things on the deceased—those that can't fight back—which is exactly why I had to be Tamla's voice.

I have attempted to file complaints against Agent Aldrich for defaming me and my daughter after the judge's ruling and after reading the DFCS records that I did not make up allegations to hurt the police or my ex-husband. I have been denied the opportunity to file a complaint by Inspector Adkins of the GBI, who told me she simply "spoke" to Aldrich and REFUSED to file any formal complaint. Neither the head of Internal Affairs at the GBI nor the GBI attorney have allowed me to file a complaint. I was told by Internal Affairs he would have to get with his legal team to take my complaint. I never heard back. Corrupt does not begin to describe what is going on in the state of Georgia.

Bexley harassed my real estate agent the day before my closing on January 19, 2021. He wanted to identify my closing attorney and title company to steal money from me and my seventy-year-old mother upon the sale of our house.

Mandy, whom Jeanne did not like and made her leave her home when we were there November 5, 2018, was my real estate agent. Once Bexley was done performing his shakedown, he marched over to the probate court to file a lien on my home. Mind you, to date, I had never received a bill from either counsel to try to collect the attorney fees previously mentioned. One can only assume the "exercise trainer" gone real estate, Nichole, found out my closing was the following day, so they had to work fast.

As a result of the multiple motions the attorneys kept filing to quash my attempts at gathering evidence and properly defend myself, we had multiple court hearings. Judge Harris finally told the plaintiffs' attorneys to stop filing motions to get this case to move forward. A few of the ridiculous motions filed included a motion to quash my subpoenas filed and protective orders so I could no longer email the police about the inconsistencies in this case. The county attorney who represented the sheriff's office also filed a protective order to stop me from obtaining anymore open record, Freedom of Information Act evidence. I sent the sheriff's office pictures of Detective Christian at the scene on the balcony of Jeanne's home, even though he'd told the family he was not at the scene in a recorded conversation. The attorney general in Georgia, Chris Carr, filed a protective order so I could not subpoena the medical examiner for the GBI, Andrew Koopmeiners, who was a public government employee. As a constituent of the state, I had the right to speak to this man. Another firm in Forsyth County represented Deputy Coroner Keith Bowen and filed a protective order so I could not subpoena the deputy coroner, who was the only person who provided a time of death and time of injury in Tamla's case. If none of these people did anything wrong and they wanted to prove I was on some sort of witch hunt, then why duck and run? Why not shove the information I wanted in my face to prove my theory wrong?

Ironically, the questions and inconsistencies I directed at the GBI medical examiner have since been answered and/or withdrawn to justify proof contrary to his findings. The C2 fracture has been withdrawn, and the wrist was broken at the exact time of death, so that was why there was no blood, according to Dr. Koopmeiners.

That is scientifically impossible considering the heart was still pumping at the time of this supposed "fall" he indicated happened, so there would have still been blood pumping through her body. Blood does not dry up as soon as the heart stops, and we know Tamla did not die until 10:47 a.m. according to Deputy Coroner Keith Bowen.

The night before one of our court hearings, in an effort not to withhold evidence, counsel provided a lengthy report on the investigation into Jose accessing my information and Tamla's case information, which resulted in his termination. According to the report, Jose used his work computer to write a bogus letter to the sheriff's office claiming I was stalking him and ruined his good reputation by my Facebook posts, again on my private, personal Facebook account. Jose also admitted in this report he'd shared my driver's license number with Jeanne, who gave it to the others. A computer invasion of privacy is a felony, but DA Penn refused to allow me to press charges against Jose for another crime against me. By tarnishing his good name, that would be tarnishing the DA's office since he'd worked for them, and they'd recommended him for this job. They were not about to admit guilt or wrongdoing. I am sure he was not trying to see what injuries they found to cover his ass and come up with a story before his interview. Jose, according to police, was simply "curious."

Tamla's family attended all the hearings and supported me throughout this grueling process. It was clear the plaintiffs in this case had no empathy or remorse for what happened to Tamla, which continued our suspicions as to what really happened. Jeanne, Paula, Stacy, and Nichole could be heard and seen during the court hearing laughing and giggling. They even had to be reprimanded by Judge Harris after their phones began ringing during open court all in front of Tamla's family.

I was deposed on July 31, 2019, during which I endured three hours of questioning and was asked if my relationship with my best friend's husband, Leander Horsford, was romantic or platonic? I was questioned about which doctor at my job I questioned about Tamla's injuries, how I knew the woman who interviewed Jeanne's neighbor who told her in a recorded conversation Jeanne's Ford Expedition went missing following the party, about my interview with Mike Petchenik from WSB-TV Channel 2, Atlanta, regarding my statement that "this was not an accident," and Bexley tried to get me to say murder, but I did not. The only person who has been "interrogated" in this case was me.

Georgia Statute 16-10-26 is the false reporting of a crime, which Detective Christian, Officer Haff, Investigator Kalin, and all but three partygoers violated through the false reports of stalking November 23, 2018, and on November 30, 2018, via magistrate arrest warrant applications. As usual with DA Penn at the helm, I was not afforded the right to press charges against those that clearly committed more crimes against me. The arrest warrant applications stated in bold black lettering that it is a crime punishable by law for making knowingly false claims on court documents.

Prior to Judge Harris recusing himself, Bexley attempted to request the judge demand I provide all my messages in my Facebook messenger, which was denied. However, the judge did request I provide a download of all my posts made to Facebook onto a flash drive and hand deliver it to the clerk of court's office to ensure privacy. I complied with this request and hand delivered a flash drive to the clerk's office and put it in the hands of the clerk of court employee. Two days prior to the deadline, I called the court administrator to ensure my flash drive made it to his office in the sealed envelope I'd delivered it in labeled evidence for Judge Harris with the case number. My flash drive mysteriously disappeared. And never made it from the clerk of court's office on the first floor of the Courthouse to the second floor where the court administrator was housed. I filed a police report with the sheriff's office about the disappearance of a sealed, classified envelope addressed to the judge with the case number, which should not have been mistaken for anything else. The sheriff's office told me they "checked cameras, elevators, and stairwells" and found or saw nothing. Another example of how inept the Forsyth County sheriff's office is. Mike Petchenik of Channel 2 WSB-TV Atlanta ran a story about it, and the courthouse spokesman stated they were going to "change their policy" for receiving evidence. Now that we know how much "everybody" in the courthouse "loved" Jose and all the friends he had that worked there I found on his Facebook, I am not surprised the flash drive grew legs and vanished into thin air. Fortunately, all the underhanded, shady attempts this town attempted against me ALL FAILED MISERABLY. I made a new flash drive and walked it to the court administrator himself so that there was no way this one could be stolen again. My theory is the counsel for the plaintiffs was trying to have me found in contempt of court for not providing the evidence the judge requested. At the end of the day, the judge found nothing incriminating in my Facebook posts and denied the plaintiffs' motion for reconsideration in the matter.

After Judge Harris dismissed the claims for damage and recused himself from the case, another judge was assigned to the case from the Mountain Judicial Circuit where Detective Christian's brother, George Christian, was the district attorney.

In a continued effort to get to the truth, I sought out a private forensic investigator named Chris Robinson. I sent this individual $2,000 of my own money to review the evidence I had in hopes I would get the real story of what a professional thought happened to Tamla. Unfortunately, this man had worked eleven years prior for the GBI. I'd specifically inquired via email if his past employment would alter his investigative efforts and I was assured "No ma'am." That was, in fact, not the case. After anxiously waiting several months for his outcome and results, I was told he spoke to Dr. Eisen stat, who was the chief medical examiner for the GBI, and he agreed with the autopsy results. His reason was Dr. Eisenstat would not lie and knew what he was talking about. I was told Mr. Robinson made a video of a "dummy" he'd used that he hoisted off his own balcony weighing in at more than Tamla's weight of 156 pounds, and this "dummy" landed exactly like Tamla did. I said, "Oh really?" I asked him how this "dummy" got off the balcony, and Mr. Robinson replied, "He threw it over." So, for the "dummy" to get off the balcony and supposedly land in the same position, it was "thrown off." I asked for a copy of this video he'd made to verify this information for myself, and I was refused the video. In fact, I was refused even a written report until I badgered this man with multiple emails for a week. Then I received a bogus report and no video after sending him $2,000. Thankfully, I learned early on to record EVERYTHING, and I recorded his verbal report I'd received June 5, 2020. Mr. Robinson said Tamla's last moments were not good and that she'd "suffered" were his words, suffocating to death. In fact, Mr. Robinson said he hoped she'd lost feeling at the end with the C2 fracture, but we know she did not have a fracture, so she felt everything. I inquired about someone holding her head down to suffocate her with the deep indentations of grass embedded in her face, and he "could not rule that out" were his words. I inquired about the huge hematoma in the right temple with the indention in the side of her head. He could not explain that either. I asked if she fell face-first off the balcony, how did the hematoma get there, as it was on the right temple? Could someone have punched her prior to the fall? Mr. Robinson again answered, "It is possible." Yet, he agreed with the "accidental fall" determined by the GBI medical examiner. How could someone who fell off a balcony land back underneath it? Tamla's legs were perfectly positioned together with both feet pointed to the right, and her right arm was broken and behind her, with her left arm out to the side of her in a closed fist-like position. Tamla's outfit was perfectly clean with no dirt or grass stains from a fourteen-foot fall onto grass. Tamla's face had grass stuck to only her lips to conceal the shredded bottom and top lips that were still bleeding in the crime scene photos but not reported on the autopsy, along with most of her injuries like the broken nose, the abrasions between her thighs, the abrasions on her arms, the compound fracture of the wrist and many more injuries Dr. Koopmeiners said were minor and he did not feel the need to document or photograph. In fact, according to Dr. Koopmeiners, the only severe injury was the dislocated arm.

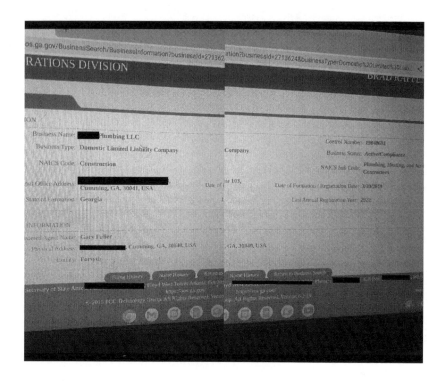

move to!!!!! Thank you to the person who sent this to me

11:05

Jeanne PM ▶ SR Homes, LLC
May 21 at 4:50 PM

I purchased a home in Concord Creek 2 months ago and it has been a nightmare ever since. The communication between the sales agent on property, the builder and the quality inspection team is lacking to say the least. The home was paid for in cash, in full at closing and now my home no longer matters to them or their trades. I would not recommend this builder to anyone. After multiple requests to speak to the builder or anyone that can help being ignored, this is one last attempt to make someone aware.

👍 Like   💬 Comment   ↪ Share

SR Homes, LLC
Jeanne, I have shared your feedback with our team and was assured that our team has communicated with you on numerous occasions. If you have specific issues with warranty, please contact them directly through our online request form http://www.srhomes.com/

September 12
12:29 PM   Edit

1d

It's official!!! I passed!!! I'm a Cosmetologist!

👍 Like   ↪ Share

Home value   Owner tools   Home details   N ⟩

Nichole Renée
3d · 🌐

Services availability

No Data

Coming Soon!

████████████████ Rd, Gainesville, GA
30506-4012, United States

Price and tax history

Coming Soon
Enjoy plenty of space on this 1.... See more

Price history

Date	Event	Price
1/8/2021	Sold	$640,000 (-1.5%)

Source: ░░░ GAMLS #8891001 Report

| 11/26/2020 | Pending sale | $650,000 |

Source: Keller Williams Realty Community Partners Report

| 11/12/2020 | Price change | $650,000 (+3.2%) |

+43

👍❤️😊 126   64 comments 8 shares

MICHELLE GRAVES

Overview   Facts and features   Home value >

X   **Zillow App** ★★★★★ 4.3M Ratings   Open App

67

This home will be featured on the Emmy nominated show The American Dream! Perfect for a single family or the perfect set up for a multi-generational family home. Enjoy plenty of space and privacy on this 1.48 acre Exquisite lake property in the new EAST FORSYTH COUNTY School District! Deep water cove just minutes from Pelican Pete's with galvanized/composite decking, single slip

Read more

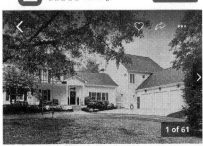

1 of 61

$2,150,000 6 bd | 6 ba | 5,000 sqft

9140 Browns Bridge Rd, Gainesville, GA 30506

● **For sale** | Zestimate®: **$2,112,545**

Est. payment: $11,403/mo $ Get pre-qualified

MODERN UPGRADES

PRIVATE SALTWATER POOL   JET SKIS

SINGLE SLIP PARTY DOCK

EASY BREEZE WINDOWS

Request a tour
as early as today at 4:30 pm

Contact

‹   **Nichole Renée**   Q

Coming Soon
Enjoy plenty of space on this 1.5 acre lake property in Forsyth County! DEEP water cove minutes from Pelican Pete's with aluminum, single slip party dock and boat lift (dock permit included). Lake views from the front of the house all year long and seasonal views from the back and sides. Plenty of parking and storage for boats, jet skis, and vehicles. No more paying for storage and NO HOA! Enjoy the convenience of a salt water pool steps from your back door and a covered porch with easy breeze windows for any season. The interior boasts 7 total bedrooms and 5.5 baths with 2 master suites on the main floor, 2 full sized entertaining kitchens, 2 laundry rooms, and 2 living rooms. Plenty of walk in attic space for storage and an approximate 1800 Sq ft barn on the property for dry storage and toys. Also included is a brand new 3 car garage. Enjoy charming, nostalgic elements kept from the original home with all the modern upgrades and designs for today's standards.

191

CHAPTER 14
"The Relationships & The Money"

⸻

It was not long after I started investigating that I figured out why the partygoers were protected by the police. One quick sweep through Facebook exposed deep-seated relationships between many at the party and the government officials involved in Tamla's case and the county in general. Combine this with Tamla being Black and she never had a chance. On the body camera at the scene, you could hear one officer telling another officer that Marcy, the one who had to work at Coach was more than good because the cop's wife was her boss. Another officer could be heard saying how he knew Jose well; they were good friends. Officer Waldrop said to another officer that it was Jose's house and how he left Jose in charge of the crime scene, and he told all those that returned to the house not to go out back. Since it was cold outside, the officer left everyone together in the dining room. Sergeant Spriggs also noted in his report on scene that he knew Jose. We know Jose, Nichole, and Mike Christian all worked out at the gym together, which was not mentioned in the county investigation, but in the GBI investigation two years later.

Sheriff Freeman was friends with Stacy. They exchanged pleasantries on Facebook, with Stacy wishing Ron a happy birthday on November 7, 2018, only three short days following Tamla's death. Ron extended the same courtesy to Stacy in October for her birthday. Prior to that post, Stacy posted about how excited she was in supporting Freeman's campaign. Through the public record, I found out A. Deblois was Freeman's campaign treasurer and Stacy's best friend, as found on Facebook. Mr. Meyers even sent me a message on Facebook messenger about how he would "back Jeanne 100% financially to get this case closed." The same Mr. Meyers I found makes $29,000 a month per his open record divorce decree with Jeanne. Stacy was friends with Officer Cannon, who was still employed by Forsyth County sheriff's office at the time of Tamla's death, before he was fired for arriving in a patrol car to a 9/11 memorial with a blood alcohol level of .31. Detective Christian had been covering for Officer Cannon's drinking problem and was demoted and taken off Tamla's case in January in the middle of her supposed investigation. Not even the coroner, Lauren McDonald, knew Christian had been pulled off the case. I of all people let him know and this is verified in text messages between McDonald and myself. McDonald is now a state representative for the House of Georgia, keeping the good ole boy system alive and well in the state of Georgia.

McDonald was the one who had his immediate family all employed at his funeral home, and they are listed as coroners for the county—double-dipping in the payroll pool.

In March, two months after Detective Christian was demoted, Sheriff Freeman promoted Christian to corporal—only a two-month demotion with a salary increase as well. Two years later, Christian was allowed to simply resign after being caught sending pictures of Tamla at the scene of her death. The story aired on Channel 2 WSB-TV Atlanta, with Mike Petchenik on February 4, 2020, and can be seen on the Channel 2 WSB-TV Atlanta's Facebook page. Another criminal in Forsyth County not charged for the crimes he committed. Not only did this man send pictures of the crime scene to his girlfriend, but he was also found to have committed a plethora of violations of his oath of office and abused his power. Forsyth sheriff's office Internal Affairs investigated Christian and found he was involved with seven women at one time. As a married man, all this was found in his open record report done by POST (Peace Officer Standards and Training) as mentioned previously. They thought what he did was bad enough to never be an officer again and took his pension, but the GBI and sheriff's office did not press any charges against him. Mind you, his friend Agent Aldrich he shares an office space with did his investigation too. There was no transparency or integrity to Tamla or any other case because of the close friendships.

Former Detective Belafi lied to me about my daughter's abuse investigation and told me the case was being sent to another DFCS investigator in Lumpkin County the day the case was closed.

Nichole is friends with Paul Holbrook, the funeral-director-gone-coroner, where Tamla was painted with blackface at her funeral, who told the family the funeral home burned Tamla's outfit with her body. According to the GBI, that was not true because they tested her outfit, not for DNA, but because of a dark spot on the back side of her pajamas that turned out to have the same chemical makeup as "semen." Of course, Agent Aldrich tried to say it was porch paint transfer from the deck and went back to the house to get a sample. Surprise. It was not porch paint, which anyone would know because the deck paint was not wet.

Aldrich did not go any further with this and never tested anyone at the scene to determine whose "semen" was on the right buttocks of Tamla's pajamas. Aldrich never stated whether any DNA was found anywhere else on the pajamas when Bridgett was adamant her DNA was on there per her statement to police November 14, 2018. Another reference of semen was found on Tamla's tank top; However, GBI specialist, said he could not tell the difference between saliva, detergent, or semen. I wonder how high and how hard the GBI had to look for these clowns?

Paula is friends with Lauren McDonald, who, as already mentioned, performed Tamla's funeral and attended the magistrate show cause hearing in disguise to spy for Sheriff Freeman, which he admitted to Tamla's father on January 31, 2019. The same man who'd told Tamla's husband, father, and me on February 6, 2019, the extent of Tamla's injuries and that they ruled her death an "accident." The same man who told me the "Unfriendlys" from Atlanta stole his county car he'd left the keys in. During that conversation he tried to convince me he was a good guy because he could have lied and said whoever took the car broke in the house and got the keys, I recorded this conversation as well. The same conversation he told me that his office and the medical examiner were holding up the autopsy results because they were busy.

Jose was friends with every officer at the scene, including Investigator Kalin, Detective Christian, the DA, and the ADA's. James Dunn, who just won the state court judge position, told the GBI how Jose got caught for lying and was fired from the City of Cumming, but was a good guy and was well-liked in the courthouse. Jose was fired for sexual harassment and an inappropriate relationship with a coworker. He also had a "fiancée" listed in his personnel file as a contact at the time.

Jeanne's father was a U.S. Marshall for the Department of Justice and was retired from the Air Force. My first two attempts to contact the Department of Justice about Tamla went nowhere as a result, I suspect. Fortunately, since the new administration took office and after waiting two years to contact the Department of Justice again, my effort was finally recognized, and I received notification from the Department of Justice that they'd sent Tamla's case to the FBI field office in Atlanta. Of course, to my knowledge, the story stopped there because Sheriff Freeman was acquainted with the FBI in Atlanta. My first two attempts to contact the Department of Justice were brought up in my deposition during the defamation case, and no one could have known I'd contacted the DOJ unless someone on the inside told them.

Jeanne is now engaged and proudly flaunted a picture of her ring all over social media. Ironically, Jeanne is engaged to a man who owns a body shop (also found on Facebook). Remember the neighbor who'd said Jeanne's Ford Expedition went missing after Tamla passed? He recalled this because they had the same vehicle and would discuss issues about the truck. After doing my own investigating through Carfax reports, the Expedition only had 11,000 miles put on it in two years, and it was serviced at an automotive shop that was in the same parking lot as Jeanne's ex-husband's business and had a right front tire replaced. Jeanne's ex-husband brought the vehicle in for her, according to their records. Previously, the vehicle had been serviced at an express oil change and tire shop in Dawsonville since they owned the vehicle, but it was never serviced at this new auto shop. The vehicle was traded in and sold shortly after the tire was replaced in July 2020 to Billy Howell in Cumming, a dealership that had a relationship with the sheriff's office. Billy Howell was where the sheriff's 9/11 memorial was held every year and where Jeanne purchased her new vehicle she bought (or mommy probably bought) after trading in her Expedition. Funny she got rid of the vehicle as soon as the GBI started their investigation in June 2020.

Not only was there relationships and money, but everyone at the party has since gotten new jobs (businesses they did not have until the year following Tamla's death), cars, and houses. Some even changed their names. They have changed their Facebook handles multiple times and even the GBI investigators changed their Facebook handles after the investigation into Detective Christian. Who was everyone running from and why? Ironically, Tom and Stacy sold their home and are now renting, and had to dissolve their company in 2018, according to the Secretary of State website. Funny that this couple was the only one who suffered from Tamla's death. They'd also secretly brought Tamla's shoes back, refused to let her leave, made her drinks, had access to Xanax, and had nightmares and needed Bridgett's meds. I guess Tamla was not the only one Jeanne should have felt sorry for. Her bestie was in financial trouble before Tamla died.

B ridgett was provided a list of officers to call if she ever needed anything, which Investigator Kalin was nice enough to provide and spoke of it in his phone interview with Bridgett during the investigation of Tamla Horsford. In fact, Bridgett was pulled over by the City of Cumming, and she refused to stop for the officer or roll down her window to speak with the officer once she finally decided to stop. There was a text from Detective Christian to one of his girlfriends about this traffic stop that I was provided a copy of. Bridgett phoned Kalin who told the police officer to let her go and even provided her with an escort home. Kalin reminded Bridgett during this conversation that they were closing the case, it was done, and there would be a press conference the next day. Bridgett was asked to take a polygraph by the GBI, but it was suggested she could not take the test as a result of her anxiety, so she pled insanity. Bridgett was a walking vending machine of medication morning, noon, and night, according to her "morning regimen" documented in the GBI file. Bridgett would start her day on four different anti-anxiety medications.

Sheriff Freeman was friends with Governor Brian Kemp, the governor who also ignored the injustices and discrepancies in Tamla's case to protect his friend. I emailed Kemp with the inconsistencies in Tamla's case, and I found out he'd sent the case to be reexamined by the GBI. Yet, the GBI refused even though the governor was one of the few people who could call on the GBI. I let Governor Kemp know Dan Kirk with the GBI told me he was happy with the autopsy and was not doing anything with the case. I never heard another word from the governor's office. I even sent certified letters, with no response. Funny, now Dan Kirk's own pathologist did not stand behind his own autopsy results and withdrew some of his documented injuries.

Jeanne was friends with Officer Haff and Investigator Kalin because they could not bend over backward enough to please her, according to her letter "Points to Sheriff Freeman."

Tamla's case was a bigger circus than Barnum & Bailey's as far as Forsyth County was concerned. A. Page, the sheriff's secretary who got a $20,000 raise in 2019 during Tamla's case, wrote in an email "for your case file." She was already trying to build a case against me to shut me up. "I spoke too soon Mike, here is one for your morning reading"! She thought she would not see another email from me. Forsyth thought they could harass me out of speaking up for my friend, but boy am I glad I did now. It is clear no one cared about Tamla's case, only protecting everyone involved because they were WHITE with MONEY and CONNECTIONS in the county. A. Page was the one who left me a voice mail on November 8, 2018, that said they'd found new information and the case was "reopened" the day after the initial autopsy results came in. This was the day the police realized they had been lied to about what happened but had no intention of investigating because they knew they'd lost all the evidence and were screwed. It was apparent from the extent of her injuries that Tamla didn't trip and fall or die from the cold like Christian told Leander, Tamla's husband.

GEORGIA BUREAU OF INVESTIGATION
REGION 8
INVESTIGATIVE SUMMARY

08-0381-01-20

On Wednesday, October 7, 2020, at approximately 3:33 p.m., GBI Special Agent KELLY ALDRICH telephonically spoke with STACY SMITH. SA ALDRICH asked SMITH if she recalled TAMLA HORSFORD being sick the day before JEANNE MEYERS' birthday party. SA ALDRICH referenced a Facebook Post on HORSFORD'S page about her feeling sick and SMITH commenting that she hoped she felt better. SMITH stated she did not recall what was wrong with HORSFORD, and added that HORSFORD was not sick at MEYERS' party the next day.

SA ALDRICH also asked SMITH if she recalled who brought an electrolyte drink to the party. SMITH stated that she was not sure. It should be noted that in pictures from the party there was an electrolyte drink that was full and in crime scene photos the next morning the bottle was partially empty.

ID DATA:

SMITH, STACY   (Previously Submitted)

SPECIAL AGENT KELLY N ALDRICH: 11/17/2020
mar: 11/18/2020   KA BW

EXHIBIT ___76___

199

CHAPTER 15

"The GBI investigation of 2020"

————

It was July 2020 when this case was turned "back" over to the GBI for a second time (which no one knew unless they listened to the body cam footage at the scene that wasn't released until after this investigation) after the Black Lives Matter Movement. Sheriff Freeman wanted to put his cape on again and make himself look like the hero by making this bold move, but the GBI was on this case at the scene and Freeman called them off!

There was a march in downtown Cumming after the George Floyd and Ahmaud Arbery cases fueled the racist hate in this country.

Those interviewed by the GBI included Jeanne's ex-husband and his new wife, the officers from the scene, Jose, Jeanne, and all the other party attendees except Jenn and her now ex-husband Mike. Upon further review of the GBI file, I learned on December 18, 2018, that Jeanne had hired a private investigator and an attorney immediately following Tamla's death. Jeanne said it was to get my personal information not provided on the false police report of stalking she filed on November 23, 2018. You don't need a private investigator for that, and she included the "people search" document she did on me, which provided my address and other personal information. Jeanne said the information on me she needed was not provided in what Detective Haff of the sheriff's office sent her. Why was the sheriff's office giving a woman involved in a death investigation at her home my information? I was not involved in Tamla's death. I was not at the party and had not stalked this woman or anyone else ever.

Jeanne said she needed my personal information to serve me civil papers so I would stop defaming her reputation. Your attorney could easily get my address without the need of a private investigator, so what was really going on was "I" was being stalked by a woman responsible for the death of my friend because of her negligence. I had no attorney and was able to serve everyone I needed to. No private investigator was required. Coincidentally, Jose gave the same lie to the GBI when he got caught and was fired for looking up my information—he wanted to know about me because I was crazy, and he wanted to serve me civil papers. I am standing up for a dead woman with five boys who was in touch with her family all night while at the party and turned up beaten to death in a backyard, and I am the crazy one for asking questions about the inconsistencies these people were circulating

These people going to the sheriff because they needed protection was a joke, as I was the one being followed. Jeanne wanting protection when she had the police in her pocket was laughable at best. You said in your letter, you were "instructed" to get your own arrest warrants. You had to miss work and pay $20. Jeanne went on to write that she was told by Investigator Kalin and Detective Haff on November 28, 2018, that they had probable cause to arrest me. Then they called her on November 29, 2018, to tell her they were not going to arrest me. November 28, 2018, was the same day Investigator Kalin contacted my ex-husband to inquire about my "mental health" so he could assist Jeanne in getting a temporary protective order on me. Too bad that did not work. I have every reason to believe that was the case because Jeanne attempted the protective order on November 29, 2018. There is nothing wrong with my mental health. It is the police with the mental health issues thinking they would get away with this. So, the police had a spoiled little brat waving her finger and throwing all her weight around much like her attorney she added to her case in April 2019.

I never stalked or harassed anyone, which was explained in detail to the five who filed these erroneous warrants in court. Jeanne even demanded the police put out a statement that nothing criminal took place to clear up the rumors and that she was sure the toxicology would bring closure to the case. How was Jeanne assured by police on December 18, 2018, that no charges would be filed, nothing criminal took place, and that toxicology would help them just close the case just like that? Why was Jeanne so sure the toxicology results would give insight to how Tammy died? Jeanne obviously was aware of the Xanax given to Tamla that everyone has denied doing. Tamla was clearly not drunk in any videos or texts I had seen, so Jeanne making a statement about the toxicology like that would be impossible unless she knew more than she told the police. Jeanne said they "NEVER" changed their story and the police needed to make a statement clearing their names. There was not a single statement that was consistent in the police or GBI files or that can be heard on body cam footage. So, for her to say they "never" changed their story is another lie.

What you should have said was we never gave the same story at the scene, in the initial interviews, in court, or to the GBI, Jeanne! It was amazing Jeanne could tell the police how to handle their investigation of a DEAD woman at her home. Jeanne tried to defend her boy toy, Jose, by telling the sheriff that he never gave her or anyone my information and tried to stay out of the case because of his job. The same man who was fired for accessing Tamla's case file, my personal information, and admitted in the investigative report about his accessing my information that he did in fact "share" my information with Jeanne, who shared it with others.

Georgia statute 16-10-26 reads "a person who willfully and knowingly gives or causes a false report of a crime to be given to any law enforcement officer or agency of this state is guilty of a misdemeanor with charges of $1,000 fine or a year in jail or both." I wonder what the punishment is for a law enforcement officer who assists a person in making knowingly false police reports of a crime.

Jeanne said I was portraying myself as the victim and that I claimed my personal information was accessed and shared because Jose was her boyfriend. My information was accessed, admittedly by your boyfriend and Sheriff Ron Freeman, and I knew he shared it because it was on all five knowingly false arrest warrant applications you and your friends from the party filed, but they were all denied.

Jose was interviewed by the GBI six times, all at home, and he refused a polygraph. Jose and Bridgett were the only ones asked to take a polygraph. No one else except Bridgett, Jose, and Stacy were interviewed multiple times throughout the GBI's investigation. Bridgett and Stacy were interviewed several times because they were caught lying about their drug use. Jeanne also lied about her drug use but had a criminal defense attorney present for her interview, so she was interviewed only once. I wonder why she needed a criminal defense attorney for her interview. She denied any crime was committed at her home, right? Nichole was also interviewed by the GBI with a criminal defense attorney present. What were these women afraid of? No one else needed an attorney to speak to the GBI.

Jose told the GBI agent he would "try his best" not to delete anything off his phone. Agent Glasco, another GBI agent, went on to explain that he needed Jose to not delete anything, and he would be able to see if things were deleted when they downloaded his phone during the search.

Jose was found to have deleted everything from his phone from 2018 and tried to blame the "mob mentality" of myself and Tamla's family for losing his last two jobs. Jose told the GBI agent it was December when he accessed my information and Tamla's case, which was not true. He'd accessed Tamla's case file for the first time on November 7, 2018, and the magistrate arrest warrants were filed on November 30.

Jose admitted he did not check Tamla's pulse, he did not roll her over, he did not want to see that. He said, "Death freaks me out." How did he know if she was dead or not since he never checked? Jose took a death investigation class, according to his personnel file, and was CPR-certified but did not know how to properly assess someone to see if they were dead or alive. Jose told the GBI he bent Tamla's left leg to determine her dead. Amazing after two years and only looking at the body when frantically calling 911 that he could recall such detail. Like how he was the only one who knew her wrist was "cut," and it was on the right arm. According to Jose, he put his hand on Tamla's back to see if she was breathing and did not feel anything. Also, her leg was stiff, so he "assumed" rigor mortis. Instead of letting the ambulance determine time of death and attempt any lifesaving measures, Jose without any determination or verification Tamla was dead, told the arriving Sergeant, C. Miller, Tamla was dead. This officer cancelled Tamla's ambulance after he wrote in his report that he saw what "appeared to be" a deceased female, so he went inside and started questioning people. Mind you, his body cam was not on because the only officer questioning people and making notes at the scene was officer Waldrop, who was the actual officer dispatched. It is unheard of for an ambulance to be cancelled when you call 911 and know the person is dead. The ambulance always comes anyway. I have worked in health care twenty-four years and know how things work.

Jose told the GBI that what he accessed of mine could be found in probate court on the computer. Freeman also tried to tell Tamla's family that what Jose accessed could have been obtained through open record, but that was a lie. Open record only works when the case is closed, not three days into the investigation that he was part of. Investigator Kalin was adamant during his conversation with the GBI that Jose told him he moved the arm when he checked her pulse, yet Jose said he did not check her pulse or ever move her arm. In fact, Jose told the GBI that was "bullshit!"

Detective Roe and Detective P. Simpson from the sheriff's office called the magistrate court to find out what information was written on the knowingly false reports of stalking and harassment, so they knew exactly what Jose had done. Tyler Sexton put in this same report that I did not provide evidence of what Jose accessed. Your coworkers called and got the evidence themselves, Sexton. Detective Roe and Detective P. Simpson covered up that fact along with the DA and Freeman in their report to protect Jose.

Investigator Kalin was interviewed by Agent Aldrich who started the conversation off by laughing and joking about technicalities—not a surprise since she was office mates with Kalin and was probably staring at him across her desk during this conversation. Kalin said the pulse being checked was in the 911 report, except it was not nor was it in the autopsy. Kalin did not do his job as lead detective of all investigations in the county and check for the thoroughness of the report. Investigator Kalin spoke to Jose three times on Jose's personal cell phone about the position of the body and arm, none of which were recorded or heard by anyone else, nor included in the case file. Kalin said he did not need to record those conversations. Is that why Jose deleted everything on his phone from 2018 so no one could find where the almighty Kalin helped Jose stage the scene? According to one of Christian's girlfriends, there was a twelve-minute phone call that took place between Jose and A. Kalin the morning of November 4, 2018, prior to calling the police. Of course, because evidence was destroyed by those at the party and the police, there is no record of this call. Kalin told the GBI he and Jose were not good friends, but Jose said they were, and he called him by his first name.

Agent Aldrich told A. Kalin that Sergeant C. Miller said he moved Tamla's arm when he checked her pulse, but he did not. He only observed Tamla in the yard but never made contact. Sergeant Miller suddenly recalled he "may" have moved her arm when he checked her pulse after Aldrich turned off the recorder at the end of his interview, so she turned her recorder back on and he said this on record. There is no documentation anywhere of Miller checking Tamla's pulse. Sergeant C. Miller admitted to Aldrich that he did not even know Tamla's arm was broken until they rolled her over. Clearly this man made no contact with my friend at all, did not attempt to even roll her over or check for breathing. I cannot for the life of me understand why NO ONE TURNED THIS WOMAN OVER!! Every cop on the force showed up to Jeanne's house that day and NONE of them checked a pulse or rolled Tamla over. Every one of those officers knew how to assess a person, and they all had AED devices in their patrol cars. You could see no one was examining the crime scene in the picture of Detective Christian and Sergeant Miller leaning over the deck looking down at Tamla, who was still face down and not rolled over. Mind you, they were leaning over the deck in the exact place they said Tamla fell, again disturbing the crime scene. Mike Christian, detective, did not arrive until 10:15 a.m., so all that time, no one examined the scene around the body or the body itself?

Pictures on scene began at 10:10 a.m. by Jimmy Brown from the GBI, per the Forsyth County sheriff's office report. However, Fujimura, crime scene investigator, who worked for the sheriff's office, said the body wasn't rolled over until she finished photographs. Tamla did not die until 10:47 a.m. according to Keith Bowen, the deputy coroner. This is consistent with my belief Tamla was alive based on the bubbles seen in the photos.

The GBI agents listened to the lies spewing from everyone involved in this case and did "NOTHING." You wasted tax dollars just like the police did on a "fake" investigation that DA Penn had no intention of prosecuting because her friend Jose was involved along with her sheriff's office friends Investigator Kalin and sheriff Freeman.

Jose tampered with evidence, obstructed justice, committed felony computer invasion of privacy, and who knows what other laws he broke. Yet, all went unpunished because Jose was friends with all the higher-ups in the county. In my opinion, Jose was directly involved in whatever happened that evening. A person who talked in circles, avoided yes/no answers, refused a polygraph, accessed the case file, gave all the possible "scenarios" for what happened and told lie after lie is guilty of something. Jose told Agent Glasco that he and Jeanne dated from July 2017 until spring 2019, and it ended because of the case. Jeanne told the GBI their relationship ended because of me, lol! According to the divorce records, Jeanne was not divorced until July 2018. During the defamation case when the plaintiffs were trying to fight to get a motion for reconsideration, they dropped Jose from their fight to not be considered public figures to attempt to win their case. Highly suspicious.

Jose told Agent Glasco that Jeanne's ex-husband did not like him and after Tamla passed, he did not want the man around his kids. I wonder why. Did he know something we did not?

Jose told the GBI he installed the Arlo cameras at Jeanne's but did not know how to access the camera footage. Jose had installed the same system at his own house, and we know Jeanne was not smart enough to know how to manipulate the system (my opinion). If you installed the system, you had to set it up for notifications to go to her phone. Jose said the reason he said there were cameras on the 911 call was because he did not know the cameras were not working. He found out later. Jeanne told the GBI Jose knew the cameras were not working because he helped her look for the charger in August. The door notifications also stopped that evening at 4:10 a.m., that was a completely separate system from the Arlo cameras. Jose said Jeanne never told anyone that she had cameras that saw where Tamla fell, yet according to the neighbors, she did. Jose said Jeanne went to the neighbor to her right to ask them if they had cameras. My friend went and questioned the neighbor after the first time the case was closed, and he said no officers ever spoke to him or asked about his Ring doorbell camera. This was recorded. The same neighbor said he and other neighbors called the police multiple times and were never given any information.

The police closed this case the day it happened. Officers that day said "it was an accident" because that is what they were documenting with no investigation whatsoever. This explains why one of the plaintiff's attorneys and the people at the party were screaming "accident" and sending me threatening letters about an "accident"—because police were communicating with the perpetrators and made the victim's family feel as if they did something wrong to bother these twelve-innocent people.

Forsyth County ran the criminal background check on Tamla provided in the GBI case file. Why did you run a criminal history report on the victim? They searched Tamla and Leander's Facebook pages with a warrant as well but did not run a background on anyone else or search their Facebook pages. The police and the GBI did everything in their power to blame Tamla and/or her husband for her death but not the ones really involved.

Whether Tamla was a criminal or not (which she was not) does not negate the fact that twelve residents of your community were involved in a highly suspicious and controversial case. Mind you, several of those at the party had liens by their HOA, lawsuits by credit cards, DUI, seat belt violation, and a hands-free violation. Jeanne had no problem telling everyone via text that Jose had the case number and was pulling the file. Jeanne said she even gave Tamla's family Jose's number in a text in case anyone needed to ask him questions since he was the first with Tamla. The aunt was the first to see Tamla and Jose, and Jeanne went to see Tamla together when the aunt woke them per their statement.

Agent Aldrich sent a search warrant to Verizon to get Leander's location from his phone at the time Tamla was "injured." There was no information on anyone at the party. No one asked where they worked, what they did for a living, how long they worked there, etc. Detective Sexton and Detective Christian drilled me and Tamla's father with those questions. Tyler wanted to know where Tamla worked, how long, what location, asked me what her husband did for a living, where he worked, how long, etc. Tamla's family included judges and high-ranking officials in her country of St. Vincent and the Grenadines where she was born.

DA Penn and Sheriff Freeman were more worried about their county's reputation than the life of a decent human being because she was BLACK. How would things have gone if Jeanne had been found face down in Tamla's backyard? I can tell you Tamla's mother would never have told Jeanne's family and friends how to grieve, and I am sure Tamla, and her husband would have gone straight to jail, no questions asked. The racism that still breeds in Forsyth needs to be stopped and the roots are deep among the DA and sheriff's office, much like the Ahmaud Arbery case. I had the opportunity to speak to Patrick Phillips, who authored the book *Blood at the Roots* in 2017, about Forsyth County. I suggest you familiarize yourself with that book too, to get the full understanding of the depth of corruption and the cult of people that encompass it.

I found emails in the GBI file between Jeanne, and her attorney, all regarding me, my emails to the police about the discrepancies etc. It was clear from the get-go that police collaborated with these individuals to protect the county's image.

There was a letter from Detective T. Connor, who was requested to put the case file together from Forsyth County's joke of an investigation. Connor was also involved in the case against my ex-husband for abuse against his youngest child. Detective T. Connor was the one who said the case was being turned over to the GBI (Kelly Aldrich) because of my mistrust of the county.

Detective Sexton went on to tell a government agency I was "not cooperative" with the police. In fact, Detective Sexton, it was the police who were not cooperative. I did everything I was asked and tried to provide you with facts you chose to ignore. It is still amazing to me the way I was ostracized in my own community for speaking the truth, which everyone who attacked me knew.

To accuse an innocent child of lying is deplorable. My daughter was harassed and bullied by Agent Aldrich of the GBI throughout the investigation so she could attempt to pin the abuse on someone else to protect my ex-husband. As mentioned earlier, I was not allowed to file any complaint about Kelly's behavior toward my daughter. A constituent for the state of Georgia unable to file a legitimate complaint against an agent who violated her oath and works for the state agency I pay taxes on.

There were several emails from multiple concerned citizens about Tamla's case, which all were buried in the GBI file I searched to find. Thankfully I am smart enough to know how to decipher a flash drive. There were even emails from Jenn, who was emailing Detective Christian to tell him about my posts on my private social media protected by the first amendment, which their attorney knew before he took their money. Jenn told Mike Christian she never said it was stupid for her to sit with coroners and detectives and how I wanted "justice." Then she quoted Tamla's aunt, who posted "revenge come soon." I have the text from Jenn telling our friend Tina how it was stupid for her to sit and talk to coroner and detectives, that the family may not ever share all the details. Why would she say something like that about a woman who just fell over a balcony or tripped on a garden border?

I recently was sent a picture from Bridgett's Facebook where she donated to the Go Fund Me account back in 2018. It was amazing how split the community became to protect their reputations and image in the community. Women became afraid and ran to the other side so they would not be ostracized by their community and the people they were acquainted with through football and cheer.

Every one of those women knew Tamla would never jeopardize her relationship with her children, had never seen her "drunk," and knew she always handled herself with proper etiquette. It was not Tamla who was falling drunk and dancing alone in a corner that night.

I found an email from Detective Sexton to the magistrate court administrator asking for the audio of the hearing—no mention of the notes Judge Boles said she was sending the sheriff about this case because it was still open, and she heard for herself the discrepancies on the stand.

The GBI did NOT interview the coroner, Keith Bowen, during their investigation, nor did the police. Don't you think his testimony was relevant since he gave the only time of death in the case and to question why he thought the Tequila bottle should be tested for poison, specifically he said antifreeze?

I nor any of Tamla's other friends or family were interviewed by the GBI. They only interviewed those that spoke poorly of Tamla to skew their case.

Dr. Eisenstat, who did not complete Tammy's autopsy and was the chief medical examiner of the GBI, was interviewed along with Dr. Koopmeiners, who did Tamla's autopsy, if you want to call it that. No pictures, video, X-rays, rape kit, fingernail clippings, etc. The police and the medical examiner stated initially the injuries sustained resulted in her death, specifically the broken neck. Two years later, the broken neck was withdrawn by the GBI and diagnosed as only a "hyperextension." Dr. Koopmeiners let off most of Tamla's injuries evident from the GBI photos taken at the scene. Tamla's broken nose, shredded top and bottom lip, abrasions on her nose, eyelids, thighs, arms, chin, cheek, cuts on her left wrist, finger, and forearm, etc. Dr. Koopmeiners called Tamla's injury to the right wrist a dislocation, not the "post-mortem" Smith's fracture it was. I requested an anonymous autopsy from the GBI just to see the details and how a "real" autopsy is done, and the difference was astounding. There was even a time of death.

Dr. Eisenstat made a comment about the possibility of Tamla "bouncing" when she hit the ground. Where was the grass stain on Tamla's outfit from this "bounce?" And that does not explain the hole in her shin, no blood at the scene, the cuts, abrasions, the huge hematoma in her right temple, etc. Neither Dr. Koopmeiners, Eisenstat, or Sergeant C. Miller documented a time of death, and since no ambulance came, the only time of death was provided by Keith Bowen, who determined 10:47 a.m. The GBI chose to completely ignore this significant fact, as did the Forsyth County sheriff's office. Dr. Koopmeiners said he could not determine if the scratches were fresh or old. Where did the GBI find these circus clowns? How do you work for the GBI and can't distinguish old and new scratches? You are not qualified for the job then Dr. Koopmeiners, but we knew that when we saw your autopsy results, at least the ones you documented in 2018 and 2019.

Agent Aldrich brought up my email correspondence to Dr. Koopmeiners when she "interviewed" him. I questioned him about Tamla's C2 fracture that he'd documented had "minimal hemorrhaging." He refused to answer my questions and now has withdrawn the injury completely. Aldrich asked Dr. Koopmeiners if the family ever gave authorization for the GBI to release anything to me and/or speak to me. Dr. Koopmeiners told Agent Aldrich, his coworker, that the GBI never received authorization to release anything to me. I kept a copy of the notarized letter from Leander Horsford giving permission to release whatever I requested for my defamation case from the GBI and sheriff's office. Additionally, a HIPPA letter was attached and signed, and Tamla's father, Kurt St. Jour, called the GBI and gave them permission to speak to my forensic expert I'd hired.

The GBI and the police never cared to go back and compare the interviews and written statements against the body camera footage to see all the discrepancies.

However, the second interviews were recorded and transcribed, so the detectives listened to these people tell stories that were all over the place and ignored it. Both agencies apologized for having to interview these people in their homes. The twelve never saw the inside of an interrogation room or police station unless they were there to file false complaints about me. Jose was the only one who saw the inside of the sheriff's office for his first interview. Along with the body cam footage, three sets of statements are in the GBI file, and they all differ.

Jeanne was heard on the body camera saying only Tamla drank heavily, but in her written statement a little while later at the scene, she put they were all drinking heavily. Jeanne told Agent Aldrich, "No one was falling down drunk, not even later in the night." Jeanne recalled a lot of details during her GBI interview that she either was not asked or did not provide to the police. No one ever mentioned that Jeanne's ex-husband was allowed on the scene and spoke with law enforcement, but not the husband of the deceased. Leander requested to go to the scene and the officer said Tamla was en route to the GBI, but you can hear the officer on his body camera a few minutes before being told they were still processing the scene.

Jeanne was interviewed by the GBI with three attorneys present—criminal defense attorneys. Why the overkill? Jeanne told the GBI that when she and Jose came running down the stairs with the aunt, Jenn was up and had her shoes on waiting for her husband to get her. Jenn told the police she had to get her shoes on, and then she went to look over the deck to see Tamla. That was why she could not remember what door Jeanne went out of to see; however, Jeanne and Jenn both recalled the back door being open. Jeanne even put herself on the deck with Jose when he picked up the cigarette, the first time he went to the body. That has never been mentioned by anyone else except Jeanne ever until this GBI interview. Much like Jeanne recalled she and Jose were having sex when he got back "quicker than expected" from getting his charger during this interview. Jeanne told Kelly Aldrich her neighbor, who worked for Silver City Elementary, claimed Tamla fell off the balcony. Jeanne told her that was not true. Jeanne was not liked by any of her neighbors. Another said they had a falling out as soon as they moved in. Another said she was fake crying in her driveway the morning Tamla died.

The aunt told the GBI that Tamla's body was "not far from the porch." In my opinion, that does not indicate she was under the deck as photographed, but in the yard where I saw the body imprint and the only way the aunt could have seen Tamla from her window. The aunt also said Tamla was last to arrive, but Paula and Tom arrived after Tamla. The aunt could not recall who went to get ice two years later but told the police initially that she told the guys to get ice. There were only two guys documented there, should not have baffled her so.

Marcy said everyone went to lie down at 12:30-12:45 a.m., yet in the videos from the party they are playing *Cards Against Humanity*, and Jenn and Marcy are still clearly drinking with cups in hand and rolling around laughing on the couch. Marcy told the GBI that she and Jenn slept through the night and Jenn was not up when she left. She told Kelly Aldrich that she and Jenn went to bed at 11:00 p.m. Jenn was up all-night texting her husband. No one went to bed until at least 1:00 a.m. when the card game ended. Marcy said that when she got up with an alarm, which she forgot about in her phone call with Sexton, she woke up at 4:15 a.m. The pillows on couch were in order and house was cleaned up. She left at 4:10 a.m. How did you see the house clean at 4:15 a.m. if you left at 4:10 a.m.? How did you get up, grab your stuff, and tear out of there in five minutes? The 4:10 a.m. door time was a question asked by Sexton when he called Marcy the day they closed the case. It was the last door notification, and it was not 5:00 a.m. Marcy told the GBI that Jose told Tamla, "Don't bring that shit around here," referring to the marijuana. Once again, Jose was standing next to Tamla in the kitchen while Tamla had the joint in her ear. Stacy told the GBI Jeanne came out on the patio and told Tamla," put it away." Stacy was out there, and Tamla was smoking with Stacy. Stacy said this all happened before the Happy Birthday song, but that is not true because Tamla still had the joint then. Sarah was another one who told the GBI she did not know Tamla had marijuana on her but was standing across from Tamla during the birthday song. Bridgett and Marcy, both said no one was being "belligerent." Marcy referred to it to police when they were playing *Cards Against Humanity*. Bridgett told the GBI people were drinking but no one was belligerent. I find it peculiar that they reference an argument or altercation because someone got out of hand.

Jose and Bridgett both told the GBI Tamla was eating gumbo in the kitchen at the island. Bridgett left at 1:47 a.m. and told the GBI she would not have left if Tamla was not OK. It was only ten minutes between Bridgett leaving and

Tamla supposedly going out on the deck. Jose went to get his charger when he saw Tamla at 1:30 a.m. He did not see Bridgett when he noticed Tamla eating in the kitchen alone. Then Jose came up from the basement after 1:47 a.m. That was not very "quick." It would have taken him at least seventeen minutes to get his charger. Jose told the GBI he picked up the unlit cigarette and lighter before he knew what the aunt was trying to show him. The aunt told you Tamla was in the yard not moving and you had Jeanne grab her phone when you ran downstairs.

J ose told the GBI that Tom and Stacy had already gone to bed when he put Marcy and Jenn to bed, which was previously stated as 1:00 a.m. Stacy told the police she and Tamla and her husband all went to bed at 1:30 a.m. Jeanne told the police that she, Jose, Stacy, Tom, Bridgett, and Tamla were downstairs until 1:30 a.m. Jeanne told the GBI she and Marcy put Jenn to bed , not Jose as stated by Jose, Marcy and Jenn.

The horrible things that the people said about Tamla makes me wonder if her invitation was a set up? No one from the party has ever said a nice thing about her since she died. Why did they want her in their intimate group that night, according to Nichole?

Stacy had diarrhea of the mouth about the party that night and specifically her dislike for Tamla that evening. Stacy got caught in a lie with Agent Aldrich even after Aldrich told Stacy, that if she lies about drugs, she would be lying about other things. Aldrich specifically asked Stacy if she asked Bridgett to meet her in a parking lot to get her drugs, which Stacy denied. When Aldrich told her, she'd found the texts about this in her phone search, Stacy said she did not recall. Stacy said that she got meds from her own doctor, but it was not Xanax, and she did not take it. Stacy said she took the medication because she could not sleep because she was having nightmares after Tamla passed. Stacy forgot to mention she took it the morning Tamla died only after Kelly Aldrich told her she'd found that too on her phone. The GBI found texts on Stacy's phone that said "Tamla fell down the stairs and hit her head at 2:00 a.m." and Tamla fell face-first that Stacy sent in a group text to multiple friends. The neighbor told the GBI Jeanne told her she had video to prove Tamla fell face-first and did not try to stop herself. If Tamla was seen falling, then why did they not call 911? Why was the scenario of Tamla falling down the stairs never "floated" as a theory like Detective Christian liked to refer to? Jose never produced that scenario like he did all the other erroneous ones.

Stacy said she and Tamla had been hanging out for about a month before she passed. Tom, who was Stacy's husband, said the two had been hanging out for the last six months. Tamla and I were friends for five years. One party with you and her other "new friends" and she is dead. Tamla had no reason to want "new friends." In fact, Tom told the GBI Tamla had many groups of friends from sports, school, the neighborhood, etc. Stacy told the GBI she brought Tamla's boots back and did not believe Tamla wore them to the party. She said she found them in the dining room and when she brought them to Leander, he was distraught. Stacy said the police forgot them. If Stacy didn't think Tamla wore the shoes to Jeanne's that night, then what did she wear and where are those? There was a suspicious text the GBI pulled from Bridgett's phone regarding shoes. I have questioned whether her shoes were replaced for some reason. Bridgett and her husband Gary discussed shoe sizes in the same text thread of her wanting her husband to come get her that night.

Jose was interviewed six separate times by the GBI (all were hidden in the file and not marked by name, but odd number sequences). He refused a polygraph and could not give a straight answer when asked about how many times he met Tamla since he said once in the 911 call, but four times when interviewed by police on November 9, 2018. The arriving Sergeant, C. Miller, did not do his job and check Tamla's pulse or even have contact with the body before he CANCELLED her ambulance en route. Also, the fire department was cancelled upon arrival at the scene. Miller said he did not see anything strange about Tamla's death. Miller was not the one dispatched to the scene by the 911 dispatcher on the phone with Jose. Why would you not let the fire department check the body? You can see them arrive in the body camera footage and just leave. Jose admitted he accessed Tamla's case to see if it were closed and to see the reports in the file at that point. Agent Aldrich also said the neighbor she interviewed did not have a Ring camera at time of Tamla's death. Remember, when Christian was playing doorbell tag with the neighbors, the neighbor my friend spoke to had a Ring camera.

Gary was interviewed twice by Agent Aldrich; he did not mention anyone else being drunk except Tamla and he said he dropped Bridgett off at 2:00 p.m. or 3:00 p.m. in the afternoon. Tamla did not get to the party until 8:34 p.m. There were four men total at this "all-girls" sleepover party, but that was also ignored by both law enforcement agencies. Gary was asked what he'd heard when he brought his wife back to be questioned and he said he'd heard Tamla was lying just a few feet out from under the deck, like she fell straight down.

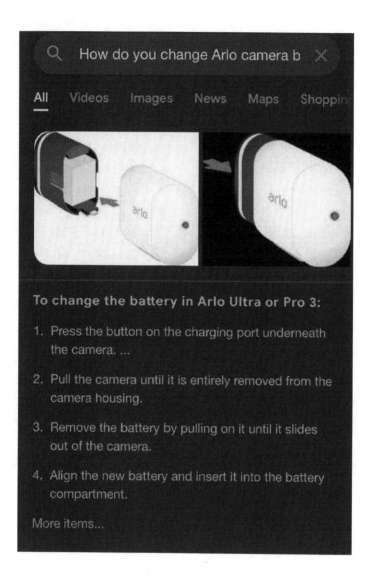

Q How do you change Arlo camera b ✕

All   Videos   Images   News   Maps   Shopping

To change the battery in Arlo Ultra or Pro 3:

1. Press the button on the charging port underneath the camera. ...

2. Pull the camera until it is entirely removed from the camera housing.

3. Remove the battery by pulling on it until it slides out of the camera.

4. Align the new battery and insert it into the battery compartment.

More items...

SA GLASCO asked MEYERS if she had ever told anyone that she had a video of HORSFORD'S death. MEYERS stated she did not, and that she only talked to the neighbors to the left of her house and had told them she wished that her cameras had been working. MEYERS only told them that because they came outside because they were mad about the news crews. MEYERS stated that she had cameras on all entry points of her house to include the front door, garage door, back deck, and basement door.

CONV WITH JEANNE MEYERS REGARDING ARLO CAMERA SYSTEM:
On Monday, November 19th at approximately 1000 hours, this detective spoke with Jeanne Meyers via telephone in regard to her camera system at her house.
Jeanne said she would forward me her camera information and password in order for me to glean whatever information I needed from her home security system.
She sent me an e-mail with her ARLO Security System information and password. This e-mail also contained a forwarded message from ARLO dated on August 18th of this year stating the ARLO battery was low and needing attention. This corresponds to Meyers statement that the cameras charger had gone missing approximately three months ago.
A copy of this e-mail will be added to the case file.
At approximately 1430 hours, I accessed Jeanne Meyers ARLO system via the information provided. The ARLO System shows that recording at the Meyers house started back on November 8th. The system also shows there was a camera which had the system been in working order on the night of the third or morning of the fourth of November would have captured activity on the back porch. Photographs of the ARLO display were taken and added to the case file.

MEYERS: NO, DID YOU GET THE NEIGHBOR'S VIDEO CAMERA?

CHRISTIAN: WE'VE BEEN PLAYING PHONE AND DOORBELL TAG. THEY,

SEXTON: (INAUDIBLE) TALK TO THEM.

CHRISTIAN: I LEFT MY STUFF, THEY CALLED ME, JUST WE HAVEN'T CONNECTED. BUT

At the end of the night when STACY and THOMAS went to bed, STACY could not recall exactly what time it was, the following people were still there: MEYERS, BARRERA, SEALS, TAMLA, MORRELL, HARDIN, BRIDGET FULLER, and MADELINE LOMBARDI who was in bed. STACY and THOMAS went to go to bed, and TAMLA tried to get STACY to stay up with her. TAMLA was making jokes about not having anyone to sleep with so STACY set her phone next to TAMLA'S and said their phones could sleep together. STACY and THOMAS then went to bed together. Everyone kind of went to bed about the same time. STACY stated that neither she nor THOMAS got up during the night and they never heard anything. STACY stated that bothered her because the bedroom they were sleeping in was above the living room which the deck is off of. When everyone went to bed FULLER and TAMLA were the only ones that were still up. STACY knew that TAMLA was going to stay the night because she had talked about going home. THOMAS told her not to drink and drive. TAMLA stated that she was going to smoke and then go to bed. When STACY went to bed TAMLA seemed fine, was having fun, and was not slurring or stumbling. STACY stated that TAMLA was laughing and having fun, and was just her typical personality.

LOMBARDI was cleaning and misplaced the charger, so the cameras were not charged. MEYERS was not worried about them being charged because she and her ex-husband were amicable at the time and she did not feel like she needed the cameras. MEYERS also had door openings monitored through Xfinity. MEYERS was only able to pull up thirty events on the door times and after that you have to request them. SA ALDRICH asked MEYERS if she was aware if Xfinity updates their time during daylight savings time since SA ALDRICH knew that the time changed on the night of the 3rd into the 4th. MEYERS was not aware if they updated their times. MEYERS was the only one that got notifications from Arlo and Xfinity, and the only one that had access to either of them. BARRERA did not have access to the cameras or the door times, but did know that the cameras were not charged because he had helped her look for the charger.

Sent 1:49 PM, SMITH: "Hey, do you have Lee's number?"
Sent 1:49 PM, SMITH: "Do you know how they are."
Sent 1:49 PM, SMITH: "?"
Received 1:50 PM, CASSIE: "Who is this?"
Sent 1:50 PM, SMITH: "Stacy"
Sent 1:50 PM, SMITH: "Tam was with us last night"
Received 1:50 PM, CASSIE: "I know Stephan is with him"
Received 1:51 PM, CASSIE: "The police was leaving"
Sent 1:51 PM, SMITH: "We were drinking and everyone went to bed and she said she was going to smoke and then to bed."
Received 1:51 PM, CASSIE: "She was found this morning?"
Sent 1:52 PM, SMITH: "Yes"
Sent 1:52 PM, SMITH: "She passed out and fell face first."
Sent 1:52 PM, SMITH: "We all thought she was in bed sleeping"
Received 1:52 PM, CASSIE: "My god!!! This is so bad...those poor babies"
Sent 1:53 PM, SMITH: "I know, I'm such a mess. She was so happy last night"
Sent 1:53 PM, SMITH: "We had so much fun"
Received 1:55 PM, CASSIE: "I don't know what to do"
Received 1:56 PM, CASSIE: "They have no family here"
Received 1:56 PM, CASSIE: "The Reynolds are over there"

11/4/18 Group message with HORSFORD, LACY, NIKKI, DENSMORE, ANNA LNU, "KC", and MELANIE:
Sent 4:34 PM, SMITH: "Everyone please pray for Tam's family. They need all the prayers they can get."

lived at their residence since March 14, 2014. MARY ANN described the female resident of 4450 Woodlet Court as the neighborhood gossip. MARY ANN could not recall the resident's name or her boyfriend's name. MARY ANN recalled the homeowner's boyfriend as being weird. MARY ANN could not provide any details of

MEYERS advised that the video showed HORSFORD went outside to smoke a cigarette. HORSFORD fell and "she didn't try to catch herself."

Approximately two days later, MEYERS came to BLAKE'S residence and advised she owed him an explanation for the large police presence at her residence. MEYERS advised BLAKE that people had been saying someone fell off her balcony. MEYERS denied this and stated the video she had proved it. MEYERS advised that one of the neighbors worked for Silver City Elementary School and was claiming that HORSFORD had fallen off of her balcony; MEYERS claimed this was untrue.

Later that morning BLAKE and his family went to breakfast at around 9:00 a.m. BLAKE recalled seeing a white male and a white female leaving 4450 Woodlet Court at that time. One of the individuals was holding a crockpot. The male and female got into a

MICHELLE GRAVES

4465 Woodlet Court is located in the cul-de-sac adjacent to 4450 Woodlet Court where
HORSFORD died. SA ALDRICH asked LAMY if she recalled the morning that
HORSFORD was found deceased. LAMY stated that she did, but that she did not
realize that anything was going on at 4450 Woodlet Court until approximately 11:00 a.m.
on November 4, 2018. After LAMY saw what was going on across the street she
checked the video from her Ring doorbell. LAMY stated that at approximately 3:00 or
3:30 a.m. a vehicle pulled into the cul-de-sac and went right back out. LAMY was not
able to tell where the vehicle came from or what kind of vehicle it was. LAMY stated
that you could only see headlights circle around the cul-de-sac. SA ALDRICH asked
LAMY if she had by chance saved the video, and LAMY stated that she had not.

On Tuesday, December 29, 2020, at approximately 11:08 a.m., GBI Special Agent
KELLY ALDRICH received an email from JEANNE MEYERS attorney, ZACK SMITH
(attached). SA ALDRICH had previously spoken to SMITH to request MEYERS
inform SA ALDRICH which door on her Xfinity door alerts was the back door, which was
the garage door, who went into the garage on the morning of November 4, 2018, and if
MEYERS had an official copy of the door alerts from Xfinity from November 4, 2018.

SMITH stated that he had spoken to MEYERS regarding her Xfinity door alerts.
MEYERS stated that on the alerts the back door was the door to back deck, and the
garage door was the door from the house to the garage. BRIDGETTE FULLER was
the one who opened the garage door around 1:40 a.m. on November 4, 2018, according
to MEYERS. MEYERS did not have records from Xfinity, and only had the screenshot
of the door alerts that she previously provided to the Forsyth County Sheriff's Office.

GEORGIA BUREAU OF INVESTIGATION
REGION 8
INVESTIGATIVE SUMMARY

<u>08-0381-01-20</u>

On Thursday, September 10, 2020, at approximately 2:15 p.m., GBI Special Agent
KELLY ALDRICH was located at the Forsyth County Adult Detention Center for the
purpose of speaking with STEVEN REYNOLDS. SA ALDRICH had to interview
REYNOLDS using an attorney/client video booth at the Adult Detention Center, and
therefore was not able to record the interview with REYNOLDS.

SA ALDRICH asked REYNOLDS if there was any information he could provide
regarding the death of TAMLA HORSFORD, who died on November 4, 2018.
REYNOLDS stated essentially the following:

TAMLA'S husband, LEANDER HORSFORD, is REYNOLDS' best friend. Their kids
play football together. LEANDER and TAMLA were close, and according to
REYNOLDS were soulmates. TAMLA and LEANDER had normal disagreements but
always agreed to work things out. REYNOLDS and his wife considered LEANDER and
TAMLA relationship role models.

TAMLA and LEANDER'S house was always used for football parties and get togethers.
TAMLA was not a confrontational person and got along with everyone.

TAMLA did not get along with JEN MORRELL and had said that she did not like
MORRELL's "vibe". REYNOLDS was told by his wife and MICHELLE GRAVES that
TAMLA said that day that if MORRELL was at JEANNE MEYER's party, she was not
going to stay. REYNOLDS' wife and GRAVES also said that they told TAMLA they did
not want her to go because they felt like the girls that were going to be at the party were

EXHIBIT 74

223

08-0381-01-20

In the above mentioned conversation DENSMORE stated that HORSFORD, "...fell down steps and hit her head". SMITH stated that HORSFORD, "...passed away this morning around 2am. It is very tragic and a huge shock to all." SMITH then stated that HORSFORD, "...tripped over mulch". SMITH then said, "We don't know the exact cause of death yet. She was happy as could be last night and having a blast.", and "...we had a sleepover at Jeanne's to celebrate Jeanne's birthday." SMITH added that she and JEANNE MEYER's were the last one's to see HORSFORD. The conversation continues regarding everyone being shocked and LEANDER HORSFORD needing their help and support.

SA ALDRICH did not observe anything else of significance related the investigation into HORSFORD's death in the Facebook records.

Sent 2:46 PM, BRIDGETTE: "Jose has me"

11/21/18 Messages with MEYERS:
Received 8:39 PM, MEYERS: "How mg/strength is your Xanax?"
Sent 8:41 PM, FULLER: "I have 1mg ones"
Received 8:42 PM, MEYERS: "Ok my cousin takes those too"

11/25/18 Messages with KATE ANDERSON:
Sent 2:28 PM, FULLER: "Because of all the damn bullshit still going on with the Tam thing"
Received 2:18 PM, ANDERSON: "What's the current update on all that?"
Sent 2:32 PM, FULLER: "Murder & coverup conspiracy with the police force involved its great"

SA ALDRICH informed FULLER that she had follow-up questions regarding information found on STACY SMITH'S cell phone. SA ALDRICH reminded FULLER that during her initial interview she stated that she never shared her Xanax with anyone. SA ALDRICH then informed FULLER that SA ALDRICH found text messages on SMITH'S cell phone that led SA ALDRICH to believed that FULLER had given SMITH and possibly JEANNE MEYERS medication. FULLER stated that she gave MEYERS medication when MEYERS was going through her divorce. FULLER stated that she gave SMITH a smaller milligram of Xanax then what FULLER normally takes the morning of HORSFORD'S death because SMITH was upset. FULLER stated that she only gave SMITH and MEYERS medication because she knows them well and would not have given HORSFORD any of her Xanax. FULLER stated she especially would not have given it to HORSFORD not knowing what her reaction would be to it and because she was drinking.

GEORGIA BUREAU OF INVESTIGATION
REGION 8
INVESTIGATIVE SUMMARY

<u>08-0381-01-20</u>

On Monday, August 3, 2020, GBI Special Agent KELLY ALDRICH reviewed BRIDGETTE FULLER's cell phone download, and noted the following messages:

It should be noted that all times listed are UTC -4.

11/3/18 Messages with JEANNE MEYERS:
Sent 2:01 PM, FULLER: "Hey sweets What's the time to come to your house"
Received 4:23 PM, MEYERS: "7:30"
Sent 4:24 PM, FULLER: "K"
Sent 7:36 PM, FULLER: "Is there anything u need b4 i get there"
Received 7:47 PM, MEYERES: "Maybe blueberry vodka"
Sent 8:02 PM, FULLER: "Well gary got a big one for u"

11/4/18 Messages with GARY FULLER:
Sent 1:13 AM, BRIDGETTE: "I don't want to stay here"
Sent 1:20 AM, BRIDGETTE: "Baby please"
Sent 1:20 AM, BRIDGETTE: "Its to much"
Received 1:23 AM, GARY: "Why did you even act like you were gonna stay then"
Sent 1:27 AM, BRIDGETTE: "Plz baby"
Received 1:27 AM, GARY: "I'm fucking coming"
Received 1:45 AM, GARY: "Let's go, I am here"
Sent 2:42 PM, BRIDGETTE: "U can get me"
Received 2:43 PM, GARY: "Ok"
Sent 2:45 PM, BRIDGETTE: "Never mind i got it covered"

EXHIBIT ___56___

The following morning LAWSON received a phone call from MEYERS around 9:30 or 10:00 a.m. MEYERS was hysterical and told LAWSON that she had to come back to her house because they had found HORSFORD deceased in the backyard. LAWSON waited for her dad to get to her house to watch her daughter, approximately three minutes or so, and left to go back to MEYERS. On the way LAWSON called COCKERHAM to tell her. LAWSON believed that she was the first one back at MEYERS' residence of the people that had left the residence already. LAWSON met with law enforcement outside the residence, and never went back inside.

The following morning FULLER received a phone call at approximately 9:00 a.m. from MEYERS saying, "she's dead", MEYERS told FULLER to come back to the house and said, "I can't believe TAM'S gone".

CHRISTIAN: RIGHT.

FULLER: IT WASN'T LIKE INTENTION, NOT WHAT SO EVER, I'M JUST TELLING YOU FROM MY PERSPECTIVE.

INTERVIEW, BRIDGETT FULLER:
On Wednesday, November 14th, 2018 at approximately 1015 hours, Bridget Fuller was interviewed at

Present for this interview was Bridget Fuller and this Detective. FCSO Cpl. Sexton was present in the office. Cpl. Sexton did not sit in on the interview due to Fuller's agitated state. This interview was recorded in audio. A copy of the interview will be placed in the case file. What follows is a transcription.
INTERVIEW WITH:
BRIDGET FULLER
11/14/18

CHRISTIAN: IN THE PICTURE I'VE SEEN YOU'RE IN THERE ON YOUR LAPTOP.

FULLER: YEAH BUT I DO IT ALL THE TIME, I MEAN I WORK ALL WEEKEND.

CHRISTIAN: YEAH.

FULLER: ALL WEEK, MY SHIT DOESN'T STOP. NOW DO I DO IT FOR LONG LENGTHY PERIODS NO BUT I DO HAVE TO KEEP UP ON THINGS.

CHRISTIAN: YEAH.

FULLER: SO I WAS SITTING THERE DOING THAT AND EVERYTHING AND SHE GOES I JUST DON'T THINK YOU'RE IN THE FULL SWING OF THIS AND SHE COMES OVER AND SHE JUMPS ON MY LAP AND SHE STRADDLES MY LAP AND SHE GOES, YOU NEED TO RELAX. MEANWHILE I HAD A BOTTLE IN MY HAND AND I'M LIKE JOSE WAS BESIDE ME AND I'M LIKE HERE. THIS IS GOING TO END UP ON THE CARPET AND IT'S GOING TO PISS JEANNE OFF. I'M CONSTANTLY CHASING CUPS AND STUFF UNDER PEOPLE'S ASSES I'M LIKE YOU'RE GOING TO KNOCK IT OFF, IT'S GOING TO MAKE A STICKY MESS. SEE, MOTHER HEN.

SA ALDRICH asked FULLER if he recalled what time he dropped his wife BRIDGET FULLER off at JEANNE MEYERS' residence on November 3, 2018 for MEYERS' birthday party. FULLER stated that he believed he dropped BRIDGET off around 2:00 or 3:00 p.m. SA ALDRICH asked FULLER how often he and BRIDGET spent time with MEYERS and her boyfriend JOSE BARRERA. FULLER stated that it was approximately once or twice a month for maybe three to six months prior to HORSFORD'S death. FULLER stated that BRIDGET knew MEYERS from work and they only knew BARRERA from him dating MEYERS.

marijuana and was not a part of any of that. SA ALDRICH specifically questioned FULLER as to whether or not she gave Xanax to HORSFORD. FULLER stated that she did not give HORSFORD Xanax, and there is no way that HORSFORD would have gotten one of FULLER'S Xanax pills without FULLER noticing. FULLER did not have any Xanax with her other than what was in the vial she wears around her neck.

226

FULLER first met HORSFORD at the Halloween party at JEANNE MEYERS' residence the weekend before HORSFORD's death. FULLER carved pumpkins. HORSFORD was there with her sons. HORSFORD was drinking that night but seemed to be fine. FULLER stated that HORSFORD was very nice to her.

It should be noted that FULLER'S parents, BRENDA BONEBREAK and BLAINE BONEBREAK were present during this interview. FULLER stated that she has anxiety and would be more comfortable speaking with SA ALDRICH with the BONEBREAKS' present.

GARY went back to MEYERS' residence the next morning with BRIDGET. GARY had to take BRIDGET because she was upset. BRIDGET only told GARY that there was an accident or something, and that HORSFORD had passed away.

08-0381-01-20

11/4/18 Messages with LAWSON:

Received 4:59 PM, LAWSON: "How are you holding up?"

Sent 4:49 PM, SMITH: "I'm ok, what about you?"

Received 5:01 PM, LAWSON: "Emotionally drained, as the rest of us I'm sure. I'm so glad we all have each other. I'm so glad we could show her a great time before she passed."

Sent 5:01 PM, SMITH: "Yes, me too"

11/4/18 Messages with BRIDGETTE FULLER:

Sent 5:53 PM, SMITH: "I hate to ask but can I please get more meds? It really helped me."

Received 5:56 PM, FULLER: "Yes where r u or even Tom we went to eat in cumming i can bring it to you or if he's out i can meet him its totally up to u I'm completely flexible"

Sent 5:59 PM, SMITH: "He is about to run to Zaxby's at 17"

Received 6:02 PM, FULLER: "I'm down at texas Roadhouse if u give me your address I will come to u if that's ok"

Sent 6:03 PM, SMITH: "That's perfect 4935 Rose Creek dr cumming ga 30040"

Sent 7:47 PM, SMITH: "If it makes it easier I can meet you"

Received 7:49 PM, FULLER: "Where did u want to meet"

Sent 7:49 PM, SMITH: "What ever is good for you"

Received 7:49 PM, FULLER: "U off matt hwy"

Sent 7:50 PM, SMITH: "369"

Sent 7:50 PM, SMITH: "How about tat gas station off of exit 16"

Sent 7:50 PM, SMITH: "That we stopped at the other day on our way to get mine and Jeanne's cars?"

Received 7:51 PM, FULLER: "Yes that works"

08-0381-01-20

no............ out love Tam and that cunt and all of them can ROT IN HELL."

2........ messages with LAWSON, COCKERHAM, STACY SMITH, FULLER, JOSE BA.......RA, HARDIN, SEALS, and TOM SMITH:

Re..... ..d 4:13 p.m., LAWSON: "Btw, my husband works with a guy. His wife is very clo.. . on Tam's neighbor. She told him that Tam was known in the neighborhood for tak........ything people would give her. Apparently not well liked by many neighbors b.. .... .. she was always high or drinking."

R........ 4:16 p.m., SEALS: "Like pills? Drugs? Alcohol? All the above ?"

R....... .d 4:17 p.m., LAWSON: "Yep! All of the above!!!"

2........ messages with MATTHEW MEYERS:

R.......ed 7:41 p.m., MATTHEW: "What did Tam drink that night tequila vodka? Did sh............ he. own?"

S... 7.41 p.m., JEANNE: "Tequila & she brought her own"

R......... 7:42 p.m., MATTHEW: "What was the brand? American? Did anyone know the....hot proof and content?"

R.......ed 7:44 p.m., MATTHEW: "Wow. Some good shit."

R.......ed 7:45 p.m., MATTHEW: "38% ... that is a lot"

S... 7:47 p.m., JEANNE: "Yep!"

3/....... messages with FULLER:

S... :02 p.m., MEYERS: "Stacy said if she could have 1 too please. We are losing it!"

R.......d 7:02 p.m., FULLER: "Got u covered"

S... :03 p.m., MEYERS: "Thank you!!"

EXHIBIT   98

08-0381-01-20

not aware of issues anyone had with HORSFORD. HORSFORD was very involved with football.

On the night of JEANNE'S birthday party, November 3, 2018, MATT was at home with his fiancée, AMANDA O'BRYAN, and his and JEANNE'S four children. MATT said they would have gone to dinner or the movies because that is what they did on weekends, but he could not recall exactly what they did on that particular night. MATT was not at JEANNE's house that night.

The next morning, JEANNE'S mother called MATT, and told him that JEANNE had a party and one of the girls died. JEANNE'S mother told MATT that he needed to go over to the house. MATT recalled that he was at Waffle House with his son BO when he received the phone call. MATT traveled to JEANNE'S residence where he spoke with law enforcement. MATT had very limited information about that morning, and stated that he observed the women were separated at the house. Everyone was horrified looking, and MATT was just trying to figure out who died. MATT talked to JEANNE while he was at the residence. JEANNE was shaking and told him that it was HORSFORD that had died. JEANNE stated that HORSFORD was lying face down in the backyard and she could not believe that it happened. HORSFORD'S husband, LEANDER, kept calling JEANNE'S phone and JEANNE was upset because she was not allowed to answer the call. JEANNE was upset that LEANDER did not know that HORSFORD was deceased.

MATT stated that he built the deck on the back of JEANNE'S house for their children not to get hurt, so he was surprised to hear that HORSFORD had fallen off of it.

EXHIBIT   75

08-0381-01-20

MATT stated that he is aware that MICHELLE GRAVES felt that HORSFORD'S death was not an accident. MATT did not think that MICHELLE understood the extent of HORSFORD'S friends. GRAVES was good friends with HORSFORD, but HORSFORD had other friends too.

SA ALDRICH asked MATT if he was aware that JEANNE had cameras in the house. MATT admitted that when he and JEANNE were first going through divorce he would walk into JEANNE'S house, and that was why she put cameras up. MATT stated after things calmed down between the two of them JEANNE did not worry about the cameras since they were no longer needed for him.

MATT never had any concerns that anyone at the party did anything to HORSFORD. MATT is familiar with all of the women that were at the party and said they were all happy drunks. MATT stated that he knew JENNIFER MORRELL the least out of the women. MATT stated that he was not even concerned that JOSE BARRERA did anything to HORSFORD. The only concern he ever had about BARRERA was that he was dating JEANNE. MATT did not like his children knowing that JEANNE was dating someone so much younger than her. MATT stated that if he ever had any concerns about BARRERA, he would not have allowed BARRERA to be around his children.

MATT stated that when he and JEANNE were married, they always entertained at their house and it was not abnormal for them to go to bed while the guests were still up. Everyone would just go to sleep when they wanted to.

MATT added that it was well known that HORSFORD was a partier, and he was not surprised by her toxicology results. MATT also stated that JEANNE'S aunt, MADELINE

Page 3 of 4

PROPERTY OF GBI
Further dissemination is prohibited
without written approval of a GBI Supervisor

789058

EXHIBIT   75

In October of 2018, HARDIN met JEANNE MEYERS at HARDIN'S birthday dinner at Marlowe's Tavern. HARDIN and MEYERS were both friends with JENNIFER MORRELL, and MORRELL had invited MEYERS to have dinner with them. HARDIN had seen MEYERS prior to that at the cheerleading gym, but did not actually know her. While at Marlowe's Tavern, they started planning MEYERS' birthday party for November 3, 2018.

HARDIN was not sure if she could go to MEYERS' party, and did not remember getting an e-vite. HARDIN stated she was invited verbally, but did not remember who gave her the details of the party.

You made yourself a public figure. Good job with that. Legally doing some fact searching in public records, wow, I found

Your right. All for the wrongs reasons. The Toxicology report will be examined even futher. That why the sheriff's depart deflected on this in the press conference. Not to disparage tam and tried to be classy about the way it qas done. She brought her own bottle and drugs to the party. Lee was aware of this

Sequence	1
Offense Date	8/9/2020
Charge	Unlawful Use of Wireless Device

1   DUI - Alcohol - Less Safe

2   Failure to Maintain Lane

08/11/2008

Paternity /
Legitimation

McClelland, T.
Russell, III

1   SEAT BELT VIOLATION

On Monday, August 10, 2020, at approximately 10:15 a.m., GBI Special Agent KELLY ALDRICH was located at the Forsyth County Sheriff's Office for the purpose of meeting with Forsyth County Sheriff's Office Sgt. TYLER SEXTON. SEXTON provided SA ALDRICH with four compact disks containing Forsyth County Sheriff's Office patrol car video from the response to TAMLA HORSFORD'S death on November 4, 2018 (BB56757). This videos will be reviewed in a separate summary.

It should be noted that SA ALDRICH had requested these videos from Sgt. SEXTON on Wednesday, August 5, 2020. SA ALDRICH had also requested that Sgt. SEXTON check to see if Sgt. MILLER was testing a body camera on November 4, 2018. Sgt. SEXTON informed SA ALDRICH on this date that he had checked, and Sgt. COREY MILLER was not wearing a body camera on the date of HORSFORD's death.

08-0381-01-20

SA ALDRICH asked CHRISTIAN if he went to HORSFORD'S autopsy and CHRISTIAN stated that he did not because he did not feel like there was foul play in her death. CHRISTIAN tended to only go to autopsies when he felt like there was foul play

In the first recording ROBINSON informed GRAVES that it appeared HORSFORD suffocated, but GRAVES stated that she felt HORSFORD was alive when the Forsyth County Sheriff's Office arrived because she could see "spit" ROBINSON stated that you could see bubbles in the picture, but that he was hoping she lost feeling when her vertebrae cracked. GRAVES then pointed out that the Medical Examiner said there was minimal hemorrhaging, and you would expect to see hemorrhaging if she was alive with a fracture in her spine. GRAVES also stated that the second autopsy did not even reveal a fracture.

On Thursday, September 10, 2020, at approximately 9:36 a.m., Crime Scene Specialist Special Agent ELAINA HONEA was located at 4450 Woodlet Court, Cumming, Forsyth County, Georgia, in reference to obtaining evidence in the death investigation of TAMLA HORSFORD. SA HONEA met with the current home owner, ROD REEVES, and obtained written consent to obtain a known paint sample from the back porch of the residence, specifically the porch railing (see attached). SA HONEA was previously requested by the GBI Crime Lab to obtain the known sample to compare to a substance on the back of HORSFORD's clothing at the time of her death. The paint sample was collected as evidence and assigned GBI Barcode BB63217.

how HORSFORD was found and if anyone had touched the body, but did not see where it affected the investigation. Lt. KALIN did not cover for anyone and did not falsify a report.

Lt. KALIN stated that he did know of BARRERA prior to this case from working with BARRERA at the Forsyth County Courthouse. Lt. KALIN had BARRERA'S cell phone number because he was given it after BARRERA was fired from the State Probation Office. Lt. KALIN stated that BARRERA and another female were fired from State Probation for lying, and Forsyth County District Attorney's Office ADA JAMES DUNN talked with Lt. KALIN about trying to get BARRERA a job with the Sheriff's Office. DUNN told Lt. KALIN that BARRERA should not have lied, but that he was a good guy and had a good reputation around the Courthouse.

Lt. KALIN is not sure why BARRERA would say that he never said that he moved HORSFORD'S arm nor was he sure why BARRERA would tell him he moved HORSFORD'S arm if he did not move it.

Lt. KALIN stated that he called BARRERA regarding this case two or three times.

GEORGIA BUREAU OF INVESTIGATION
REGION 8
INVESTIGATIVE SUMMARY

08-0381-01-20

On Tuesday, August 11, 2020, GBI Special Agent KELLY ALDRICH received a telephone call from GBI Chief Medical Examiner JONATHAN EISENSTAT and Medical Examiner ANDREW KOOPMINER. Dr. EISENSTAT stated that he and Dr. KOOPMINER had listened to the Murder Squad Podcast on Spotify relating to TAMLA HORSFORD's death that SA ALDRICH had previously requested that they listen to.

Dr. EISENSTAT and Dr. KOOPMINER stated the following in regards to information from autopsy that was discussed in the podcast:

It was mentioned in the podcast that the independent autopsy that was conducted showed an absence of a hematoma and hemorrhage surrounding HORSFORD's Smith's fracture of her right wrist. Dr. EISENSTAT stated that there was blood around the fracture, and that HORSFORD did not survive long enough after the fracture for a hematoma to form.

The absence of subcutaneous subgaleal hemorrhage or lacerations of the scalp was also mentioned. Dr. EISENSTAT said that was not surprising to him due to HORSFORD landing on a grassy surface.

Dr. KOOPMINER addressed the scratches on HORSFORD's arms. He said they were minor, and there was no way to tell if they were from HORSFORD's fall or occurred prior to the fall.

EXHIBIT____67____

Prior to HORSFORD'S autopsy, Dr. KOOPMEINERS was told that HORSFORD was found deceased in a backyard below a balcony that was 25 to 30 feet high. HORSFORD may have fallen or been pushed and had been drinking heavily. No one from the Forsyth County Sheriff's Office attended the autopsy, but Dr. KOOPMEINERS did speak with Forsyth County Sheriff's Office Detective MIKE CHRISTIAN the day after the autopsy.

Dr. EISENSTAT stated that the fact that HORSFORD was so close to the base of the porch suggested a fall. Dr. EISENSTAT stated that if she had jumped or been pushed she would have been further out from the base of the porch.

Dr. EISENSTAT stated if there was ever any new evidence related to HORSFORD'S autopsy that suggested anything more than a fall, he would be happy to review it but due to what Dr. KOOPMEINERS saw during the autopsy Dr. EISENSTAT still agreed with HORSFORD'S death being an accidental fall.

Dr. EISENSTAT had reviewed HORSFORD'S autopsy and agreed with GBI Medical Examiner Dr. ANDREW KOOPMEINERS findings that HORSFORD'S death was an accident. It should be noted that Dr. KOOPMEINERS conducted HORSFORD'S autopsy. HORSFORD'S death was ruled an accident due to her intoxication, injuries, and lack of certain injuries. All of HORSFORD'S injuries could have come from a fall off of a balcony. As far as a lack of certain injuries, Dr. EISENSTAT stated that for signs of any kind of struggle they look for certain external injuries. HORSFORD did not have any broken fingernails, and her fingernails were clean and short. There was no evidence of her grabbing or scratching anything. HORSFORD did not have bruises to her knuckles or external injuries to her neck. There were also no injuries that suggested that HORSFORD had been hit prior to contact with the ground. Dr. EISENSTAT stated that evidence of bruising and bleeding suggested that HORSFORD was alive when she impacted the ground. Dr. EISENSTAT stated it would have been possible for HORSFORD to have bounced slightly when she hit the ground due to the ground not being a completely flat surface.

SA ALDRICH asked Dr. KOOPMEINERS if there were more photographs than what were given to the Forsyth County Sheriff's Office. Dr. KOOPMEINERS stated there were not and that was all of the photographs that were taken. The reason there were not more photographs was due to a miscommunication with their photographer, and that it is not standard practice to take pictures of minor injuries. SA ALDRICH again questioned Dr. KOOPMEINERS in regard to photographs and there not being pictures with a scale of any of HORSFORD'S major injuries. Dr. KOOPMEINERS stated again that there was a miscommunication with the photographer, and it seemed pretty straight forward in regard to the fact that HORSFORD had fallen and was not pushed, so he did

The audio recording was stopped. At this time SA ALDRICH informed Sgt. MILLER that she was inquiring about the body camera due to an inconsistency between statements and scene photographs of the position of TAMLA'S arms. Sgt. MILLER stated that he had something to add in regard to that, so SA ALDRICH turned her recorder back on. Sgt. MILLER stated that he did check TAMLA'S pulse at the scene but did not recall if it was her neck or arm. Sgt. MILLER stated that if it was her arm, he may very well have moved her arm when he checked her pulse. Sgt. MILLER stated

a standard autopsy. Dr. KOOPMEINERS did not do a sexual assault kit or fingernail clippings on HORSFORD due to it being a standard autopsy. SA ALDRICH asked Dr. KOOPMEINERS why he felt that HORSFORD had fallen instead of being pushed and did a standard autopsy when the information he received was that she could have fallen or been pushed. Dr. KOOPMEINERS stated there was an absence of injuries to multiple surfaces of the body, there were no signs of strangulation, and there were minimal external injuries. Dr. KOOPMEINERS did not see any evidence of her being pushed and did not make a final decision until he got toxicology back. Dr. KOOPMEINERS stated that HORSFORD'S level of intoxication led him to believe that she fell.

Dr. KOOPMEINERS stated that his opinion had not changed and he still believed that HORSFORD'S death was an accidental death. Dr. KOOPMEINERS stated that he wished he had taken more photos during the autopsy. Dr. KOOPMEINERS heard through media that the autopsy had been reviewed. Dr. KOOPMEINERS stated that nothing he saw during the autopsy would say that HORSFORD was pushed.

Dr. KOOPMEINERS stated that he has only had contact with law enforcement, the Forsyth County Coroner, and MICHELLE GRAVES in regard to the autopsy. Dr. KOOPMEINERS stated that GRAVES sent him emails asking questions, and he tried to have the Forsyth County Coroner deal with GRAVES. Dr. KOOPMEINERS stated that he never responded to GRAVES due to the fact they can only talk to people who are not family if they have consent from the family to do so. Dr. KOOPMEINERS provided SA ALDRICH with two copies of physical letters that GRAVES sent him and two emails that she sent him (see attached).

RESPONSE TO MOTION FOR CONTEMPT

COMES NOW Dr. Andrew Koopmeiners, employee of the Georgia Bureau of Investigation (GBI), who is not a party to this action, by counsel, Christopher M. Carr, Attorney General for the State of Georgia, and files this Response to the Motion for Contempt[1] filed on or about June 13, 2019, by counter-plaintiff Graves regarding a purported "subpoena" for May 1, 2019, showing this Court as follows:

PATHOLOGICAL DIAGNOSES

A. Blunt Force Injuries of the Head and Neck
    1. Abrasions of the face
    2. Subgaleal hemorrhage
    3. Soft tissue hemorrhage of the right temporalis muscle
    4. Subarachnoid hemorrhage
    5. Subdural hemorrhage (approximately 150 milliliters)
    6. Fracture of the 2nd cervical vertebra

B. Blunt Force Injuries of the Torso and Extremities
    1. Laceration of the right ventricle of the heart
        i. Hemopericardium, 100 milliliters
    2. Dislocation of the right wrist
    3. Laceration of the right wrist and right lower leg
    4. Abrasion of the left arm, left hand, and left leg

Blunt Force Injuries of the Torso and Extremities

There is a ¾ inch linear laceration of the right ventricle of the heart, with associated hemorrhage of approximately 100 milliliters into the pericardium. There right wrist is dislocated. There is a 1 inch laceration of the anterior right wrist. There is a 1/4 x 1/8 inch superficial abrasion of the anterior left forearm. There is a 1/8 x 1/8 inch abrasion of the tip of the left index finger. There is a ½ inch laceration of the proximal anterior right lower leg. There is a ¼ inch abrasion of the proximal anterior left lower leg.

Dr. Koopmeiners 11/7/2018 at 1450

Discussed case with Investigator Mike Christian (404-925-6825) who is the lead investigator in the case. Per Investigator Christian, the house has a balcony which is approxmiately 13-15 feet above the ground. There is a stairway which leads from the balcony to the ground. The decedent was drinking heavily and smoking marijuana at the residence. At approximately 0145 the decedent tells the homeowners that she is going out to the balcony to smoke. The homeowners then go to bed. The next morning they discovered the decedent unresponsive in the back yard. The position of the body does not appear that she had fallen directly from the balcony on to the ground. Rather, she appeared to have fallen from ground level, with the grade of the yard adding approximately

On Mar 18, 2019, at 2:52 PM, Wilson, Laura <laura.wilson@georgia.gov> wrote:

Thanks for providing the additional details, Michelle. The following request is out of the jurisdiction of the Governor. However, I have forwarded the information along to the Georgia Bureau of Investigation.

Laura Wilson
Assistant Scheduler
Office of Governor Brian P. Kemp
laura.wilson@georgia.gov | (404)291-6031

235

Case: 2018-1029773 User: BENHAMD 11/19/2018

CASE: 2018-1029773

STATE OF GEORGIA

GEORGIA BUREAU OF INVESTIGATION

RECORD OF MEDICAL EXAMINER

CITY CUMMING			COUNTY FORSYTH		
NAME OF DECEASED TAMLA HORSFORD					
RESIDENCE OF DECEASED 4465 AMBASSDOR WAY**CUMMING, GA					
AGE/DOB 40 YEARS - 10/10/1978		SEX F	RACE B		
	NATURAL	HOMICIDE	SUICIDE	ACCIDENTAL	UNDETERMINED
MANNER OF DEATH					

CAUSE OF DEATH	SIGNOUT
PENDING TOXICOLOGY	PENDING PD INVEST
PENDING ME Investigator	

PRONOUNCED DATE: 11/04/2018	HOUR: 10:47	PLACE: SCENE - 4450 WOODLET CT.	
NOTIFIED BY KEITH BOWEN		DATE 11/4/2018	HOUR 10:10
BODY IDENTIFIED BY FRIEND		PHOTOGRAPHS BY JIMMY BROWN	
INVEST. OFFICER M. CHRISTIAN			
EMPLOYED BY FORSYTH CO. SHERIFF'S OFFICE - (#)			

CASE AGENCIES:	Forsyth Co. Coroner	#(2018110379)
	Bell-Forsyth Judicial Circuit	
	Forsyth Co. District Attorney	
	Forsyth Co. Sheriff's Office	#(2018110177)
	GBI-Medical Examiner-HQ DOFS	#(KOOPMEINERS)

OTHER AGENCY	
DATE IN 11/4/2018	TIME IN 14:23
ME INV.: FELICIA FARMER	FUNERAL HOME MCDONALD AND SON 770-885-9899
PROC: AUTOPSY DATE: 11/6/2018 TIME:	BY: ANDREW KOOPMEINERS, MD

DATE _____

SIGNED _____

MEDICAL EXAMINER

Mail - michelle graves - Outlook

50-18-70 et seq, received on April 23, 2019 regarding certain records pertaining to Tamla Horsford.

GBI does not have any Photos we did not investigate this case; you will need to check with the Forsyth County Sheriff Office for these items.

Sincerely.

Brad Parks
Special Agent in Charge
GBI Office of Privacy & Compliance

DAwATEBYzEwLWUrMzAiYzVrhN0wMAltMDAKAEYAAAMGpF6Fd/l6ZFARbuPfz5vZLsnBwDoAl6N4z9... 4/4

236

Sgt. MILLER heard a call come out regarding an unresponsive female that was not breathing. Sgt. MILLER was the first officer on the scene. Sgt. MILLER could not recall who all was outside when he arrived but was told by JOSE BARRERA to go around the side of the house to the back of the house. In the backyard Sgt. MILLER saw a female, later identified as HORSFORD, face down in the backyard wearing an animal outfit. One arm was underneath HORSFORD, and MILLER could not recall what position the other arm was in. HORSFORD'S feet were towards the house with her head pointed away. Forsyth County Sheriff's Office Crime Scene Investigator MARIKO FUJIMURA took photographs and then the Coroner rolled HORSFORD over. That was the first time Sgt. MILLER saw HORSFORD'S arm that was underneath her and observed that there was an injury.

CONVERSATION WITH SKYE MULLARKEY, GBI:
On January 7th, 2019 I spoke with Skye Mullarkey, GBI in regards to this case. Skye stated they do not usually test for THC in Post Mortem cases. I replied that in this case we needed a complete Toxicology report in order to complete the case file. She stated that she would get with her supervisor and order the test.

pending the autopsy results. I stated that depending on what the medical examiner's report says it will tell us which direction to go from here. Leander wanted to know if we had given everyone at the party a polygraph test. I told him no and that we typically don't do that and at this point there was not a need to do it. I also explained that we couldn't force someone to take a polygraph test. Leander turned the conversation into race and money. He made several comments about Forsyth County being a racist county and even mentioned that people with money have a lot of influence. He wanted to know if a white woman had died at a all black party would we be investigating it the same. I told Leander that his allegations of race and money having anything to do with this actually offended me. I assured him that race and money had absolutely nothing to do with this case or how it was being investigated. Leander continued to talk over me and would not let me speak. I warned him several times that if he continued I would not continue the conversation. Leander continued to be hostile and would not let me speak so I ended the call. [02/04/2019 13:08, TRSEXTON, 122, FCSO]

INTERVIEW DR. A. KOOPMEINERS ASSOCIATE MEDICAL EXAMINER, GBI:
On Friday, November 9th, 2018 at approximately 1130 hours, FCSO Det. T. Sexton and this Detective met with Dr. A. Koopenmeiners, GBI at the GBI Headquarters on Panthersville Road in Decatur. We brought Dr. Koopenmeiners the incident photographs on a DVD-R which we turned over to him. While with Dr. Koopenmeiners we reviewed the pictures and the anecdotal evidence from the case. Dr. Koopenmeiners stated Tamla's injuries were consistent with a fall from that height. He stated that externally her body showed little signs of trauma. He stated a broken neck like Tamla had suffered would not be immediately fatal but would be incapacitating within a minute or so.
Dr. Koopenmeiners said that he would need to wait until Tamla's Blood Alcohol Report and Toxicology were completed to finish his report. However, if there was a large amount of alcohol or drugs in her system, he felt this would be listed as an accidental death.

HORSFORD was found and that she had her face profusely, but did not see where it affected the investigation. It was the his not come to anyone and did not finally a report.

LT KALIN stated that he did know of BARRERA prior to this, you have working with BARRERA at the Forsyth County Courthouse. LT KALIN had BARRERA's cell phone number because he was given it by LAZRO-GA a cousin from the State Probation Office. LT KALIN stated that BARRERA and his cell phone were fired from State Probation for lying and Forsyth County District Attorney's Office ADA JAMES Dunn talked with LT KALIN about trying to get BARRERA a job with the Sheriff's Office. DUNN told LT KALIN that BARRERA should not have said, but that he was a good guy

F14   1/2

7/5/22, 6:53 PM — michelle graves - Outlook

and had a good reputation around the Courthouse.

LT KALIN is not sure why BARRERA would say that he never said that he moved HORSFORD'S arm nor was he sure why BARRERA would tell him he moved HORSFORD'S arm if he did not move it

GEORGIA BUREAU OF INVESTIGATION
REGION 8
INVESTIGATIVE SUMMARY

08-0381-01-20

On Wednesday, October 7, 2020, at approximately 3:33 p.m., GBI Special Agent KELLY ALDRICH telephonically spoke with STACY SMITH. SA ALDRICH asked SMITH if she recalled TAMLA HORSFORD being sick the day before JEANNE MEYERS' birthday party. SA ALDRICH referenced a Facebook Post on HORSFORD'S page about her feeling sick and SMITH commenting that she hoped she felt better. SMITH stated she did not recall what was wrong with HORSFORD, and added that HORSFORD was not sick at MEYERS' party the next day.

SA ALDRICH also asked SMITH if she recalled who brought an electrolyte drink to the party. SMITH stated that she was not sure. It should be noted that in pictures from the party there was an electrolyte drink that was full and in crime scene photos the next morning the bottle was partially empty.

ID DATA:

SMITH, STACY   (Previously Submitted)

SPECIAL AGENT KELLY N ALDRICH: 11/17/2020
mar: 11/18/2020   KA   BW

EXHIBIT ___76___

239

SA ALDRICH had contacted SMITH in regard to follow-up questions that had come up during this investigation. SA ALDRICH reminded SMITH that during her initial interview she had informed SA ALDRICH that HORSFORD was going to visit a friend who was going through a bad divorce prior to coming to MEYERS' birthday party. SA ALDRICH asked SMITH if she was aware of who that friend was. SMITH stated that she did not know at the time, but now believed that it was MICHELLE GRAVES. It should be noted that GRAVES was interviewed by the Forsyth County Sheriff's Office after HORSFORD'S death and had informed them that she went to HORSFORD'S residence and left prior to HORSFORD getting ready for MEYERS' party.

SA ALDRICH asked SMITH if BRIDGET FULLER had ever given her any medication. SMITH stated that her goddaughter committed suicide in December of 2018, and FULLER gave her some Xanax at that time. SA ALDRICH asked if FULLER had ever given SMITH any medications after HORSFORD'S death, which SMITH stated she had not. SA ALDRICH confronted SMITH with the fact that there were text messages on SMITH'S cell phone relating to FULLER giving SMITH medications the morning of HORSFORD'S death and the evening after. SMITH stated that she did not recall FULLER giving her anything after HORSFORD'S death.

IN THE SUPERIOR COURT OF FORSYTH COUNTY
STATE OF GEORGIA

Michelle Graves,	§	
	§	
Plaintiff,	§	CIVIL ACTION
	§	
vs.	§	FILE NO.: 09-CV-1346
	§	
David Graves,	§	
	§	
Defendant.	§	
	§	

FINAL ORDER

The Husband and Wife in the above styled case were married on August 14th, 1999;

There are three minor children born as issue of this marriage, to wit: Emily Graves, born February 11th, 2000, Matthew Graves, born August 6th, 2003, and Julia Graves, born September 5th, 2006.

Because of certain domestic difficulties, the Husband and Wife are now living in a bona fide state of separation and the Wife has filed a Complaint for Divorce in the Superior Court of Lumpkin County, Georgia.

A final hearing was held in this matter on April 1st, 2010. Defendant had proper notice and failed to appear. The Plaintiff was present and appeared with counsel, Ridge Rairigh. Following evidence being presented and argument of counsel, the Court issued the following FINAL ORDER:

1.

The parties shall live separate and apart, each being free to choose his or her place of residence and employment and each shall be free from interference, molestation,

Page 4 of 23

240

CHRISTIAN: MADELINE WE TALKED A COUPLE OF TIME BEFORE BUT WE'RE GETTING A RECORDED STATEMENT THIS TIME. TELL ME ABOUT THIS WEEKEND, I GUESS STARTING SATURDAY ABOUT THE PARTY AND THEN PROCEED INTO SUNDAY MORNING, IF YOU DON'T MIND AND IF I HAVE SOMETHING IN PARTICULAR, I'LL STOP YOU AND ASK YOU BUT.

started arriving before dark. At first it was just females, and then JOSE BARRERA and THOMAS SMITH arrived. BARRERA and SMITH said their hellos and went to watch football downstairs. LOMBARDI went to bed after they cut the cake for MEYERS' birthday. LOMBARDI recalled someone going to get ice after the cake was cut, and then she went to bed.

FORSYTH COUNTY SHERIFF'S OFFICE
STATEMENT FORM

CASE NUMBER: 2018110177

Name: Madeline Lombardi   Employer: Retired

Address: Address: N/A

City: State: City: State:

Zip: Phone: Zip: Phone:

DOB: Sex: Fe   Place of Birth: Email:

Race: Native   Height: 5'2"   Weight: 130   Hair: Brown   Eyes: Brown

DESCRIBE, IN DETAIL AND IN YOUR OWN WORDS, THE EVENTS OF THE INCIDENT OR ACCIDENT:

We had a party celebrating Jeanne's birthday. The first person to arrive was Nicole. Jeanne and Stacey arrived and after guest trickled in. Everyone gathered around the bar, eating & fixing drinks @ the bar. When the LSU game started, everyone except for a couple of ladies who stayed @ the bar. We watched the game. Everyone was drinking and having a good time. At half-time Jose and Tom were downstairs until half-time, they were watching the game in the basement. They came up @ half-time. They ate and then went to the store to get ice. Iam went outside to smoke a cigarette, I went with her. It was my first time meeting her and we were discussing my past relationship w/ Jeanne. We discussed her going through New Orleans

Madeline Lombardi
ON MAKING STATEMENT SIGNATURE   11-4-2018 11:00 Am
   TODAY'S DATE & TIME

CHAPTER 16
"Running Scared"

O ver the past three-and-a-half years, I have spent every waking moment trying to find someone who would help get justice for my friend. Unfortunately, this case is so deeply covered up by so many high-ranking government officials, everyone is too scared to do their job and grow a conscience! From attorneys, news reporters, activists—you name it—they appeared interested with the case, wanted the facts, and did news stories, then got too spooked to air it or take the case. I am amazed at the number of attorneys I have been in contact with that just disappear in the night over this case.

I have contacted the ACLU, Department of Justice, FBI, NBC, ABC, CBS, Oprah, *Rolling Stone*, CNN, Black Lives Matter, True Crime on MTV, Governor Brian Kemp, Ben Crump, Johnny Cochran, Lee Merritt, True Crime All the Time, Tyler Perry, WSB TV Channel 2, 11 Alive, Vice President Harris, CBS 46, Senator Warnock, John Ossoff, the Southern Center for Human Rights, attorneys I have seen on Dateline episodes—you name it and I have reached out to get help for my friend. The ACLU sent me a letter that stated they were "too busy." The Department of Justice finally sent me a letter after three attempts to get them to do something about the police corruption in this case. They sent the case to the FBI Atlanta field office. I was even contacted by the *Atlanta Journal-Constitution*. A reporter spent weeks corresponding with me via email and text and over the phone. This individual was as concerned as I was not only with Tamla's death but with the relationships and the connection between the coroner's office and the funeral home owned by Lauren McDonald, the state house representative and former coroner. Together we found that Lauren McDonald has his entire family on the payroll at his funeral home, they were all listed as deputy coroners for the county, and he was the lead coroner for the county. I suppose this is normal, but I find it odd.

I reached out to a high-profile attorney who had just retired from the Atlanta DA's office who seemed very eager to help, had appeared on Channel 2, Atlanta, and had a reputation that preceded him in the area. We had conference calls. He obtained Tamla's case file from Leander's attorney. I provided him with numerous pictures and reports to show the corruption in this case, and after weeks of working with this individual, he ghosted us like the others. Now he is a judge in South Fulton County. This same attorney was helping the family of Kendrick Johnson, the boy who was found dead rolled up in the gym mat in South Georgia. I was referred to an attorney from the Southern Center for Human Rights who seemed very motivated to take Tamla's case. She told me she was brainstorming and would get back to me. Ghosted again.

It is utterly amazing the organizations that say they are here to help. Must be nothing more than a façade. Warnock's office got back to me and said they would help. They told me someone at the GBI would help me—a Ms. Miles. Ms. Miles is their public spokesperson and she emailed me to say the GBI was not doing anything more about this case. A CNN reporter interviewed me. I provided all the facts of the case we knew at the time, and it was supposed to air in a few weeks. I provided a plethora of information to accompany my interview, so the producers had evidence to support what I said. Suddenly, my portion was pulled from the interview, just before it was to air. I cannot tell you how many times I thought I was making headway and then nothing but disappointment. No one wants to uncover the truth in this case. No one has the tenacity to stand up for what is right, and no one cares about a dead Black woman in the state of Georgia and/or specifically Forsyth County.

I recently had a reporter drive all the way to my home in Florida to do a story on the evidence that has been found in the GBI file. Tamla's father and aunt were included in the interview via Zoom. The story was to air in February, then it became May; however, this reporter did a phenomenal job. The story finally aired May 13, 2022. Thank you, Rebecca Lindstrom and 11 Alive News, Atlanta. If you have not seen the story on YouTube or the 11 Alive Facebook page, I recommend you view it. It is also on my website for this book, tamlahorsford. net. The first reporter to do what she promised and was not afraid to show the conflicts and issues with the investigation. Mike Petchenik who was with Channel 2, Atlanta, is another dedicated journalist who sees the facts and has kept on Tamla's case for four years. Mike now has his own podcast and recently interviewed myself and Wayne Beyea, retired homicide detective, about Tamla's case. Mike actually did an interview himself with a new investigative reporter for Cox Media in Atlanta where he discussed all his issues with Tamla's case. I cannot thank Mike enough for sticking with this case and continuing to help me anyway he can to get to the truth in this case. I was put in touch with a reporter from Forsyth County News who also seemed interested in Tamla's case. She had an extended conversation with me via Messenger where she shared her feelings about Forsyth County and how it is like a cult among the locals whose families have lived there for hundreds of years. This person even commented on the old cold case that happened in Forsyth County twenty-plus years ago and what she knew and what the police knew. That case is being handled by GBI Agent Kim Williams, who was on Tamla's case and who Sheriff Freeman is close with. This Forsyth County News reporter wanted to help, had a conference call with a private investigator and me, discussed the ins and outs of Tamla's case and how she did not believe she fell off the balcony either. Then of course she disappeared. I have never seen anything like it. I honestly believe people solicit me just to get information about what evidence I have or know.

The evidence is overwhelming in this case by way of audio recordings, interviews, statements, court hearings, pictures, videos, text messages, body cam, etc.

I have recorded numerous news stories that have aired on multiple news stations in Atlanta of people falling off and through balconies—all who survived.

CHAPTER 17
"The Next Step"

———

As I conclude this book, make no mistake that it does not mean my quest for justice will end with it. I have authored this book solely to get justice for Tamla and let people know who Tamla really was and how low and dirty those at the party stooped to cover their own wrongdoing (in my opinion). I want the world to know every little dirty detail and lie told by not only the people at the party, but the police and GBI who were "supposed" to investigate this case. I wanted the public to read the facts about how poorly this case was handled by all law enforcement agencies involved, how they just ignored the lies they were told and then fabricated excuses and stories to cover the inconsistencies told from one interview to another. I wanted to show every documented inconsistency throughout two laughable investigations whose investigators should be fired and charged criminally for knowing they were lied to and did nothing about it.

While the effort to bring attention to Tamla's case is appreciated, no one has gotten all the facts in the case accurate. This was another reason I wanted to write the book—so the general public can have ALL the pieces to the puzzle with this case.

Over the past three-and-a-half years, I have been through hell—not able to grieve the loss of my friend because I have had to fight off the police, the DA, attorneys, and the partygoers. Instead of protecting myself and Tamla, they helped those involved forge a war against me. I know in my heart, Tamla put this fight on me because she knew I could handle it and was not afraid to fight for the truth. Tamla was my absolute best friend—someone I spent every day with. In an instant she was gone. I put my pain aside and immediately jumped in to care for her boys every birthday, holiday, going to school, having lunch on my days off with her younger boys, sleepovers at my house every weekend, going to kids' art shows, and sporting events. You name it, I was there until the boys moved back to Florida. I was with the boys every day before Tamla passed so they were comfortable with me and my kids. I know they were comfortable and felt loved at my house.

There were nights Tamla's youngest boy would cry until he fell asleep; he always asked for "back scratches" (as he called them) like his mommy would do until he fell asleep. Holding a four-year-old boy while he cried for his mother broke my heart and continued to give me the strength to keep fighting for my friend.

I remember one night; the boys and I were drawing and coloring. Tamla's youngest drew a picture of his mom with purple earrings and a purple dress. She loved purple. I will never forget when he stopped what he was doing and looked at Tamla's other son and me and said, "My mommy is watching us." I said I know she is. I know Tamla is present. It may sound crazy to those who have never experienced the loss of someone close to you, but I feel her presence. I get chills all over my body and I know it is her. When I talk about her or am thinking about her, I will get the chills. Much like the moment I was told Tamla had passed and my immediate response was "No, and that is not what happened to her," when they told me she was found dead in the backyard. Tamla told me then that her death was no accident and was brutal. I got an overwhelming, gut-wrenching, dark feeling in my gut, and I knew at that moment Tamla died a horrible death. My feeling was proven when I saw her in the casket and viewed the crime scene photos. Of course, with everything I know now, I know the feeling I got was no coincidence. It was my friend putting this on me to seek justice.

I write this book for the sake of Tamla's children too; they need to know the truth and not the horrible things these disgusting people at the party have said about their mother. Tamla would never have jeopardized her job as a mother. She lived and breathed for her boys. She loved them with all her heart. The boys need to know just how much their mother loved them, and she did not do anything that night that would have separated her from her boys. Nothing. What amazes me is that every one of these women went home to their children, except Jose. He was the only one with nothing to lose. These people got home and crawled into bed with their significant other like nothing happened and with no conscience whatsoever. Hardly normal human behavior.

Something went down that night and after everything I know, I have one suspect in mind who is responsible for Tamla's death whom I will not state for legal reasons, but I am sure you can produce your own suspect based on the facts.

In my opinion, those involved were the ones still there in the morning. That was why everyone else was allowed to leave. If everyone there had been directly involved in the "incident" that took place and resulted in Tamla's injuries, I am sure Jeanne would not have let them leave. Jenn certainly could have Ubered home if needed (in my opinion).

Everything I have stated in this book can be found in open record from the Forsyth County Sheriff's Office and the GBI. In fact, the interviews with the GBI are all over YouTube (not posted by me). I have provided pictures throughout this book to verify and substantiate everything I have said. Nothing in this book was fabricated, exaggerated, or made to ruin anyone's reputation. Facts and opinions are stated as such. The rest of the information in this book came from Secretary of State websites, openpayrolls.com, Facebook, Instagram, etc.

I recently filed a complaint for an investigation to be done by the sheriff's office after finding evidence in the GBI file. They thought I would go away. Ha! I decided I would reach out to the county attorney. Counsel Leibel immediately responded and told me the sheriff's office would get back to me right away. He also forgot to start a new email thread and I got copied on his email to the sheriff that read, "Let's talk before you respond." These people are a bunch of blubbering idiots, and these are police and attorneys who you would think would be more cognizant than that. Doug Rainwater recently came back with a conclusion to my complaint against T. Sexton, A. Kalin, and D. Haff in regards to them "instructing" these people (the partygoers) to go after me via lawsuit and false police reports. To no surprise, he basically said the police were doing their job by helping Jeanne and the seven others who sued me and file arrest warrants.

I do not hate the police and I want people to understand that I have much respect for what police officers must do and the quick decisions they must make under stressful conditions daily. However, there are a lot of "dirty" cops out there that ruin it for the good ones, and unfortunately, the Forsyth County sheriff's office is full of "dirty" cops. I just cannot respect officers who were laughing and joking, making fun of a woman lying in a backyard, trying to hang on if she could for her boys. After all the grave injustices that have happened since the scene I have learned about, I know there is a special place in hell for all those involved in Tamla Horsford's cover-up.

I am still waiting for one agency to provide anything to prove my theories wrong. The attorneys for the plaintiffs in the defamation case filed numerous motions to quash my subpoenas, so I could not get any evidence to prove me wrong. If I were so crazy and off my rocker, then prove me wrong. Provide the evidence to shut me up. But that never happened. Instead, I was attacked, bullied, and harassed by the government agencies in place to protect us in a collaboration with the partygoers. I go back to Freeman telling me the GBI can't do anything without his or DA Penn's say. So, which one of them told the GBI to not photograph the autopsy and to call it an accidental fall before the police even started an investigation only a few hours after the half-assed autopsy. No fingerprints, no rape kit, one X-ray, no nail clippings, etc. Who told the GBI not to follow a normal autopsy procedure?

I often look and watch some of the news stories and read the articles in magazines about Tamla and it does not seem real. How could this happen, my best friend dead from going to a party? Things like that don't just happen, especially not in Cumming, Georgia, an upscale, white privilege community. It is still hard to believe it has been almost four years. It feels like yesterday because we don't have answers. We need closure and until we get that, I personally will continue to fight until we get the answers we want, and the justice Tamla and her boys deserve.

Neither investigating agency chose to get a true "victimology" on Tamla, only what the partygoers said. I have never once watched any TV show from *Dateline, 20/20, True Crime, CSI*, etc. where the police investigating a crime just believe everything the people with the dead body say without hesitation and with no need to check up on their stories. Why did no one talk to Tamla's friends and family to get a real picture of Tamla? When the police spoke to any member of the family or me, for instance, they were hardly trying to get any "victimology" or "advocating" in any way for Tamla. That was evident by Heather Wheeler in my interview. The police ignored our statements that conflicted with the partygoers' stories about Tamla's mannerisms, habits, etc. T. Sexton and Mike Christian were too busy running toxicology screens on marijuana for some reason, but not the bottle of Tequila. Mike Christian and

Kelly Aldrich were too busy running background checks and location history for Leander Horsford and his wife than conducting a true "victimology." T. Sexton was too busy badgering Tamla's family during their meetings and insulting their intelligence with his *Paw Patrol* theories of what happened to Tamla to receive any information pertinent to the case.

Now that you have finished this book, I hope you agree the biggest takeaway from both investigations is there were at least five stories or versions of what happened to Tamla. None of them, in my opinion, were consistent with her injuries and were just that: stories. From falling down the stairs and hitting her head, to tripping over the metal garden border, falling face-first down the steps without bracing herself, standing on a propane tank to light a cigarette, suicide, or falling while throwing up. What I don't understand is, if any of these things happened, why did no one call 911 when the incident occurred?

If you want to witness for yourself the blatant inconsistencies and lies told to the police and the GBI that were ignored by DA Penn for prosecution, file an open records request with the GBI and the Forsyth County Sheriff's Office. The office file lacked all the audios. I had to get those from an attorney. The GBI buried the information in their file as well. The body cam videos are hidden as an auto play icon. Court records and business records referenced are all available with a quick search online at the Secretary of State and the Forsyth County Court records websites. Personnel files are always available open record for any government employee via the county, city, or state where they are employed.

Acknowledgments

To the Horsford boys, you have continued to give me the strength to fight for your mom whether you know it or not. The pain I've watched you endure along with that of Tamla's parents over the loss of their daughter is unbearable. A parent should never have to bury their child, and a child should never bury their mother. Though Tamla was only a friend and not a family member, someone had to have Tamla's back, and while everyone else was grieving, I turned my pain into finding out why this happened.

This book is not only for the Horsford family, but for the others who suffered tragic losses in Forsyth County: Linda Henderson and Kenny Brown to name a few. I write for those who may have also suffered tragedy in Forsyth County but were too afraid to do anything about it. Tamla and the others deserved better whether Black, White, or otherwise, everyone deserves to get the same investigation our officers and agents took an oath to provide.

Thank you to Wayne Beyea for supporting me and unknowingly giving me motivation. Most of all thanks for Chapter 4 from your book *Blind Justice*. Thank you to my new friend, Darcy, who introduced me to Wayne and has become a huge support system for me whether she knows it or not. It is amazing how tragedy can bring people together, however unfortunate that we share in the grave injustice done to our loved ones in Forsyth County, Georgia.

Thank you to the complete strangers who have heard about Tamla's case and supported me on social media. To those who have helped get her story out there with your podcasts and blogs, thank you.

Most of all, thank you to my friends and family who have supported me and dealt with all the time that was taken from them while I worked on this book and Tamla's case. My kids sacrificed a great deal of time with their mother while I worked hard defending myself in court, defending my own child, deflecting felonies being committed against me, etc., you will read about.

Thank you for those who did not get spooked and run away like the others.

Thank you to Nile Capello from *Rolling Stone* who did two very good stories about Tamla's death and the inept investigation attempted by the Forsyth County sheriff's office. I know she is continuing to work, as the others are, to figure out how to get justice for Tamla!

I want to thank all those who have supported me and encouraged me along this long and difficult journey. Your messages have kept me going at times, so continue to send those encouraging words. Those doing readings, podcasts, etc., to see if you can get to the truth and get the story out there, THANK YOU! Together we can figure out the TRUTH about WHAT HAPPENED TO TAMLA HORSFORD.

Please check out the author's website, tamlahorsford.net
for more details about the case.

Email: contact@tamlahorsford.net

Made in the USA
Columbia, SC
11 July 2024

38471570R00146